The
Arab
City

The Arab City:
Architecture and Representation

EDITED BY
AMALE ANDRAOS and NORA AKAWI
with CAITLIN BLANCHFIELD

The Arab City: Architecture
and Representation

Edited by
AMALE ANDRAOS
NORA AKAWI
with
CAITLIN BLANCHFIELD

Robot jockey racing a camel in Kuwait.

The Arab City in Representation
AMALE ANDRAOS

The symposium "Architecture and Representation: The Arab City" was held at Columbia University's Graduate School of Architecture, Planning and Preservation (GSAPP) in November 2014, as a second iteration of an event by the same name that took place in Amman in 2013, with the collaboration of Studio-X director Nora Akawi. The topic was a result of the seminars and studios I held at GSAPP from 2011 to 2014, which all revolved around the question of representation in architecture and urban design, as seen through the lens of the architectural and urban production in the Middle East and North Africa region over the past decade. "Representation" is a multiple term for architects, evoking the act of architectural drawing or the affordances of participation in a society, but perhaps most significantly for these discussions, it is understood as the capacity for buildings to hold *meaning* or to be iconic. The seminars in particular were focused on situating this contemporary conversation and production within a larger historical context, starting with the fall of the Ottoman empire and its division into colonized territories and extending to the rise of the "Gulf cities," an ascension in which architecture and real estate development played a critical role.[1]

The focus on the "Arab City" came first as a personal interest in reexamining the various constructions of this term historically. Such constructions have spanned the scales of architecture and urbanism, with architecture always carrying the many ideas about the "city," even in its details. Acknowledging the ludicrousness of reading cities as essentially defined or categorized along ethnic lines, the term "Arab" can nevertheless connote unique aspirations and evoke particular images, rendering the city specifically other to "Islamic" or "Arab-Islamic," as the latter's two adjectives are decoupled to uncover a history that is today too often forgotten, or even erased.[2] Those aspirations were awakened in a hopeful moment during the events of the Arab Spring and its "retaking of the public square."[3] They seem to have continued to live and grow, if not in the realities of the "Arab Street" (now sadly bloodier and more repressive than ever), then in the minds and work of a new generation of highly engaged architects, historians, and scholars. With many of them joining the symposium, the conversation was charged not only with great intensity and a sense of urgency but also with a feeling of irreverent optimism in the continued power of the ideas embodied by a secular, transnational, progressive, and intellectual "Arab" that attempted to articulate modernity, and indeed politics, on its own terms.

The second reason for taking the Arab City as a focus was to probe under-examined issues raised by the notion of "global practice" in architecture today. The term has been generating hype for over a decade now, yet the discussion surrounding it has been stymied by its inevitable clichés.[4] Over and over the terms to be negotiated have been reduced to the assumed opposition between "local" and "global," with architecture bestowed the role of bridging "tradition" and "modernity," even as it further conceals the very modernity of "tradition" as a construction and an effect of modernity itself.[5] These contradictions have given us many of the most notable icons of the twenty-first century, on the one hand, often conceived as built metaphors, with the power of brand.[6] On the other hand, they have provided a new kind of socially motivated architecture that brings together local craft, labor, and materials with imported western technology, and where words such as "authenticity" and "heritage" are embraced unselfconsciously as architects talk earnestly about expressing cultural specificity and difference.[7] In both instances, otherness is usually enshrined in sound bite motifs, easily digested by our virtual, twenty-four-hour infoscape of architecture-as-image.

In many ways, what contemporary global practice ushered back is the question of architecture as symbolic form, engaged in representation rather than limited to performance. This return has succeeded despite the heated debates of architectural postmodernism, which ran from the pleasures of signs and symbols reintroduced by Venturi, Scott Brown to the disarticulated and voided architectural bodies and processes of the Museum of Modern Art's 1988 deconstructivist show, to the more recent debates around affect or procedure.[8] As representation came back largely in the form of branding—a strategy imported from graphic and product design—it enabled the expediency required to serve the speed and scales of global practice and global capitalization, as well as the production of architectural icons.[9] Yet the encounter of those representations with the realities of local contexts has not always been pleasant, inviting us to consider the impossibility that architecture could ever exist outside of either context or content and to engage instead in a more critical reading of the content and contexts being produced.[10] When we continue to hear of identity building through architecture, whether for a corporate client, an institution, a city, or a state, what are the meanings produced?[11] What identities are being constructed, and how can that knowledge allow us (architects) some margins in which to resist?

There is probably no context more pregnant for this investigation than that of the Arab City, as site of imagination and projection, in a region at once feared and exoticized. The Arab City has witnessed simultaneously, and not coincidentally, the devastation of its old centers and the rise of new ones. The old centers—Beirut, Baghdad, Damascus, Cairo—represent a long, rich, and complex dialogue with, struggle over, and embrace of modernity, not only through art, literature, poetry, and intellectual and political thought, but also through the architecture and urban experiments launched during the last stretch of the Ottoman rule.[12] What the new centers offer is a seeming blank slate—"no context," as many architects might say.[13] This seeming contextual void is fast-tracking from tradition to modernity as it gives rise to new urban centers of great power and influence. This is the typical narrative: Only recently inhabited by fishermen and Bedouins roaming the desert and living in tents, these instant cities today boast the financial skyscrapers, luxury lifestyles, and cultural centers of the post-industrial city, led by visionary rulers who are single-handedly lifting their citizens and cities toward the future while respecting the traditional and religious values of the past. This harmonious coming together is set in contrast to the narrative of politicized Islam and the violent clash of civilizations we are said to be experiencing, even as it is intimately connected to it.[14] For even as we move beyond the narrative of an East/West civilizational divide, we are nevertheless witnessing a struggle for regional power through the rise of these new cities. On one side is a progressive attempt to engage modernity; on the other, a conservative pull to modernize without democracy. And in this struggle, ethnicity, tradition, and religious identity are set as the foundation for new transnational formations, however moderate or extreme they may be.

Standing as the skillful diplomat is the architect, weaving together "tradition" and "modernity" in a mashup of signifiers for both. Among the most notable and successful examples of the past decade are the twin proposals of Foster + Partners' Masdar in Abu Dhabi and OMA's new eco-city for Ras-El-Khaimah, both of which were designed to echo the traditional medina, with its high-density, low-rise built form that so inspired Alison Smithson's 1974 manifesto for the mat building.[15] Masdar in particular presents a sophisticated language of traditional Islamic architectural motifs-turned-high-tech devices for green energy performance, such as the use of the *mashrabiya* to screen the sky and as part of building façades, a strategy also embraced in Jean Nouvel's Abu Dhabi Louvre and in I. M. Pei's Islamic Museum in Qatar.[16] Other strategies involve layering calligraphy onto the bold forms of contemporary expression, such as for the new Qatar Faculty of Islamic Studies designed by Ali Mangera and Ada Yvars Bravo.[17] Finally, there are the proliferation of architectural metaphors referring to traditional life in the desert and on the ocean, exemplified by buildings such as Burj Al Arab (a building in the form of a sail), Zaha Hadid's Dubai Opera House ("the gentle winding form evokes images of mountains or sand dunes"), Morphosis's King Abdullah Petroleum Studies and Research Center ("the new KAPSARC master plan is rooted in the historical model of the oasis village"), OMA's Jeddah International Airport proposal ("both the main terminal and

Royal pavilion with their crescent-like shape enclose an internal oasis that can accommodate different forms of use"), and Nouvel's National Museum of Qatar, which "crystallizes" the Qatari identity, in "a building that, like a desert rose, appears to grow out of the ground and be one with it."[18]

In many ways, this approach is not dissimilar to that of camel racing, which has regained popularity among young Emiratis. Anthropologist Sulayman Khalaf traces the genealogy of this sport and its significant revival starting in the mid-1990s, demonstrating how it was reinvented, expanded, and promoted by the United Arab Emirates' ruling family and President Shaikh Zayed as a means to construct the Emirati identity as stable and continuous in the face of significant transformation of its society.[19] The camels signify tradition and the historical Bedouin lifestyle, but they are driven by highly developed robot-jockeys, which embody the Emirates' embrace of modern technology and progress. This bringing together of camels and robots demonstrates the ruling family's visionary approach to developing its city-state, with a commitment to reconciling traditional lifestyle and values with the modern, technologically driven western world. This bridging of tradition and modernity enacts a kind of harmony as it produces a unique, highly specific cultural experience that reinforces the strength and preservation of local identity in the face of global homogenization.

This last point, that of the construction of identity, becomes the most interesting, for it is a particular identity that is being constructed, one that is not only stable but also exclusive and exclusionary. The Emirati identity is here narrowly defined as stemming from the pure lineage of Bedouins, the only original inhabitants of the *watan* (homeland), staged as bearers of the "authentic" culture of this land and place, at the exclusion of many of the other populations and cultures that in fact rendered the historical populations of the Gulf States much more hybrid over time.[20] This narrative also serves as a political and cultural performance meant to reassure the Emirati nationals, to whom the newly created population in which they have become a minority is alarming. Set against the reality of a highly diverse people—from young western expats, to Arab refugees, to Southeast Asian construction workers—is the representation of authentic cultural heritage that groups all non-Emirati together as a never-to-be-integrated "other."

While enlisting cultural heritage to construct an exclusive, and purportedly authentic, identity is one way the UAE's ruling family has engaged in statecraft, another is the seemingly opposite: as a narrative of a nation-state engaged in a kind of "reverse Orientalism," as anthropologist Ahmad Kanna has brilliantly argued in *Dubai: The City as Corporation*.[21] Building on Edward Said's theory of Orientalism as an essentialist reduction of a people depicted as frozen in static religious beliefs and cultural practices, Kanna renders Dubai and the Gulf

States as equally and miraculously suspended outside of history or politics, but this time as hypermodern states driven by futuristic and visionary development purveyed by urbanists and starchitects.[22] In this narrative, Dubai becomes the fantastically glittery city-as-spectacle, emerging from the desert as the twenty-first-century incarnation of the *One Thousand and One Nights,* which inspired Frank Lloyd Wright's vision for Baghdad in the middle of the last century.[23] As the old centers of Arab struggles for modernity make way for the new centers of global entrepreneurial neoliberalism, Dubai asserts the promise of a new future that constitutes a radical break from "Arab traditions and pathologies."[24]

Set against the representations of authentic and original culture as embodied by the Bedouin lifestyle and the imaging of futuristic hypermodern cities is "the real," whether the desert, the crumbling modernist old town, the new shopping malls, or the relentlessly generic housing and commercial buildings of the prebranded neighborhoods.[25] Deemed inauthentic and uninspiring for architects, this banal reality ushers in the typical question of "how do you build in a place with no context?"[26] Inviting context to become a fantasy that brings together the golden age of a mythical Islamic empire with the promise of new technological utopias. Naturally, this narrative is made to resonate with another, that of a mythical historical golden age of Islam, now a reconstituted archive that groups together, undifferentiated in space or time, the traditional medinas of Fez and Aleppo, the lush palaces of Andalucía, the golden buildings of the caliphate of Baghdad, or the domes and pixelated refracting surfaces of Sinan's mosques.[27] This construction of a mythical context, at once nostalgic and futuristic, produces a powerful narrative: Islam is not against progress because it was once the driver of progress. What we are witnessing is in fact a new Islamic renaissance, that of an emerging society at once deeply religious and conscious of belonging to a broad "Islamic nation"—a concept that has possibly never been as complex or charged as today—and at the cutting edge of a visionary, global, urbanized future.

The most undeniably successful (and quite beautiful) architectural embodiment of this narrative is, Ateliers Jean Nouvel's Louvre Abu Dhabi. Situated on Saadiyat Island, the building takes inspiration from the organic patterns of the traditional medinas to create a landscape of building-scaled rooms, whose nonhierarchical relationships are made legible by a shallow dome with a diameter close to that of the Louvre's Cours Carrée in Paris. As a layering of fractal three-dimensional patterns, the dome filters light to create microenvironments of dreamy mist, echoing at once rays of sunlight trickling through the palms of an oasis and the refraction of light produced by the ornate surfaces of mosques. As with many of Nouvel's projects, architecture is dematerialized, blending with the scenarios and atmospheres of its context both real and imagined. Nouvel, a self-declared contextual architect, is a no kitsch designer, his sophisticated knowledge rendering him an orientalist of the highest caliber.[28] Such has been Nouvel's reputation since his Institut du Monde Arabe, where the mechanical façade of sun-sensitive lenses is a technological interpretation of the Islamic geometric pattern that calibrates light to render vision as both optics *and* experience in a multilayered and complex configuration.[29]

So what, then, is the problem if these constructions are able to produce exemplary architecture? A first problem is that this montage of signs and symbols usually leads to reductive meanings and experiences, the essentializing of an entire society, which, as Said's thesis demonstrated, was not only offensive in its representations but also instrumental in advancing the colonial project.[30] The construction of cultural specificity is all too often reduced to a simplistic identity, defined in opposition to, and at the exclusion of, others (a difficulty inherent in architecture's reductiveness). A second and possibly larger problem lies with a tendency toward a type of pan-Islamism. While art historians like Oleg Grabar have thoughtfully probed the boundaries of Islamic art (and its continued influence), others still believe that if particular architectural features were developed during the technological advancement that took place in sixteenth-century Istanbul under the genius of the architect Sinan, it is equally contextual to use them in the desert of Qatar or Abu Dhabi because they belong to a unified history of Islamic architecture. Regardless of place and time, politics or economics, material advancements and technologies, Islamic architecture is constructed as the principal unifier that extends from the lands of Syria to Iraq—a form of cultural displacement that strangely makes possible the conception of a romanticized, cohesive Islamic people, nation, or empire. At its most dystopic, this is the same mythical Islamic empire claimed by (and marked by the horrific violence of) ISIS, where an overgeneralized idea of Islamic culture is used to legitimize the brutal murder of innocent others as well as the destruction of any symbol of ancient architectural hybridity or contaminated progressive modernity.

This kind of essentialized identity should in fact be seen as the construction of a particular archive, which at once renders if not impossible then at least quite difficult the possibility of uncovering and reconstituting any alternatives. The endless focus on the expression of Islamic culture in all its forms—whether scholarly, in popular culture, or in architecture, and even cities—has produced powerful and all-encompassing noise that has rendered invisible the knowing and uncovering of another past, that of the endlessly rich and varied intellectual, political, literary, and artistic dreams and discourses that attempted to build a modern, progressive (and secular) Arab nation. It is those two visions—and histories—that collided again for a brief hopeful moment in the streets of Cairo, inflamed by a youthful and disenfranchised population whose memory and appropriation of Nasserian slogans was not coincidental—though neither was its violent silencing by the Muslim Brotherhood's singular Islamic vision.[31]

This alternative history has driven many of the intellectual, political, and artistic practices that have emerged from the region in the past two decades, and that have questioned "identity" as an interpretive lens. A seminal recent account is that of historian and political economist Georges Corm in his *Pensée et politique dans le monde arabe*. Starting from his disappointment with the Arab Spring's denouement, Corm brilliantly traces the evolution of Islamic and Arab intellectual and political thought in its encounter with modernity from 1850 to today. Looking to early religious reformists such as Sheikh Tantawi and, later, Taha Hussein, both emerging from Al-Azhar University in Cairo, and early Arab secular thinkers such as Yassin El-Hafez, Mahdi 'Amel, the poet Adonis, the economist Samir Amin, and the feminist poet May Ziade, to name but a few, Corm generates an archive that counteracts the dominant "Jihad vs. McWorld" narrative that is fueling much scholarly research on, and architectural rhetoric in, the region today.[32] Faced with such a long and complex account of modernist progressive thought, one can only wonder why this line of critical engagement with an Arabic modernity could not constitute an alternative archive from which to construct new architectural possibilities in the face of the conservative social and political structures we are most often invited to serve.

Institutions such as the Arab Image Foundation (AIF) and the Arab Center for Architecture, both based in Beirut, are engaged in this same project in historical memory and Arab modernity, at times secular and at times stemming from religious reforming forces.[33] Founded in 1997, the AIF houses a unique collection of over 600,000 photographs taken between 1850 and 1950—precisely the same time frame of Georges Corm's account of the *Nahda*, or Arab Renaissance—by professional, amateur, and anonymous photographers. The images encompass a wide range of subjects, genres, and styles that capture everyday life during an age of transformation, progressive thinking, and optimism about the future of Arab nations. While the AIF's stated mission is to shed light on the practice of photography in the region over that century, it acknowledges that "inevitably, the research projects raise questions about how images are used or their relationship to notions such as identity, history, and memory." With powerful collections such as Akram Zaatari's "The Vehicle," which splices through family albums "the infiltration of modernity into the Arab world through the representation of the vehicle"; or "Arts et Couleurs," which depicts "a time of economic growth, hula hoop parties, beehive hairdos and the Beatles"; or the Rafik Chadirji collection, which documents Baghdad's ebullient intellectual and artistic renaissance in the 1950s, the AIF presents modernity in its multifaceted and complex layers, in contrast to the common narrative of a region stuck in time and mindless conflict.[34] For architecture, the Chadirji collection is particularly important, as it documents a time when Iraqi architects, poets, and writers were welcoming modernist ideas and styles, hybridizing them not with

Islamic references but rather with a playful mix of Babylonian ancestry and contemporary critical discourse.[35] This was a time that brought the talents of architects such as Mohammed Makiya and Hisham Munir together with Walter Gropius, Josep Lluís Sert, and Marcello d'Olivo.[36] Even Hassan Fathy, whose language has come to embody the quintessential regionalist architecture, never referenced Islamic motifs in his seminal 1958 New Gourna project but rather freely wove together abstract modernist forms with pharaonic imagery.

This embrace of modernity helped Arab nations shed the shackles of colonialism and build new, independent institutions.[37] The writing of certain architects, urban theorists, and scholars resists the notion that modernity was experienced as an imposition, arguing instead that it adopted a unique form (architectural and otherwise) in every city it took root in.[38] This narrative is one that the Arab Center for Architecture is painstakingly documenting as a collection of buildings and projects whose traces are recorded through photography, drawing, and texts. Gradually, these valuable documents are becoming available in an online archive, as well as a collection of original drawings at the center in Beirut. As with the Arab Image Foundation, the archive collapses the distinctions between generic structures and exquisite buildings, private houses and public monuments, and makes palpable the many-layered complexities of the modernist project in the region. Like the AIF, the archive also carefully traces authorship, documenting collaborations between local and international architects as well as temporary and permanent residents of the region. CETA, a collaborative of French and Lebanese architects and engineers (J. Aractingi, J. N. Conan, J. Nassar, P. Neema), for example, was responsible for the design of the perfectly proportioned Electricité du Liban building (1965–72) in Beirut.[39] Today, many of these jewel-like buildings have been destroyed by either conflict or development, fallen in complete disrepair or "pimped up," hidden behind Orientalizing arches and a depressing pastiche of the architectural tropes commonly used to signify identity.

In fact, to visit the old centers of Cairo, Beirut, Damascus, or Baghdad is to see disproved the notion of an "authentic" culture brutally displaced by its encounter with modernity. To this day these cities embrace modernism with little doubt. Instead, it is with the rise of the new centers of oil economies that the supposed weaving together of "tradition" and "modernity" developed. Critical regionalism in the Middle East can be traced alongside the rise of socially conservative states, gaining significant traction in the late 1960s and early 1970s as the emerging oil economies of the Arabian Peninsula built new centers of regional power.[40] To implement this new mandate, Saudi Arabia turned to new and fruitful collaborations with Japanese architects, whose respect for tradition, consciousness of cultural specificity, and commitment to creating a specific national identity through architecture rendered them a desirable partner in the construction of a conservative rather than progressive form of modernism. From the elegant lines of the Dahran airport designed by Minoru Yamazaki (1961) to the numerous state buildings of Kenzō Tange, places like the Royal State Palace in Jeddah (1980–83) or Alkhaira, the King Faisal Foundation (1976–84) in Riyadh, this new architecture borrows oriental, Bedouin, or "Islamic" motifs—patterned surfaces, arched openings, courtyards, medina-like cityscapes, tent-inspired structures—to demonstrate origin stories and authenticity with modern statehood.

Following these early collaborations, the new alliances with American oil and construction companies such as Aramco and Bechtel led to increased commissions for American corporate firms. Their architectural language further coupled conservative social and political values with modern technologies. Today, this narrative can be read across buildings such as Skidmore, Owings & Merrill's National Commercial Bank of Jeddah (1977–84), which boldly weaved together modernist abstraction with Orientalized patterns and courtyards; the firm's Abdul Azziz International Airport in Jeddah, also known as the Hajj Terminal (1982); and HOK's King Saud University (1984), as well as King Khaled International Airport (1975–84) in Riyadh, designed in collaboration with Bechtel.[41] This representation of tradition and modernity—and it is always a *representation* of synthesis rather than an actual mediation of past and future—was not limited to the architecture but also manifest in urban planning: from Constantinos Apostolou Doxiadis's plan for Riyadh (1971) to Georges Candillis's plans for Dahran and Al Khobar (1974) developed for Aramco, in which modernist approaches to zoning and a focus on infrastructure in plan were combined in section with particular privacy concerns, leading to strict guidelines that controlled views, height, and setbacks.[42]

At the same time, ironically, local forms of settlement were replaced by suburban-style gated communities. In the 1930s Aramco introduced the compound typology as a gated community or "company town" for its employees, attracting middle-class Americans to spend a few years in the desert of Arabia with a vision of suburban comfort. These detached homes and surrounding yards inverted the local courtyard housing typology which connected rooms and houses around extended kinship and tribal relationships. As Aramco built suburban-style compounds for its Arab staff—segregated from its American employees yet with the same trappings of consumerist lifestyle—the company struggled to define family boundaries, turn women into a labor force, and attract occupants through its home ownership program (seen by Arab women in particular as socially isolating).[43] Today, as the Gulf States' sprawling luxury gated communities are built alongside invisible camps for imported labor, one is reminded of the oil company's original experiments to promote an American brand of modernity through the single-family home and its consumerist lifestyle.

It is this narrative of conflicting modernities, of forgotten cultural heritage, and of political, social, economic, and technological transformation that the Bahrain Pavilion of the Fourteenth Venice Architecture Biennale so powerfully told. Designed as a rotunda of shelves, the pavilion staged a library filled with thousands of copies of the same book. An archive of seminal architectural buildings from the Middle East and North Africa region built between 1914 and 2014, the book stood as a manifesto for the region's ability not only to "absorb modernity," as Biennale curator Rem Koolhaas's polemical invitation suggested, but to find in the generic and abstract nature of the modernist architectural language and within the universal qualities of its social ambitions, highly specific and various forms of invention and adaptation.[44] As visitors flipped through books while seated around a large circular table, the white dome above displayed an endlessly multiplied identical image: a man dressed in white and absorbed in what seemed a trancelike prayer—an assumption visitors inevitably made as a result of his speaking in Arabic. The speaker was in fact simply reciting the names of the nations from which the buildings had been selected.

The pavilion's scenography presented the long-standing opposition between an Arab progressive and modernist nationalism—as represented by the collected buildings and the map on the table—and an Islamic conservative nationalism as suggested by the speaker's incantation above, even as it undermined the simplicity of this binary narrative. The pavilion's sponsor, Bahrain, supported the vision of Lebanese architects Bernard Khoury and George Arbid, who modeled the multiple, varied, and complex Arab modernity asserted within the pages of the book itself.

This desire to resist single narratives, reveal other histories, and produce multiple meanings has motivated architects working in the region, and in Lebanon in particular, where much of this debate played out during the civil war and throughout the reconstruction of downtown Beirut.[45] The Solidere project, named after the private company that led the reconstruction and continues to oversee the development of the heart of the Lebanese capital, embodied not only the transition from the old centers of power and influence to the new ones in the Gulf but also the reshaping of an Arab secular nationalism to the predominant narrative of religious and embattled identities.

Founded in 1994 by Prime Minister Rafik Hariri, a self-made man who had risen to fortune and power working as Prince Fahd's personal contractor in Saudi Arabia, Solidere soon became a model for the region and beyond, inspiring new development structures from Mecca to Mumbai.[46] Despite the attacks on its procedures—from the use of eminent domain to the pressure to forfeit property rights to the redrawing of property lines to allow larger parcels to be developed—within a few years Solidere had produced significantly more destruction than fifteen years of war.[47] This destruction represented nothing less than a political editing of history, demolishing certain buildings while restoring and recasting the significance of others. With the goal of reviving Beirut as a tourist destination and the "Paris of the Middle East," Solidere turned the buzzing, tightknit, and messy fabric of downtown—with its street vendors, layered histories, and secular modern fabric—into a city of icons, where mosques, churches, and a single temple have been excavated and preserved as ruins while the active cityscape around was wiped out.[48] Transformed into freestanding objects, these religious buildings became at once monuments and meaningless clichés standing in for religious pluralism and gutted of the real life and endless daily transactions that shaped them.[49] Using as its alibi the preservation of memory, Solidere constructed a fiction instead: that of religious pluralism as the only possible foundation of Lebanese identity. As religious icons punctuate shopping streets with alternating Haussmanian and Ottoman flavors, downtown Beirut is today a successful tourist destination for wealthy Gulf and Saudi nationals. Emptied of local population, it becomes a ghost town the minute those countries declare its grounds unsafe for their citizens to travel to.

It is this complex and contingent understanding of the Arab City that makes clear the impossibility of architecture to exist outside of its own context. Yet this context is not the monolithic set of formal devices that have come to represent the Arab City in so much contemporary architecture. Rather, it is a multilayered, messy, and multiple history that brings together the opposites we inevitably continue to construct—the secular and the religious, tradition and modernity, the local and the global. Examples such as the reconstruction of downtown Beirut or the Louvre Abu Dhabi tell a larger story of contemporary global architectural and urban production. They are a testimony both to architects' powerlessness in the face of development forces and to architecture's power in continuing to embody concepts, produce content, and shape its context, as Bernard Tschumi once said.[50] And yet, at a time of wrenching violence, unbearable displacement, and devastating conflict across the Middle East, it seems important for architects to contribute a greater understanding to the historical, social, political, cultural, and economical complexities at hand, taking responsibility to articulate and engage both the real and its representation in more complex and incisive ways. The concepts we enlist, the contexts we shape, and the content we produce matter. As a site at once imaginary and real, the Arab City sits at the intersection of much of what is at stake today for architects and for architecture. To engage in its complexity is to acknowledge the renewed urgency of historical knowledge while also embracing the responsibility to project much needed alternate futures.

1   On "Gulf Cities" see Rem Koolhaas/ AMO's exhibition on the Gulf at the Tenth Venice Architecture Biennale, in 2006, which presented "an overview of urban developments in the Persian Gulf and the combined impact of these developments on the region and beyond," http://oma.eu/news/ amo-exhibition-on-the-gulf-at-venice-architecture-biennale.

On process of capitalization, see Timothy Mitchell's keynote for "Architecture and Representation: The Arab City," Columbia Graduate School of Architecture, Planning and Preservation, New York, November 21, 2014, included in this volume as "The Capital City," page 258. See also Omar Jabary Salamanca and Nasser Abourahme, "City Talks: Timothy Mitchell on the Materialities of Political Economy and Colonial History," *Jadaliyya*, November 17, 2015, www. jadaliyya.com/pages/index/23182/city-talks_timothy-mitchell-on-the-materialities-o.

2   On the deconstruction of the the terms "traditional," "Islamic," and "cities," see Janet Abu-Lughod's scholarship. In particular, see Janet Abu-Lughod, "The Islamic City—Historic Myth, Islamic Essence, and Contemporary Relevance," in *International Journal of Middle East Studies,* vol. 19, no. 2 (1987): 155–76, and "What Is Islamic about a City? Some Comparative Reflections," in *Urbanism in Islam: The Proceedings of the International Conference on Urbanism in Islam,* volume 1 (Tokyo: Middle Eastern Culture Center, 1989), 193–217. See also André Raymond, "Islamic City, Arab City: Orientalist Myths and Recent Views," *British Journal of Middle Eastern Studies,* vol. 21, no. 1 (Autumn 1994): 3–18.

On erased histories see Nicolai Ouroussoff in conversation with Jorge Otero Pailos, Daniel Betrand Monk, Laurie Rush, and Ian B. Straughn during the "Culture and Heritage after Palmyra" panel discussion, Columbia Low Memorial Library Rotunda, New York, October 29, 2015. See also Nasser Rabbat, "They Shoot Historians Don't They?," *ArtForum,* vol. 54, no. 3 (November 2015).

3   On the relationship between the mosque and the square, see Nasser Rabbat, "The Arab Revolution Takes Back Public Space," *Critical Inquiry,* vol. 39, no. 1 (Autumn 2012): 198–208.

4   A Google search for "global practice in architecture" yields 146,000,000 entries. Among the recent conversations, one can note the "AIA Entrepreneur Summit 2015: Global Practice," the 2013 AIANY presidential theme "Global City/Global Practice," and the ACSA 2014 Annual Meeting "Globalizing Architecture / Flows and Disruptions." One of the most interesting critical approaches to contemporary global practice has revolved around the questions raised by the project "Who Builds Your Architecture?" led by professors Mabel Wilson and Kadambari Baxi.

5   For a critique of the constructed opposition of "tradition vs. modernity," situating tradition as an effect of modernity, see Timothy Mitchell, "The Stage of Modernity," in *Questions of Modernity,* ed. Timothy Mitchell (Minneapolis: University of Minnesota Press, 2000), 1–34.

6   Examples of such metaphors: the Beijing stadium by Herzog and deMeuron as a bird's nest; BIG's REN Building, which takes the form of Chinese character for "person"; or the Taipei 101 tower by C. Y. Lee Architects, in the form of stacked vernacular pagodas. For more on branding, see Robert E. Somol, "12 Reasons to Get Back in Shape," in *Content,* ed. Rem Koolhaas (Cologne: Taschen, 2004).

7   See David Adjaye on the Aïshti Foundation in Beirut, "with its aluminum tubular structure applied to the building as an exoskeleton, the distinctive red façade envelops the edifice in a scrim of multiple layers and patterns, reminiscent of the perforated woodwork typical of traditional arabic architecture." Philip Stevens, "First Images of David Adjaye's Completed Aïshti Foundation Revealed," *Designboom,* October 30, 2015, www.designboom.com/architecture/ david-adjaye-aishti-foundation-beirut-leb-anon-tony-salam-10-30-2015. See also the mission of the Aga Khan Architecture Award, which while promoting the important work of preservation and preserving heritage works to move beyond the criteria of Islamic identity. And see also Michael Juul Holm and Mette Marie Kallehauge, eds., *Arab Contemporary: Architecture & Identity* (Humblebaek: Louisiana Museum of Art, 2014).

8   See interview with Ali Mangera in this volume (page 198) on supergraphic calligraphy being reminiscent of Venturi, Scott Brown. And see, for example, the recent lecture by Farshid Moussavi on "affect" in Wood Audtitorium, Columbia University Graduate School of Architecture, Planning and Preservation, New York, November 16, 2015, and the "Postmodern Procedures," symposium organized by Sylvia Lavin, Princeton University School of Architecture, December 4-5, 2015. See also Jeffrey Kipnis, *A Question of Qualities: Essays in Architecture* (Cambridge, MA: MIT Press, 2013).

9   On branding see Somol, "12 Reasons to Get Back in Shape." This is also the legacy of the work of Rem Koolhaas and OMA/ AMO where the question of "identity" and "brand"—starting with the Universal Headquarter building—began to take shape. See also "The Other Architect" exhibition at the Centre for Canadian Architecture curated by Giovanna Borasi, October 2015–April 2016.

On capitalization, see note 1.

10   Viewers' expectation of meaning have led to interpretations of Zaha Hadid's Qatar stadium as a vulva or OMA's CCTV Headquarters in Beijing as the silhouette of man sitting on toilet.

For such a critical reading on architecture and its contexts, see Reinhold Martin, "Financial Imaginaries," in *Mediators: Aesthetics, Politics, and the City* (Minneapolis: University of Minnesota Press, 2014).

11   See BIG's design for Two World Trade Center for 21st Century Fox and News Corp. "And what a radical idea: to produce an architecturally ambitious skyscraper whose shape actually expresses the needs of the building's tenant." Paul Goldberger, "How 2 World Trade Center Was Redesigned Exactly for Rupert Murdoch's Media Empire," *Vanity Fair,* June 10, 2014.

12   The Ottoman empire was called "the sick man of Europe" and is often described as lagging, a characterization that also served as a justification for its dismantling and the subsequent colonization of its former territory. In fact, industrialization was already starting under Ottoman rule, such as with the construction of the German-Turkish railway connecting Baghdad to Europe, which brought new materials and techniques like steel-frame construction to the empire.

13   See interview with Hala Wardé in this volume, page 190. See also Ahmed Kanna, *Dubai: City as Corporation* (Minneapolis: University of Minnesota Press, 2001), in which he quotes Frank Gehry regarding Saadiyat Island: "It is like a clean slate in a country full of resources…it's an opportunity for the world of art and culture that is not anywhere else because you're building a desert enclave without the contextual constraints of a city," 89.

14   See Timothy Mitchell, *Carbon Democracy* (New York: Verso, 2011).

15   "Masdar City combines state-of-the art technologies with the planning principals [*sic*] of traditional Arab settlements to create a desert community that aims to be carbon neutral and zero waste" ("Masdar Development," www.fosterandpartners.com/projects/masdar-development).
       "Mat Building: How to Recognize and Read It," *Architectural Design,* vol. 44, no. 9 (1974): 573.

16   "The perforations for light and shade are based on the patterns found in the traditional architecture of Islam." "Masdar Institute/Foster + Partners," *Archdaily,* November 23, 2010, www.archdaily.com/91228/masdar-institute-foster-partners. See also Laurie Balbo "Modern Mashrabiya is Arab Architecture Made in the Shade," *Greenprophet,* June 25, 2010, www.greenprophet.com/2014/06/modern-mashrabiya-is-arab-architecture-made-in-the-shade.

17   "Her Highness Sheikha Moza Bint Nasser Officially Opens New Qatar Faculty of Islamic Studies Building," March 20, 2015, www.qf.org.qa/news/qfis-building-opening.

18   "Dubai Opera House by Zaha Hadid," *Dezeen,* June 6, 2008, www.dezeen.com/2008/06/06/dubai-opera-house-by-zaha-hadid.
       "King Abdullah Petroleum Studies and Research Center," http://morphopedia.com/projects/king-abdullah-petroleum-studies-and-rese.
       "Jeddah International Airport," http://oma.eu/projects/jeddah-international-airport. For a convincing snapshot of recent clichés, as of 2013, see A. J. Armatel, "Hey Middle East: Enough with the Regional Architectural Clichés, Already," *CityLab,* August 16, 2013, www.citylab.com/design/2013/08/hey-middle-east-enough-architectural-cliches-already/6573/. See also Holm and Kallehauge, *Arab Contemporary.*
       "Jean Nouvel's design manifests both the active, dynamic aspect of the museum's program and its crystallization of the Qatari identity in a building that, like a desert rose, appears to grow out of the ground and be one with it" "National Museum of Qatar by Jean Nouvel," *Dezeen,* March 24, 2010, www.dezeen.com/2010/03/24/national-museum-of-qatar-by-jean-nouvel.

19   Sulayman Khalaf, "Camel Racing in the Gulf: Notes on the Evolution of a Traditional Cultural Sport," *Anthropos* 94 (1999): 85–106.

20   Like many port cities in the Gulf, Dubai has been home to a mix of African, Arab, Persian, and South Asian cultures since the early nineteenth century, when the region came under British control. Kanna, *Dubai: City as Corporation,* 10–11. See also the transformation of Bastakieh, "cleaned" from its Persian roots.

21   See "Theorizing Statecraft and Social Change in Arab Oil Producing Countries," in *Statecraft in the Middle East: Oil, Historical Memory, Popular Culture,* ed. Eric Davis and Nicolas Gavrielides (Miami: Florida International University Press, 1991), 1–35.

22   Edward Said, *Orientalism* (New York: Pantheon Books, 1968).
       Brian Ackley, "Permanent Vacation: Making Someplace out of Non-Place," *Bidoun* 4, http://bidoun.org/articles/permanent-vacation.
       Kanna, *Dubai: City as Corporation*; see especially the chapter "'Going South' with the Starchitects: Urbanist Ideology in the Emirati City."

23   Magnus Bernhardsson, "Modernizing the Past in 1950s Baghdad," in *Modernism and the Middle East, Architecture and Politics in the Twentieth Century,* ed. Sandy Isenstadt and Kishwar Rizvi (Seattle: University of Washington Press, 2008), 88.

24   See Thomas Friedman on the Arab World: "The problem is much deeper—we're dealing with a civilization that is still highly tribalized and is struggling with modernity. Dubaians are building a future based on butter not guns, private property not caprice, services more than oil, and globally competitive companies, not terror networks. Dubai is about nurturing Arab dignity through success not suicide. As a result, its people want to embrace the future, not blow it up." "Dubai and Dunces," *New York Times,* March 15, 2006.

25   Timothy Mitchell, *Colonizing Egypt* (Cambridge, England: Cambridge University Press, 1988), 1–34. See also Yasser Elsheshtawy's essay in this volume, page 56.

26   Kanna, *Dubai: City as Corporation,* 1–42, 77–194.

27   See note 3.

28   Jean Nouvel, *Louisiana Manifesto* (Humblebaek: Louisiana Museum of Modern Art, 2008).
       See the rehabilitation of Orientalism post-Said in the work of Georges Corm, among others.

29   On vision and knowledge, as opposed to optics, as a way of seeing, see Hans Belting, *Florence and Baghdad: Renaissance Art and Science* (Cambridge, MA: Harvard University Press, 2011).

30   Said, *Orientalism.*

31   Georges Corm describes the return to favor of the Nasserian thought during the Arab Spring during which the main reforming party, "nasseriste uni" of Hamdeen Sabahi, openly aligned itself with the Nasserian political thought. Portraits of Nasser were also visible during demonstrations. Georges Corm, *Pensée et politique dans le monde arabe* (Paris: Découverte, 2015), 178.

32   Benjamin Barber, *Jihad vs. McWorld* (New York: Ballantine Books, 2001).

33   Arab nationalism was not only anti-imperialist but often Marxist in its critique, socialist in its ambitions, and nonaligned, thus threatening to the West.

34   "The Vehicle: Picturing Moments of Transition in a Modernizing Society," Arab Image Foundation (1999), www.fai.org.lb/projectDetails.aspx?Id=19&ParentCatId=2; "Arts et couleurs" Arab Image Foundation, (2004), www.fai.org.lb/projectDetails.aspx?Id=14&ParentCatId=2.

35   In the fall of 2013, Iraqi architect Hisham Munir came to speak to my students as part of the "Arab Cities in Evolution" seminar at Columbia University's Graduate School of Architecture, Planning and Preservation, sharing stories about the time he spent with architects such as Rafik Chadriji and Mohamed Makiya in the ebullient Baghdad of the 1950s.

36   Munir collaborated with several European architects and became close friends with Marcello d'Olivo, with whom he collaborated on the Unkown Soldier Monument in Baghdad.

37   "Traditional" and vernacular styles had been indexed, codified, and then hijacked toward a more assimilative form of occupation, as brilliantly described in Gwendolyn Wright, *The Politics of Design in French Colonial Urbanism* (Chicago: University of Chicago Press, 1991), 53–84.

38   See Jad Tabet, "From Colonial Style to Regional Revivalism: Modern Architecture in Lebanon and the Problem of Cultural Identity," in *Projecting Beirut*, ed. Hashim Sarkis and Peter Rowe (New York: Prestel, 1998), 83–105.

39   See George Arbid's presentation at the "Architecture and Representation: The Arab City," Columbia University Graduate School of Architecture, Planning and Preservation, New York, November 21, 2014.

40   This narrative of a "return" to concerns about regional identity starting in the mid-1960s and expressed through architecture can be traced in Gwendolyn Wright, "Global Ambition and Local Knowledge," in *Architecture and Politics in the Twentieth Century*. Some, however, approach the idea as if "Islamization" of this regional identity were a natural evolution. See, e.g., Hasan Uddin-Khan, introduction to *World Architecture, 1900-2000: A Critical Mosaic*, Volume 5: Middle East, ed. Kenneth Frampton and Hasan-Uddin Khan (New York: Springer, 2000).

41   See the US pavilion (*OfficeUS*) at the 2014 Venice Architecture Biennale.

42   Saleh al-Hathlool, *The Arab-Muslim City: Tradition, Continuity, and Change in the Physical Environment* (Riyadh: Dar Al Sahan, 1996), esp. 195–235.

43   Nathan Citino, "Suburbia and Modernization: Community Building and America's Post–World War II Encounter with the Arab Middle East," *Arab Studies Journal* 13–14 (Fall 2005–Spring 2006): 39–64.

44   This narrative transpired across all of the pavilions.

45   Architects working in the region include Bernard Khoury, Hashin Sarkis, and L.E.FT, among others.

46   Solidere was exported as the public-private company Millennium to lead the redevelopment (and destruction of much of the settlement fabric) in Mecca. Solidere also employed UAE-based companies such as Emaar Properties to develop heavily in downtown Beirut. Emaar can be found now across India.

47   See Samir Kassir, *Histoire de Beyrouth* (Paris: Fayard, 2003), especially 630–40.

48   "The plan proposes to demolish 80 percent of the town center and increase the density fourfold. Effectively, a fatal blow has been dealt to the memory of this very ancient city, one better suited for oil-rich Arab countries, with a wealth of new buildings, perhaps, but a dearth of architectural traditions. In a city such as Beirut, which has more than two thousand years of history, the idea of memory must not be belittled. To pretend to protect this memory by preserving a few monuments while obliterating the context onto which they were inscribed can only diminish their real nature. They will be like desecrated tombs, witnesses to the death of the city." Assem Salam, "The Role of Government in Shaping the Built Environment," in *Projecting Beirut: Episodes in the Construction and Reconstruction of a Modern City*, ed. Peter Rowe and Hashim Sarkis (New York: Prestel, 1998), 132.

49   See Nada Moumtaz, "The Knotted Politics of Value: Beirut's Islamic Charitable Endowments between Islam and Capital," unpublished manuscript.

50   Bernard Tschumi, *Event-Cities 3: Concept vs. Context vs. Content* (Cambridge, MA: MIT Press, 2004).

The Case of the Traveler:
Claims for a Post-Identitarian Representation

NORA AKAWI

Amale Andraos's invitation to work on cocurating a conversation on "Architecture and Representation: The Arab City" presented a tremendous opportunity. In the first iteration of the conference at the Columbia Global Center Amman in 2013, we began the conversation with colleagues from Jerusalem, Dubai, Beirut, Cairo, and Amman. There, discussions on the work of Yasser Elsheshtawy, Bernard Khoury, Senan Abdelqader, and others presented many possibilities for further exploration, particularly on questions on representation and identity, citizenship, participation, and conflict. The 2014 conference, which convened in the Graduate School of Architecture, Planning and Preservation's Wood Auditorium on November 21, was an intensive encounter of historical studies and future imaginations for Arab cities from across the campus and the world. The works presented were authored by, and discussed with, a group working in diverse forms of architectural and spatial practice (designers, historians, artists, educators) and of different generations: from the authors who have set the tone for the dominant architectural discourse on Arab cities today to the emerging voices working to build on, or even challenge, such terms. Beyond these differences, however, the participants in the auditorium shared a collective sense of urgency: a coupling of frustrations and aspirations that seemed to make this encounter more than important, relevant, and timely; rather, it was necessary. Here too was a shared reckoning of, and stake in, "the situation" in our cities, which Adrian Lahoud illuminates in his contribution to this volume, and the possibility for this common interest to produce, in solidarity, alternative futures for the Arab street.[1] Hovering in the room was the weight of the violence with which both destruction and construction are being performed in Arab cities, by local, foreign, and occupying political and corporate powers, causing immeasurable displacement and the loss of lives, livelihoods, histories, cultures, and environments.

Despite the many attempts to undermine its transformative effect, the year 2011 represents a turning point in Arab history. Although met with repressive violence by regimes in power, the uprisings across the region carried with them an alternative imaginary of how people and resources should be organized in the world. But the nonviolent protests and demands for dignity, freedom, and social justice were drowned in a bloody orchestration of violence. A united political struggle against oppression and the nature of ruling powers was replaced by chaos, in most cases deliberately choreographed by regimes facing their own collapse (like the infiltration of the *baltajiah* [hooligans] in Egypt, performing state violence in civil disguise) and maintained or exacerbated by others interested in this violence and insecurity.

The revolutionary movement had yet to reach a maturity from which alternative structures of governance could be proposed. Instead, the orchestration of chaos that followed the uprisings has set a stage for counterrevolution. On the one hand, nondemocratic, oppressive regimes are gaining or maintaining popularity with their slogans of security and stability. On the other hand, on the ruins of the weakened state structures—ones built upon a colonial past and artificially drawn borders—Arab states are left with a version of sovereignty that's particularly thin and permeable to external forces. In this context, the region becomes the battlefield of proxy wars over control and resources, uprooting millions of people and leaving them displaced in the search for temporary shelter and security. Underneath this field of deafening violence lies a parallel silence of international consensus over stable flows of money, oil, arms, and power. And across the paths traveled by war-torn populations remains a static global understanding of human rights that renders entire groups of refugees invisible once they cross the borders, as artificial or porous as those borders may be.

With all the opposing opinions and theories on what's actually shaping the future of the Arab City, there seems to be one point of agreement: we're entering an era of historical transformation, leaving a generation in a state of terrifying uncertainty. Practicing and teaching architecture in this context becomes more challenging and important than ever. In the 2011 uprisings, this same generation embarked on a collective project toward democratic change and a just reorganization of governance. It is an ongoing project within which architecture, in its various forms of practice, can reclaim agency. Representational tools in architecture can be activated, as many ideas presented at the conference demonstrate, to make visible overlooked injustice, make heard silenced narratives, make sense of ungraspable scales of infrastructure, and, perhaps, even make imaginable the spatial conditions of social justice. As Felicity Scott's contribution to this volume suggests, we want to ask how architecture can be a medium or practice that "widens the field of social and political struggles" and makes available its disciplinary tools and forms of knowledge to "bring new material to the table."[2]

In this context, this publication gathers the many efforts—particularly those demonstrating that, as Laura Kurgan reminds us, representation is always an active task—made by architects (through their practice, research, or teaching), to propose new imaginaries for this shared space, in a new organization of governance where marginalized communities can begin to take part in shaping their environments.[3]

—

> The political community is a community of interruptions, fractures, irregular and local... It is a community of worlds in community that are intervals of subjectification: intervals constructed between identities, between spaces and places. Political being-together is a being-between: between identities, between worlds.
> —Jacques Rancière, *Disagreement*

For Jacques Rancière, democracy can only exist where a community is defined through a sphere of appearance of a people, a political community. He clarifies that "appearance" is not to be understood in the sense of "illusion opposed to the real" but as an act that modifies the regime of the visible, introducing the visible into the field of experience, splitting reality to reconfigure it as double. This political community cannot be formed only by those who represent, or are considered part of, the state or society. Rather, it is composed of those "floating subjects" that deregulate and derail all authoritarian attempts at representations of places and identities.[4] So democracy can be practiced only when those who are not represented appear and challenge the image of society. The space of appearance where people emerge is the very place of dispute—not disputes between parties that constitute the state but disputes initiated by the nonrepresented subject, which Reinhold Martin refers to as struggles for "the right to representation."[5] It is the struggle for *la part des sans-part*, the claim of the share of those who are deprived of a share in the common good, excluded from recognition, dignity, rights, property, security, speech, decision making.

This insurrectional moment, according to Étienne Balibar,

> Manifests the essential *incompleteness* of the "people" as a body politic... This instable and problematic character of the civic community has been long concealed or, better said, it has been displaced because of the strong degree of identification of *the notions of citizenship and nationality*...the constitutive equation of the modern republican state, which derives its apparently eternal and indisputable character from the permanent strengthening of this state, but also, as we know, from many mythical, or imaginary, or cultural justifications.[6]

The understanding of democracy as a regime of *collective life*, as consensus on a static, united, and whole national *character* or *identity*, is the repression of politics and of democracy altogether.

Felicity Scott warns us of the dangerously common expectation of architecture to participate in the definition and production of this identity in nation-building. In the context of recently decolonized or still-colonized societies in the Arab world, she invites us to "rethink architecture's role as always facilitating stabilization or unification, particularly vis-à-vis national identity," and to understand architecture as a potentially "powerful marker of ambivalences, discontinuities, and instabilities." We are urged to "think of a type of postnationalist figuration of architecture, a paradigm that refuses to collapse into, or even actively contest assumptions informing exclusivist notions like an Egyptian architecture, a Jordanian architecture, a Lebanese architecture, and so on."[7]

—

In the same way that Scott warns us of the dangers that come when architecture is expected to produce exclusivist identities, Edward Said warns us about the pact universities make with the state or with national identity. He writes that academic freedom is at risk whenever discourse in the university must "worship the altar of national identity and thereby denigrate or diminish others."[8] In "Identity, Authority, and Freedom: The Potentate and the Traveler," a lecture he delivered at the University of Cape Town in South Africa in 1991, Said addresses the still very pressing question of academic freedom—the privileges but also the social and political responsibilities of civic institutions like the university, as well as the dangers of the relationship between the university and national identity.

Said elaborates on the notion of academic freedom in regard to the university's relationship to national identity, particularly in postcolonial states in the Arab world, where universities become nationalist political institutions. Having achieved independence after anticolonial struggles, the first changes to be made were in the area of education, which went through a process of "Arabization." For instance, national independence in Algeria meant that for the first time, youth would be educated in Arabic and learn about Algerian culture and history, which were previously either excluded or given an inferior status in a curriculum that reflected the "superiority of French civilization."[9] But this also meant that the national universities were conceived as extensions of the new national security state, with a mandate of shaping national identity, of dictating what is to be included in that identity or excluded from it, what should and shouldn't be taught. So whereas Arab students' education had been encroached upon previously by the colonial intervention of foreign ideas and norms, in the state-building process they were to be "remade in the image of the ruling party."[10] This had devastating consequences for the Arab university. Academics were encouraged to conform rather than excel, and the general result was that "timidity, a studious lack of imagination, and careful conservatism came to rule intellectual practice.… [Nationalism] in the university has come to represent not freedom but accommodation, not brilliance and daring but caution and fear, not the advancement of knowledge but self-preservation."[11]

In the larger debate on academic freedom, on the one hand we are faced with the argument that the university is to be exempt from the practicalities of the everyday world. On the other hand there is the view that directly inserts the academy into that world: the university is meant to be engaged, intellectually and politically, with political and social change and to be responsive to abuses of power. In this view, the university must not only be critical of but also overtly align itself in opposition to oppressive power regimes. The myth of the university as impermeable to the world outside, of course, no longer stands. Said reminds us that "so much of the knowledge produced by Europe about Africa, or about India and the Middle East, originally derived from the need for imperial control," and "even geology and biology were implicated, along with geography and ethnography, in the imperial scramble of Africa." He mentions both the concealed and the public instrumentalization of the American academy by the government and military during the Vietnam War, where academics and researchers were developing studies on counterinsurgency or "lethal research" for the State Department, the CIA, and the Pentagon.

More recently, according to an article in the *Nation*, the Technion—the Israeli Institute of Technology—was involved in developing remote-control capabilities for the Caterpillar D9R, "Black Thunder" armored bulldozer.[12] Referring to these unmanned bulldozers, an Israel Defense Forces officer said that the newly improved machine "performed remarkably during operation Cast Lead," the invasion and massive destruction of Gaza in 2008–2009.[13] At the time of Said's lecture in Cape Town, in 1991, Palestinian universities and schools were closed by the Israeli military, which had kept the major universities in Palestine shut since the beginning of 1988. Today, learning institutions continue to be targeted by Israel from both the air and the ground. Examples include the raiding of Al-Quds University campus by Israeli forces on November 17, 2015, when rubber-coated steel bullets and tear gas canisters were fired at students.[14] The University of Illinois professor Steven Salaita, who had joined the American Indian Studies program with a tenured offer, was recently fired on account of his statements on social media criticizing Israel's conduct of military operations in Gaza.[15] Also, the systematic prosecution of politically active students in Birzeit University by Israel and of Kurdish and Turkish "Academics for Peace" in Turkey for having signed the statement "We Will Not Be Part of This Crime" testifies to the direct involvement of universities with the political realities outside.[16]

In response to the increasing view of the university as simply an arm of the government, which reflects only the interests of corporations and establishment power, Edward Said gives an account of a "new worldliness in [the academy] that denied it the relative aloofness that it once seemed entitled to." On the contrary, it called for the university to become the place where students would be educated as reformers. He continues: "*relevance* was the new watchword."[17]

Political repression, the lack of democratic rights, and the absence of a free press have never been good for academic freedom. They are in fact disastrous for academic and intellectual practice. "To make the practice of intellectual discourse dependent on conformity to a predetermined political ideology," or predetermined canon of learning, Western or other, Said argues, "is to nullify intellect altogether." Academic freedom is the freedom to be critical, the rejection of any kind of homely comfort:

> The world we live in is made up of numerous identities interacting, sometimes harmoniously, sometimes antithetically. Not to deal with that whole is not to have academic freedom. We cannot make our claim as seekers after justice if we advocate knowledge only of and about ourselves. Our model for academic freedom should therefore be the migrant or the traveler: for if, in the real world outside the academy, we must be ourselves and only ourselves, inside the academy we should be able to discover and travel among other selves, other identities, other varieties of the human adventure.

He suggests that we consider academic freedom as an invitation to give up on identity, in the hope of understanding or assuming more than one. "We must always view the academy as a place to voyage in, owning none of it but at home everywhere in it."[18]

According to Said, there are two ways of inhabiting academic and cultural space in the university. The first is the academic professional who is there in order to reign: the king or the potentate who surveys everything with detachment and authority. This entails dictating what should and should not be taught, what should or should not be included, defining disciplinary boundaries, reinforcing existing canons. The second is based on the figure of the migrant, "considerably more mobile, more playful, although no less serious. The image of the traveler depends not on power but on motion, on a willingness to go into different masks and rhetorics…. Most of all, and most unlike the potentate who must guard only one place and defend its frontiers, the traveler crosses over, traverses territory, and abandons fixed positions, all the time."[19]

1   See Adrian Lahoud, "Fallen Cities: Architecture and Reconstruction," in this volume, page 102.

2   Felicity Scott, "Architecture and Nation-Building," in this volume, page 139.

3   Laura Kurgan, "Architecture and Representing," in this volume, page 230.

4   Jacques Rancière, *Disagreement: Politics and Philosophy* (Minneapolis: University of Minnesota Press, 1999), 100.

5   Reinhold Martin, "Remarks on the Production of Representation," in this volume, page 182.

6   Étienne Balibar, "Antinomies of Citizenship," *Journal of Romance Studies,* vol. 10, no. 2 (Summer 2010): 4.

7   Scott, "Architecture and Nation-Building," 140.

8   Edward Said, "Identity, Authority, and Freedom: The Potentate and the Traveler," *Reflections on Exile and Other Essays* (Cambridge, MA: Harvard University Press, 2000), 396.

9   Said, "Identity, Authority, and Freedom," 392.

10   Said, "Identity, Authority, and Freedom," 392.

11   Said, "Identity, Authority, and Freedom," 392–93.

12   Adam Hudson, "Cornell NYC Tech's Alarming Ties to the Israeli Occupation," *Nation,* March 1, 2013.

13   Yaakov Katz, " 'Black Thunder' Unmanned Dozers to Play Greater Role in IDF," *Jerusalem Post,* March 30, 2009.

14   "Israeli Forces Clash with Students During Raid into Abu Dis," *Maan News,* October 25, 2015, www.maannews.com/Content.aspx?id=768485.

15   Corey Robin, "Top Legal Scholars Decry 'Chilling' Effect of Dehiring Scholar Salaita," *Mondoweiss,* August 15, 2015, http://mondoweiss.net/2014/08/top-legal-scholars-decry-chilling-effect-of-dehiring-scholar-salaita.

16   Mariam Barghouti, "Birzeit University Rises Up Against Israel's Arrests," *Al Jazeera,* January 11, 2016, www.aljazeera.com/news/2016/01/birzeit-university-rises-israel-arrests-160106083537743.html; "UK Academics: We Support Academics for Peace in Turkey," Kurdish Question website, January 17, 2016, http://kurdishquestion.com/index.php/kurdistan/north-kurdistan/uk-academics-we-support-academics-for-peace-in-turkey.html.

17   Said, "Identity, Authority, and Freedom," 398, emphasis added.

18   Said, "Identity, Authority, and Freedom," 403.

19   Said, "Identity, Authority, and Freedom," 404.

For the Love of Cities and Books:
Janet Abu-Lughod (1928–2013)

LILA ABU-LUGHOD

Janet Abu-Lughod, my late mother, would have loved to be at a conference on architecture and the representation of Arab cities, and she would have loved to see the discussions that followed it in this publication. She loved cities, and Arab cities held a special place for her. We all belong to intellectual lineages. We hope that we will be remembered by those who come after. Many of us believe that books carry our legacies. Her books on Cairo and Rabat are part of her legacy. But so is her personal library, which now is housed in Amman, at Columbia University's Global Center, where new generations will have access to the books she learned from and loved.

My mother loved architecture. It was a family joke to mimic her enthusiasm about Islamic art and architecture by exclaiming, after a trip we took across North Africa in 1969, "Look at that beautiful doorway!" Yet she had little patience for "representation," except to critique Orientalist representations of "the Islamic city," whose *isnad* (chain of authority) she traced back to an article published in 1928 by William Marçais titled "L'islamisme et la vie urbaine" and whose continuing influence she feared in the misguided efforts of contemporary Arab planners to recreate "Islamic cities" by edict.[1] Later, her deep knowledge of the histories of Arab cities would make her question Eurocentric representations of the world's networks.[2] Cities were, for her, for living in, and people made cities over time within social, legal, and political contexts. That is what interested her, as well as the comparisons to be made among urban forms and functions.

In this essay, I draw from an unpublished intellectual memoir my mother wrote when in her seventies to offer some insight into how she came to work on Arab cities and what she studied about them. She traced her interest in cities to her early concerns with prejudice and poverty and her opposition to racial segregation in US cities, starting with the place she grew up, Newark, New Jersey. When she moved to Chicago as a young college student, she was horrified by the white ghetto she found herself in (Hyde Park) and remembers picketing all-white skating rinks. "Like many other young idealists eventually drawn into sociology—a field I had never even heard of when I set out for the University of Chicago in 1945, just barely turned seventeen and decidedly wet behind the ears—I wanted to fight injustice."

She explained her next move, into urban planning, as follows. She met a young man at a dance and politely asked him what he was doing. He told her about a new program being established at the university. It was 1948. The new program was in planning.

> This appealed to me because it was then believed that social pathologies were "caused" by bad housing environments (ah, innocence!). What better way to solve the problems of the world than by putting knowledge to use in action. I soon transferred from sociology to planning, filled with the hubris (and unrealistic hopes) of having found my métier. Our three-year program of study focused on two issues: first, planning housing, cities, and even river basins in the United States; and second (to me a complete revelation), planning economic development for "backward" nations. This latter was as exotic as anthropology, but I remember feeling very uncomfortable about our presumptuousness… In our small collaborative workshops we laid out ambitious research projects and, in God-like fashion, translated our values into "solutions," independent of economic constraints, the realities of political implementation, and (I am ashamed to say) the participation and guidance of those being planned for!

Fairly quickly she became disillusioned. She realized she had taken a wrong turn.

> City planners at best were "servants" of politicians and beholden to real estate interests and financiers; the "public good" I thought planning could achieve was not uppermost on their minds. This became clear when as director of research for the American Society of Planning Officials I read racialized zoning ordinances and recognized that the chief purpose of planning was to segregate people by class and to "protect" and enhance returns on investment. It was also becoming clearer that the good intentions of housing reformers who should have known better were likely to end in disaster.

It was around then that she met and married my father, a Palestinian refugee from Jaffa, an Arab city much beloved by its inhabitants. Coincidentally, one of her planning projects for "exotic" locations had been a water project for Palestine, so she was not unfamiliar with the place. A few years later, after he

For the Love of Cities and Books

finished his undergraduate degree and then his PhD at Princeton, she moved to Egypt with him and her two small children—my sister and myself. It was 1957. He had been offered a job with UNESCO. A city kid, she couldn't stand living at the rural development center in Sirs al-Layyan, where he worked. So she moved us to Cairo and began to teach urban sociology at the American University in Cairo.

> Few personal-cum-academic experiences were more pro-found! Virtually nothing I assumed I knew about cities (with Chicago the Ur prototype) had much relevance to the crowded, bustling, and to me, baffling metropolis of Cairo, whose physical, social, and cultural patterns had been laid down successively over its one thousand years of existence. How could I use the city as a "laboratory," as I had been taught to do, when I had little of the language, almost no historical background, and kept getting lost? I needed so much! I had to give myself crash courses in history (discovering my affinity to a field I had never studied). I had to gain as much language immersion as I had time for... And I had to make sense of its spatial and social patterns, so different from cities I had known... The best part, however, was explorations with an intrepid band of bright, bilingual, upper-middle-class girls who had innocently signed up for my course in urban sociology. Since their protected lives made them as ignorant as I about large areas of the city, we learned together—wandering around on foot, driving through areas such as the unique City of the Dead that they had never seen, observing housing and street life—and talking to people.

Her four years in Egypt were utterly transformative.

> Even after our return to the States in 1961, I continued to study and write until my book on *Cairo: 1001 Years of the City Victorious* was finally finished in 1967. [This was her PhD thesis, written while she had, by this time, four children.] It was not published until 1971.[3] I am deeply gratified that this book, now a "collector's item," is still considered the definitive study of that city. (At least, when I return to Cairo, I am greeted enthusiastically by many Egyptians who are unaware that I ever wrote anything before or after!)

Her interest in Arab cities broadened:

> Ever since completing my book on Cairo, I had considered comparing Cairo to other cities in the Arab world, especially those in North Africa that had been transformed under French colonial rule…. The Europeanized quarters of Cairo had been planned even before British colonial rule. No legal attempts to separate European settlers from "natives" were imposed, although class differences served to "sift and sort." The situation was quite different in Algeria, Tunisia, and especially in the cities of the French "zone" of Morocco, where planned apartheid achieved its most remarkable "success." Although my original too ambitious plan had been to compare Algiers, Tunis, and Rabat, the book I eventually wrote dealt with "urban apartheid" in Morocco.[4] I uncovered the full depth of French racism and was able to trace how law (and force) succeeded in constructing and maintaining radical segregation between "natives" and colonial settlers, thereby assuring the full exploitation of Moroccan labor and resources. I still think that this is the best book I ever wrote, although French scholars hated it.

Of her next major project, *Before European Hegemony*, she wrote:

> Ever since my self-taught courses on world history when researching Cairo, I had become increasingly annoyed by Max Weber's dismissal of Islam and, in general, and with the self-congratulatory narratives about the "Rise of the West" written by Western historians, which took the superiority of Western culture for granted. I knew that China and Egypt, inter alia, had long been innovators in culture, literature, and technology, and that long-distance trade had connected those two centers of power with one another and with a large number of intermediary points—long before the West "rose." Furthermore, I had been reading urban histories over the years, just out of curiosity, and was struck with the fact that many of these places had important connections to one another. In addition, in my various travels I had casually visited many museums in Europe and Asia and had noticed that, regardless of where I went, many of the most beautiful objects I saw had been made between 900 and 1300 A.D., a time when Europe was still in shadow. I kept hoping I could find a book that described and explained the world in this period. I never expected to have to write it.

By the time she finished *Before European Hegemony*, she had moved to New York, having taught for almost twenty years at Northwestern University. For the next couple of decades, she would turn her gaze back to the United States. She embarked on major comparative studies of America's global cities—New York, Chicago, and Los Angeles. Her final book was a comparative study of race riots in these three cities, returning her in the end to the interests that had driven her since high school in Newark: the injustices of racism and racial segregation.[5] But she never lost her love of Cairo, returning there when she could and keeping up with the literature.

In the last year of her life, when she was mostly housebound, I hired a graduate student to go to my mother's apartment and catalogue her library. She had agreed with my idea, enthusiastically endorsed by Safwan Masri, then director of the newly opened Columbia Global Center in Amman, that it would be wonderful to donate her books to the center. I had just visited and noticed that they had no books in their reading room. And I discovered that they were developing an urban studies and architecture focus, through the GSAPP's Studio-X and its director, Nora Akawi. But when it came down to it, my mother was reluctant to part with her books. "Not now," she said.

Still, I thought maybe my mother would enjoy the process of seeing her books taken off the shelves, one by one, for cataloguing. We went bookcase by bookcase. The volumes were arranged in terms of subject areas related to her shifting interests and projects. In the living room were the books she had worked on most recently. Books about American cities—particularly New York, Chicago, and Los Angeles. Berenice Abbott's black-and-white photographs of New York. Books of maps. Encyclopedias. Books on globalization. Books on race relations. Books on housing policy and gentrification. These were related to her first New York–based research—a collective study with her graduate students at the New School of the Lower East Side, *From Urban Village to East Village*.[6] Tucked in among these were a couple of precious shelves of books by her students and colleagues, personally inscribed to her.

In the front hallway were art books, mostly of Islamic art and architecture—those doorways (and carpets, mosques, and engraved metal urns) she had so admired. In the entrance to her apartment were books about medieval cities and trade networks. Her thirteenth-century world. Her bedroom held the oldest of them all. Here were the books about Cairo, Tunis, Baghdad, Damascus, and other Arab cities. Planning documents. Government statistical abstracts. Magazines from UNESCO, UN Habitat, and the Aga Khan Foundation, for which she had once served as a juror. She had given away many books to students when she retired and lost her office at the New School. These were in anthropology, psychology, and general sociology. And she had given me her very old books about Egypt—like Winifred Blackman's, *The Fellāhīn of Upper Egypt*.[7] There was no room for these in her apartment.

The final bookcase, crowding her bed, held her own publications and offprints and the books of family and family friends, from my first (*Veiled Sentiments*), to Edward Said's *Orientalism* (dedicated to her and my father), to my father's, including the groundbreaking volume in which her famous article on "The Demographic Transformation of Palestine" appeared: *The Transformation of Palestine*.[8] When he moved back to Palestine in 1992, my father had taken all the books in Arabic they had collected from the Cairo booksellers in the late 1950s and '60s. He donated these, along with the rest of his academic library (and the bookshelves!), to the Birzeit University Library.[9]

I had secretly hoped that the library would trigger memories and that my mother would be inspired to talk about her books and her life as we catalogued. Mostly she didn't feel like it. But one day when I came by for a visit, I found her sitting with a very old book on the dining table that now doubled as her desk. She touched the beige cloth cover of this large volume with loving care. She turned the pages slowly to show me, her eyes alive. Carefully she opened up the delicate fold-out maps. I could see her handwritten notes penciled in the margins. She was clearly moved by seeing this book again.

I then remembered. When David Sims, a Cairo-based urban planner, had asked her to write a foreword to his book, *Understanding Cairo: The Logic of a City out of Control*, she had been excited.[10] It was, I believe, the last academic writing she did. She loved his social-spatial approach, was impressed with the maps and statistics, and endorsed his political-economic analysis of the city's growth. It was use, function, and change in cities that interested her. She had an abiding interest in politics and finance that she had first explored as a budding urban planner, and these were the themes of David Sims's book.

She had been shocked, though, that he had not cited one work that she considered crucial. It was the only real flaw, she believed, in his well-researched work. She told him so. I now recognized that this old book she was so fondly showing me was the book she had scolded him for not citing. It was Marcel Clerget's dissertation, *Le Caire: étude de géographie urbaine et d'histoire économique*.[11] She saw herself in a lineage that went back to Clerget. She saw David as carrying forward this lineage. My mother respected history. Not just the histories of Arab cities and those who have built them—from architects to planners to ordinary people—but also the histories of those who have tried to understand and write about them.

Our family is proud that Janet Abu-Lughod's library has now found an excellent home in Amman, a city she visited many times as it was where her much-loved mother-in-law lived. Columbia's Global Center will ensure that these treasures are made available to students and researchers in the region. I had wanted to be able to donate Clerget's *Le Caire* to the library as well. But this time, it is I who find myself not quite ready to let go. I can't forget the look of love in my mother's eyes as she showed me this book about Cairo.

But I did find a few more special books and pamphlets for the library. They include some original offprints of the work of André Raymond and some works by Nezar AlSayyad, a younger Egyptian colleague of whom she was fond. These are two scholars who are very much part of that family who have been drawn to study Cairo. And we are contributing a copy of her own book, long out of print, that has become what she called "a collector's item": *Cairo: 1001 Years of the City Victorious*. May the city have many more years and emerge victorious. And may those who have studied and loved this great Arab city live on through it.

1   Janet L. Abu-Lughod, "The Islamic City—Historical Myth, Islamic Essence, and Contemporary Relevance," *International Journal of Middle East Studies*, vol. 19, no. 2 (1987): 155–76.

2   Janet L. Abu-Lughod, *Before European Hegemony* (New York: Oxford University Press, 1989).

3   Janet Abu-Lughod, *Cairo: 1001 Years of the City Victorious* (Princeton, NJ: Princeton University Press, 1971).

4   Janet Abu-Lughod, *Rabat: Urban Apartheid in Morocco* (Princeton, NJ: Princeton University Press, 1980).

5   Janet L. Abu-Lughod, *New York, Chicago, Los Angeles* (Minneapolis: University of Minnesota Press, 1999); *Race, Space, and Riots in Chicago, New York, and Los Angeles* (New York: Oxford University Press, 2007).

6   Janet Abu-Lughod et al., *From Urban Village to East Village* (Oxford: Blackwell, 1994).

7   Winifred Blackman, *The Fellāhīn of Upper Egypt, Their Religious, Social and Industrial Life To-day with Special Reference to Survivals from Ancient Times* (London: G. G. Harrap, 1927).

8   Lila Abu-Lughod, *Veiled Sentiments* (Berkeley: University of California Press, 1986); Edward Said, *Orientalism* (New York: Random House, 1978); Janet L. Abu-Lughod, "The Demographic Transformation of Palestine," in *The Transformation of Palestine*, ed. Ibrahim Abu-Lughod (Chicago: Northwestern University Press, 1971).

9   For an analysis of his library, mostly political science and Arab studies, especially the Palestine conflict, see Rashad Twam, "Ibrahim Abu-Lughod's Personal Library" (in Arabic) in *Ibrahim Abu-Lughod and the Engaged Intellectual: Resurrecting a Model* (Birzeit: Ibrahim Abu-Lughod Institute of International Studies, Birzeit University, 2011), 22–29, http://ialiis.birzeit.edu/userfiles/Ibrahim-Abu-Lughod-and-the-Engaged-Intellectual-Resurrecting-a-Model.pdf.

10   David Sims, *Understanding Cairo: The Logic of a City out of Control* (Cairo: American University in Cairo Press, 2010).

11   Marcel Clerget, *Le Caire: étude de géographie urbaine et d'histoire économique* (Cairo: Imprimerie E. & R. Schindler, 1934).

Identity

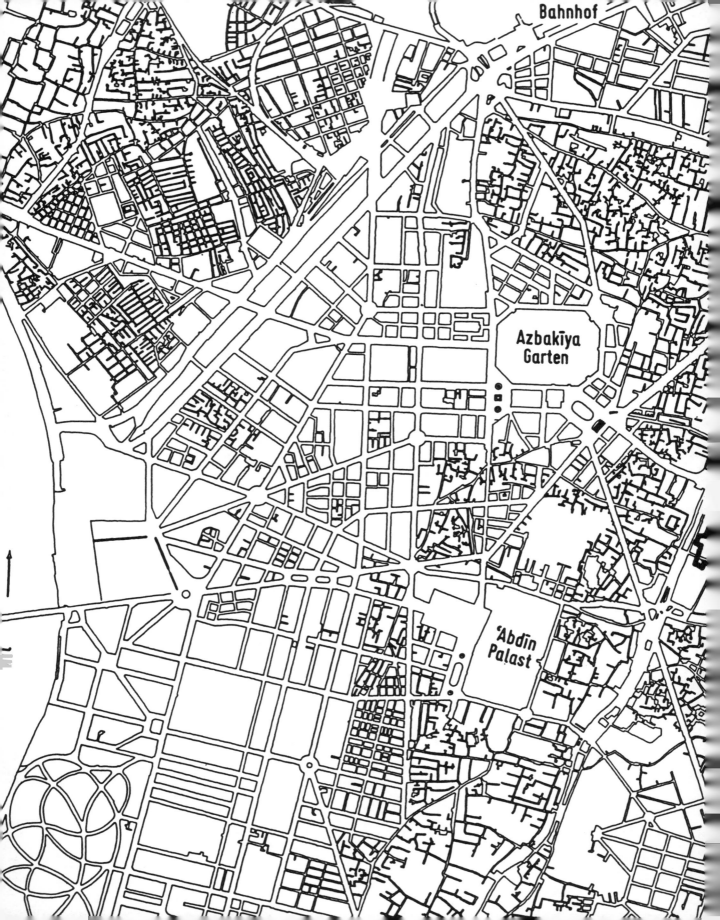

Arab Cities and Identity Crisis
NASSER RABBAT

Cities in the Arab world went through a series of existential crises in the last two centuries.[1] The romantic Orientalist conception of an Arabo-Islamic city—the medina, with its narrow winding alleyways, semi-isolated and inward-looking neighborhoods, linear and specialized souks, central congregational mosques, courtyard houses with crooked plans where large patrilineal families lived together, preponderance of ruined properties, and relentless obsession with privacy—had, by the late nineteenth century, ceased to exist.[2] In its place rose a dual city, divided between the traditional medina and a *ville nouvelle*.[3] The new cities presented a new façade of the "Orient" and a foothold for Western interests where the two sides met and cohabited despite their differences.

First to go binary, and thus to begin to experience a split personality, was Cairo. Khedive Isma'il, the impatient modernizer who ruled Egypt from 1863 to 1879 and wanted to turn it into a part of Europe despite all adverse circumstances, initiated a grand urban project, al-Isma'iliyya, which extended from old Cairo westward toward the Nile, with tree-lined avenues radiating from central squares modeled after the imperial Paris of Baron Haussmann.[4] The new city was furnished with cafés, public gardens, shopping centers, and even an opera house. Incisions in the dense urban fabric of the old city were made to provide straight vehicular access and infrastructural services and to enact a system of spatial control and surveillance. But old Cairo remained essentially premodern in its spatial and social structure, as masterfully depicted in Naguib Mahfouz's *Cairo Trilogy*, and was fronted by and hidden behind the European section, with its accouterments of modern urban living.[5]

Next came the colonial period, during which the dual city phenomenon intensified. In North Africa, where the governments of France and Italy settled colons as a means to lay perpetual claim to the land, urban strategies were implemented to separate the colonized natives from the European landowners who lived in exclusive *villes nouvelles*.[6] Such for instance was the policy promulgated by General Hubert Lyautey, the first French resident general in Morocco, whose architect, Henri Prost, produced plans for Marrakesh, Fez, Meknes, Rabat, and Casablanca. Prost's schemes mummified the historic medinas and isolated them from the *villes nouvelles*, with their wide, straight boulevards, apartment buildings, and green spaces that sometimes functioned as a *cordon vert* surrounding the old cities.[7] An extreme example of the North African colonial city is Le Corbusier's 1933 Plan Obus for Algiers.[8] It proposed

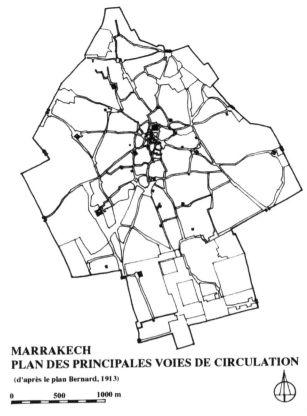

MARRAKECH
PLAN DES PRINCIPALES VOIES DE CIRCULATION

(d'après le plan Bernard, 1913)

0   500   1000 m

Plan of colonial Marrakesh, 1913.

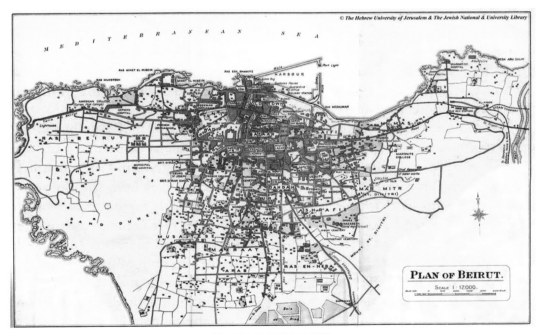

Plan of colonial Beirut, 1923.

Arab Cities and Identity Crisis

a gigantic viaduct connecting a business center on the docks to an undulating, oppressively massive residential zone on the hillside behind the city via a rapid motorway perched above the Arab City, or the *casbah*.

In Iraq, Syria, Lebanon, and Palestine—all constructed arbitrarily as colonial territories according to the secret Sykes-Picot Agreement after the dissolution of the Ottoman empire and in a softer fashion, with no European settlers (except, of course, for Palestine, but that is a wholly different tragedy)— the colonial authorities intervened directly in the old medinas of existing cities by cutting wide boulevards that connected them to the new, European-style neighborhoods developed outside for the bourgeois classes that were increasingly adopting European customs and lifestyles.[9] This was the case in cities like Damascus, Aleppo, Beirut, Baghdad, Jaffa, and other smaller cities in the region, even though the migration of the bourgeoisie to the new neighborhoods dated back to the end of the Ottoman period, when the reforms (*tanzimat*) adopted European modernization as a way to catch up with the West.[10]

Le Corbusier, Plan Obus, 1933.

With independence in the middle of the twentieth century, the Arab colonies transformed into weak nation-states, about which the late Tahsin Bashir, one of Egypt's foremost diplomats, could exclaim with deadpan seriousness: "Egypt is the only nation-state in the region, the others are tribes with flags."[11] The new bourgeois regimes deployed a blend of political liberalism, social conservatism, modernization, and laissez-faire economics as the framework of their state building.[12] They continued the urban policies of the colonial period in matters of zoning, hygiene, landscape, and traffic but tried to nationalize the cityscape by changing the names of the main streets back to Arabic, removing statues of colonial figures and replacing them with national heroes, and patronizing architectural styles for public buildings that harked back to a glorious Islamic past. But the nationalists' paternalistic form of government was shattered after the shocking defeat of the combined Arab armies in Palestine in 1948 and the *Nakba* (catastrophe) of the Palestinians, whose forcibly chased masses moved into makeshift camps around the main cities of the neighboring countries of Syria, Jordan, and Lebanon, in addition to the West Bank and the Gaza Strip.[13]

The creation of Israel caused further fissures in the already embattled Arab political culture and sense of self and led to a series of military coups in Syria (1949), Egypt (1952), and Iraq (1957), each of which took the national destiny into the army's hands.[14] But lacking some of the crucial components of legitimate governments, these incompetent military regimes overcompensated by an exaggerated reliance on the politics of class and identity.[15] New powerful concepts, such as historical identity, authenticity, and the recovery of the Arabic cultural roots, rose to the pinnacle of public interests. Cairo, Damascus, and Baghdad, the old capitals of the Arab golden ages, became the new centers of progressive national visions that wavered between a cautious territorial nationalism of the actual states and an expansive pan-nationalist Arabism, a movement that believed that all boundaries between Arabic countries would be subsumed into a mega-nation with shared language and history.[16] In the 1960s and early 1970s, Beirut, with its pro-West system and relative freedoms, became the cultural capital of the Arab world, with dissidents flocking to it from other Arab cities, whereas Cairo, Damascus, Baghdad, Tripoli, Khartoum, and San'aa fell to the control of repressive regimes that deployed pan-Arabism as state strategy, with varying interpretations of the path to (forced) Arab unity.[17]

These same regimes adopted ambitious socialist modernization programs, complete with land reforms, nationalization of industries and basic services, and an expanded administrative class.[18] The socialist framework generated new—and hastily conceived and implemented—urban, agricultural, industrial, and infrastructural projects meant to herald the new age of progress.[19] Their formal modernism, sometimes softened by symbolic references to history or formal gestures toward climate and site, was apparently predicated on the assumption that modernist projects can stand for expressions of modernity.[20]

Modernization, alas, remained an incomplete project in the face of inherited or created geopolitical, historical, and social contradictions.[21] The startling

Nasr City, Cairo, planned as part of the city's modernization following the 1952 revolution.

Arab defeat in the war of 1967 with Israel revealed the superficiality of most modernizing projects, such as the training of modern armies and the development of advanced industries, and the bankruptcy of the socialist and pan-Arabist regimes. A mood of melancholy and wounded ego pervaded the culture everywhere in the Arab world, a mood manifested in fiction, poetry, art, and even religious and historical studies.[22] But that did not translate into any serious and critical revisions of the national narrative or the political system. Instead, the regimes refashioned themselves to respond to the post-defeat conditions without loosening their tight grip on power.

Consequently, the 1970s and 1980s saw the dismantling of the faltering socialist experiments and their gradual replacement with a statist form of crony capitalism, initiated in Egypt by Anwar al-Sadat, with the misleadingly liberal name *infitah* (opening up).[23] Similar, though carefully disguised, economic reorientations followed in Syria, Iraq, Yemen, Libya, and Algeria, where the military regimes hardened into tyrannical dictatorships devoid of any political pretensions, whose sole purpose was to stay in power in order to enrich their narrow base of supporters.[24] And despite the semblance of growth that crony capitalism delivered, most of these countries experienced acute problems of urban and rural degradation, infrastructural exhaustion, demographic explosion, and socioeconomic inequality.[25]

Desperate rural migration flooded the cities in the 1980s and 1990s, which swelled uncontrollably and at an unprecedented rate to house the bursting poor population.[26] The old urban cores of the *medina*, long deserted by the bourgeois middle classes, were taken over by the new immigrants, who subdivided the old courtyard houses into multiple residential units lacking basic services. Others moved into minimally planned and badly serviced slums (with the expressive Egyptian name *'ashwa'yat*, or "haphazard areas") that grew up on the periphery, on former agricultural land, or in industrial zones.[27]

A small segment of Arab cities, however, began to flourish at that time and continue to prosper today despite the recent global economic blowout. These are the Arabian cities of the Persian Gulf: a narrow necklace of hyper-urbanized dots strung together along the vast arid and sandy coast of the Gulf from Kuwait to Oman and passing by Saudi Arabia, Bahrain, Qatar, and the United Arab Emirates.

Having lain on the edge of the desert for so long, these cities kept their modest, tribally structured, and premodern layouts until the late twentieth century. But things changed, first in the wake of oil discovery in the 1940s and then, more spectacularly, after the 1974 oil price surge. The poor countries became super rich. With the massive new wealth came the desire to develop fast and big.[28] Cities had to be modernized to serve their growing populations and to satisfy their sociocultural needs and newly acquired expensive tastes (which Beirut, mired in a nasty civil war between 1975 and the early 1990s, could no longer fulfill).

Dubai, a city-state with little oil income but with an unrestrained laissez-faire economy and aggressive pursuit of investments, led the way.[29] The entire city, its surrounding desert, and even its coastal water became the world's most phenomenal real estate laboratory, where the only check on architectural flights of fancy seems to be the ability of the designers to push the limits of size, height, eccentricity, and desire, as well as the willingness of their patrons to bankroll

Map showing the expansion of Dubai.

those fantasies. In this make-believe setting, the "utopian capitalist city," as Mike Davis called Dubai, seems to have been following a tacit design objective shared by the designers and their patrons to lure in more investors to a financial cyclical scheme that seems to have recovered most of its steam after the crash of 2008.[30]

Arab Cities and Identity Crisis

Following the model of Dubai, the Arabian Gulf cities underwent an unprecedented urban boom in the last twenty years. Gargantuan business parks and malls, towering luxury residences and hotels, showy entertainment complexes, and sophisticated museums and university campuses appeared in every Gulf city in an almost predictable and unified pattern of development.[31] In this economic scheme, design seems to function as branding instrument and spectacular wrapping for the new lavish enterprises, which broke all previous norms of size, form, function, fantasy, and, often, urban vision. Many were deliberately commissioned from international starchitects as a way to capture the glamour associated with these world-famous designers in the actual buildings they design. They are also meant to indirectly present the sensational envelope as the aspiration—and potentially the substitute—for the still unresolved tensions embedded in the monumentality, extravagance, and ambiguous social functions of the buildings themselves and the institutions they are supposed to house and serve.

The harsher effects of these extreme conditions of real estate capitalism, however, were felt in the older and poorer Arab cities that could not sustain this kind of financial, urban, or social extravaganza. As a result, they suffered a fading away of the civic qualities they had slowly acquired over the last two centuries, which were replaced by a market-driven system that split them into extremes.[32] On one end, the poor quarters were robbed of the last vestiges of civil life and turned into run-down village-like neighborhoods living by their own informal and traditional codes with no urban vision or authority, as can be observed in the districts of Imbaba, Bulaq al-Dakrur, and the Qarafa in Cairo, for instance, or in the district of Sadr City (formerly known as Ba'th City) in Baghdad, or on the southern and eastern ends of the Dhahiya in

Bulaq al-Dakrur, Cairo.

Beirut, now the domain of Hezbollah.[33] On the other end, the rich districts assumed a consumerist and globalized identity that has no local feel or sense of belonging, as in New Cairo and Qatamiyya in Cairo, the new Abdali Development in the heart of Amman, and the new residential areas around the Solidere megaproject in central Beirut.

This messy process fostered acute discrepancies in identity, ideology, social outlook, and wealth that came into the open with the popular upheavals of 2011 in several Arab countries. But the promising beginning of this so-called Arab Spring has withered away, and the unresolved problem of nationalism has degenerated into a cacophony of discordant social, sectarian, and ethnic groupings that share the same urban space and fight over the right to define and rule it.

1   William R. Polk, *The Arab World*, 2nd ed. (Cambridge, MA.: Harvard University Press, 1991), 67–92; Tarik Sabry, *Cultural Encounters in the Arab World: On Media, the Modern, and the Everyday* (London: I. B. Tauris, 2010), 1–42, 95–155.

2   Janet Abu-Lughod, "The Islamic City—Historic Myth, Islamic Essence, and Contemporary Relevance," *International Journal of Middle East Studies*, vol. 19, no. 2 (1987): 155–76; André Raymond, "Islamic City, Arab City: Orientalist Myths and Recent Views," *British Journal of Middle Eastern Studies* 21 (1994): 3–18.

3   On all colonial cities, with a focus on Algiers, see Zeynep Çelik, "New Approaches to the 'Non-Western' City," *Journal of the Society of Architectural Historians*, vol. 58, no. 3 (September 1999): 374–81. On Morocco, see Gwendolyn Wright, "Tradition in the Service of Modernity: Architecture and Urbanism in French Colonial Policy, 1900-1930," *Journal of Modern History*, vol. 59, no. 2 (June 1987): 291–316.

4   Janet Abu-Lughod, "Tale of Two Cities: The Origins of Modern Cairo," *Comparative Studies in Society and History*, vol. 7, no. 4 (1965): 429–57; Heba Farouk Ahmed, "Nineteenth-Century Cairo: A Dual City?" in *Making Cairo Medieval*, ed. Nezar AlSayyad, Irene A. Bierman, and Nasser Rabbat (Lanham, MD: Lexington Books, 2005), 143–72.

5   The Cairo Trilogy, *Bayn al Qasrayn*, *Qasr al Shawq*, and *al-Sukkariya*, completed in Arabic in 1957, is available in an English edition as *The Cairo Trilogy: Palace Walk, Palace of Desire, Sugar Street*, trans. William M. Hutchins et al. (New York: Everyman's Library, 2001).

6   On Morocco, see Gwendolyn Wright, *The Politics of Design in French Colonial Urbanism* (Chicago: University of Chicago Press, 1991), 85–160. On Libya, see Vittoria Capresi, "Architectural Transfer, Italian Colonial Architecture in Libya: 'Libyan Rationalism' and the Concept of 'Mediterraneity,' 1926–1942," in *Colonial Architecture and Urbanism in Africa: Intertwined and Contested Histories*, ed. Fassil Demissie (Burlington, VT: Ashgate, 2012), 33–66.

7   Paul Rabinow, "Governing Morocco: Modernity and Change," *International Journal of Urban and Regional Research* 10 (1989): 32–46; Hassan Radoine, "French Territoriality and Urbanism: General Lyautey and Architect Prost in Morocco (1912–1925)," in Demissie, *Colonial Architecture and Urbanism in Africa*, 11–32.

8   Michele Lamprakos, "Le Corbusier and Algiers: The Plan Obus as Colonial Urbanism," in *Forms of Dominance: On the Architecture and Urbanism of the Colonial Enterprise*, ed. Nezar AlSayyad (Aldershot, England: Avebury, 1992), 183–210; Jean-Pierre Giordani, "Le Plan-Obus, 1931–1932: Du sublime aux réalités," in *Le Corbusier, visions d'Alger*, ed. Jean-Lucien Bonillo (Paris: Fondation le Corbusier, Éditions de la Villette, 2012), 102–29.

9   Edmund Burke III, "A Comparative View of French Native Policy in Morocco and Syria, 1912–1925" *Middle Eastern Studies*, vol. 9, no. 2 (May 1973): 175-186; Vilma Hastaoglou-Martinidis, "Urban Aesthetics and National Identity: The Refashioning of Eastern Mediterranean Cities between 1900 and 1940," *Planning Perspectives* vol. 26, no. 2 (2011): 153–82; Eric Verdeil, "Michel Ecochard in Lebanon and Syria (1956–1968): The Spread of Modernism, the Building of the Independent States, and the Rise of Local Professionals of Planning," *Planning Perspectives*, vol. 27, no. 2 (2012): 249–66. On the British social and urban policies in Palestine and the consequent Israeli policies, see Daniel Monk, *An Aesthetic Occupation: The Immediacy of Architecture and the Palestine Conflict* (Durham, NC: Duke University Press, 2002), 99–127, and Sari Hanafi, "Spacio-cide: Colonial Politics, Invisibility, and Rezoning in Palestinian Territory," *Contemporary Arab Affairs*, vol. 2, no. 1 (January 2009): 106–21.

10   Christoph K. Neumann, "Ottoman Provincial Towns in the Eighteenth to the Nineteenth Centuries," in *The Empire in the City: Arab Provincial Capitals in the Late Ottoman Empire*, ed. Jens Hanssen, Thomas Philipp, and Stefan Weber (Würzburg: Ergon in Kommission, 2002), 131–44.

11   Charles Glass explains that he borrowed the title "tribes with flags" from Bashir. Charles Glass, *Tribes with Flags: A Dangerous Passage through the Chaos of the Middle East* (New York: Atlantic Monthly Press, 1990), 3. Keith D. Watenpaugh, *Being Modern in the Middle East: Revolution, Nationalism, Colonialism, and the Arab Middle Class* (Princeton, NJ: Princeton University Press, 2006), 1–31.

13   Arnold Hottinger, "How the Arab Bourgeoisie Lost Power," *Journal of Contemporary History*, vol. 3, no. 3 (July 1968): 111–28; Roger Owen, *State Power and Politics in the Making of the Modern Middle East* (London: Routledge, 2002), 1–22.

14   Owen, *State Power and Politics*, 198–221.

15   George Lenczowski, "Radical Regimes in Egypt, Syria, and Iraq: Some Comparative Observations on Ideologies and Practices," *Journal of Politics*, vol. 28, no. 1 (February 1966): 29–56.

16   Eugene L. Rogan, *The Arabs: A History* (New York: Basic Books, 2009), 277–318; Youssef M. Choueiri, *Arab Nationalism, a History: Nation and State in the Arab World* (Oxford:, England: Blackwell, 2000), 65–100.

17   Clement Henry Moore, "Authoritarian Politics in Unincorporated Society: The Case of Nasser's Egypt," *Comparative Politics*, vol. 6, no. 2 (January 1974): 193–218.

18   James M. Dickinson, "State and Economy in the Arab Middle East: Some Theoretical and Empirical Observations," *Arab Studies Quarterly*, vol. 5, no. 1 (Winter 1983): 22–50.

19   James Gelvin, "Modernity and Its Discontents: On the Durability of Nationalism in the Arab Middle East," *Nations and Nationalism*, vol. 5, no. 1 (Spring 1999): 71–89; Timothy Mitchell, "The Stage of Modernity," in *Questions of Modernity*, ed. Timothy Mitchell (Minneapolis: University of Minnesota Press, 2000), 1–34.

20   Gwendolyn Wright, "Global Ambition and Local Knowledge," in *Modernism and the Middle East: Architecture and Politics in the Twentieth Century*, ed. Sandy Isenstadt and Kishwar Rizvi (Seattle: University of Washington Press, 2008), 221–54.

21   Gehan Selim, "Instituting Order: The Limitations of Nasser's Post-Colonial Planning Visions for Cairo in the Case of the Indigenous Quarter of Bulaq (1952–1970)," *Planning Perspectives*, vol. 29, no. 1 (Spring 2014): 67–89.

22   Trevor J. LeGassick, "Some Recent War-Related Arabic Fiction," *Middle East Journal*, vol. 25, no. 4 (Autumn 1971): 491–505.

23   Relli Shechter, "From Effendi to Infitāhī? Consumerism and Its Malcontents in the Emergence of Egyptian Market Society," *British Journal of Middle Eastern Studies*, vol. 36, no. 1 (April 2009): 21–35; Clement H. Moore, "Money and Power: The Dilemma of the Egyptian Infitah," *Middle East Journal*, vol. 40, no. 4 (1986): 634–50.

24   Owen, *State Power and Politics*, 113–30; Eva Bellin, "The Robustness of Authoritarianism in the Middle East: Exceptionalism in Comparative Perspective," *Comparative Politics*, vol. 36, no. 2 (January 2004): 139–57. For an examination of the Syrian case, see Anja Zorob, "Reform without Adjustment: The Syrian Style of Economic Opening," in *The Arab Authoritarian Regime between Reform and Persistence*, ed. Henner Fuertig (Newcastle: Cambridge Scholars Publishing, 2007), 57–86.

25   Basheer K. Nijim, "Spatial Aspects of Demographic Change in the Arab World," in *The Middle East: From Transition to Development*, ed. Sami G. Hajjar (Leiden: Brill, 1985), 30–53; Valentine M. Moghadam, "Population Growth, Urbanization, and the Challenges of Unemployment," *Understanding the Contemporary Middle East*, ed. Jillian Schwedler, 4th ed. (Boulder, CO: Lynne Rienner Publishers, 2013), 287–314.

26   Janet Abu-Lughod, "Recent Migrations in the Arab World," in *Human Migration: Patterns and Policies*, ed. William H. McNeill and Ruth Adams (Bloomington, IN: Indiana University Press, 1978), 225–40.

27   Samia Mehrez, "From the *Hara* to the *'Imara*: Emerging Urban Metaphors in the Literary Production of Contemporary Cairo," in *Egypt's Culture Wars* (London: Routledge, 2008), 161–85, republished in *Cairo Contested: Governance, Urban Space, and Global Modernity*, ed. Diane Singerman (Cairo: American University in Cairo Press, 2009), 145–74.

28   The process is traced with ironic flair in Abdelrahman Munif, *Cities of Salt*, trans. Peter Theroux (New York: Vintage, 1987). Only the first three volumes of a quintet, gathered together under the Arabic title *Mudun al-Malh* (*Cities of Salt*) and published in Arabic between 1984 and 1989, are translated into English. The story follows the fate of a fictitious country, clearly modeled on Saudi Arabia, as the consequences of the oil discovery unfold over a half a century affecting everything. See Nelida Fuccaro, "Visions of the City: Urban Studies on the Gulf," *Middle East Studies Association Bulletin*, vol. 35, no. 2 (Winter 2001): 175–87.

29   Mike Davis, "Fear and Money in Dubai," *New Left Review* 41 (September–October 2006): 46–68.

30   Esra Akcan, "World, Open City?" *Architectural Design*, vol. 74, no. 6 (November, 2004): 98–104; Yasser Elsheshtawy, "Redrawing Boundaries: Dubai, the Emergence of a Global City," in *Planning the Middle East City: An Urban Kaleidoscope in a Globalizing World*, ed. Yasser Elsheshtawy (New York: Routledge, 2004), 169–99; Samer Bagaeen, "Brand Dubai: The Instant City; or, the Instantly Recognizable City," *International Planning Studies*, vol. 12, no. 2 (Summer 2007): 173–97.

31   Khaled Adham, "Rediscovering the Island: Doha's Urbanity from Pearls to Spectacle," in *The Evolving Arab City: Tradition, Modernity, and Urban Development*, ed. Yasser Elsheshtawy (New York: Routledge, 2008), 218–57; Sean Foley, *The Arab Gulf States: Beyond Oil and Islam* (Boulder, CO: Lynne Rienner Publishers, 2010), 144–52, 273–82; Miriam Cooke, *Tribal Modern: Branding New Nations in the Arab Gulf* (Berkeley: University of California Press, 2013), 77–98.

32   Hilary Silver, "Divided Cities in the Middle East," *City & Community*, vol. 9, no. 4 (December 2010): 345–57; Hassan-Uddin Khan, "Identity, Globalization, and the Contemporary Islamic City," in *The City in the Islamic World*, ed. Renata Holod, Attilio Petruccioli, and André Raymond (Leiden: Brill, 2008), 1035–62.

33   For an analysis of the Egyptian case, see Nabil 'Abd al-Fattah, "The Anarchy of Egyptian Legal System: Wearing Away the Legal and Political Modernity," in *Legal Pluralism in the Arab World*, ed. Baudouin Dupret, Maurits Berger, and Laila al-Zwaini (The Hague: Kluwer Law International, 1999), 159–71.

Teaching a Course on the Contemporary Arab City…for 5,700 People

MOHAMMAD AL-ASAD

Late in 2013, I was approached by Edraak, a project of Jordan's Queen Rania Foundation for Education and Development. Edraak was embarking on developing a series of what are known as massive open online courses (MOOCs) in Arabic on a variety of subjects. The word "massive" refers to the fact that these courses are intended to attract thousands of students. "Open" indicates that they are accessible to all, regardless of financial ability, because they are free. And, of course, these courses are offered online.

The course was on the Arab City, and one thing that was particularly striking was the students' perceptions of their role in the contemporary Arab city. Course participants have come from just about every country of the Arab world, including Arabs in diaspora. Most, if not all, of them have lived in an Arab City at least part of their lives. The subject of the contemporary Arab City is one that they have experienced intimately. They all have a strong interest—and one also would expect strong opinions—about it. In spite of this, I noticed an unexpected and surprising level of homogeneity in their research methodology. The students seemed to accept uncritically the discourse and narrative that official institutions, such as a municipal government or a ministry of information, provide about the various cities they wrote about.

I could not help but notice this acceptance, if not adoption, of the official line. Perhaps it predominated because official publications are readily available sources for the students, or because they had no other resources at their disposal, or even because the subject of urbanism was still new to many of them. I nonetheless found it concerning how almost none of the students ever referred to their personal engagement or the engagement of civic society groups such as neighborhood associations, for example, with the city. Even though they probably know their cities relatively well, may feel a strong sense of affinity to them, and likely have strong opinions regarding them, they still gave the impression that what the city was, what it is, and what it could be, in both its positive and negative manifestations, are the result of the proclamations, decisions, and actions of the relevant authorities, not the city residents. Moreover, those who chose to write their reports about the city of Dubai presented it as the realization not even of official bodies but of a specific person: its ruler, Sheikh Muhammad bin Rashid Al Maktoum. Needless to say, they all presented Dubai positively. This association of cities with official bodies—and in some cases with individual rulers—was the norm for all the reports written for the course.

One may attribute this rather passive view of the city to the exclusion of citizens and residents from decision-making processes. This is an expression of how the residents of cities in the Arab world have little, if any, say in how their cities are run. They are marginalized and disconnected from decision making and often are alienated from city government and civic life. This marginalization of course is intimately connected to the serious challenges Arab countries face regarding the development of participatory political systems. What surprised me, however, is that rather than showing any signs of resistance to such a state of affairs, the course participants seem to have normalized it, internalized it, and accepted it. Moreover, they seem to have abdicated their responsibility toward their cities to the state. Accordingly, they have come to believe that whatever happens to their city, both the good and the bad, is the responsibility of the state, and their role has been reduced to that of passive observers.

This marginalization and exclusion from the decision-making process is an issue I emphasized in the course. It also corresponds to the results of a study we carried out at the Center for the Study of the Built Environment in 2012 as part of a project on city management in Jordan.[1] We distributed a survey in which we asked participants if their municipality ever consulted them on any issues relating to the city. Of the over 300 survey participants, only 5 percent answered that it did. Of that 5 percent, most said that the municipality asked them about general services such as street paving, rodent problems, or garbage collection. Only three respondents (i.e., 0.01 percent) mentioned that their municipality consulted with them about issues of a more strategic nature, such as the future directions they feel their city should take.

More than 5,700 students had registered for the course. This is a relatively small enrollment for MOOCs, but it is overwhelming in comparison to the number of students that most of us have taught for any given traditional course. I should add that the engagement rate (i.e., those who watch any of the online lectures or carry out any of the homework) for MOOCs is relatively small. For this course, about 2,000 students showed a level of engagement, although it is difficult to quantify the exact nature of their engagement. The number of those who satisfactorily complete the requirements for MOOCs is even smaller. Only 254 completed this course, which is still sizable in comparison to conventional university classes. In order to fulfill the requirements, students had to listen to the online lectures, carry out readings, answer questions about the lectures and the readings, and write reports. Most students find this too much work for a free course that does not provide them any certified credit hours, particularly since many of them are employed and pursue the course outside their working hours. As a teaching platform, the MOOC can provide a superior medium in comparison to conventional classroom-based courses for delivering information to students, but I also should add that I find the MOOC platform an abysmal mechanism for interacting with students in comparison to classroom-based courses, unfortunately.

In preparing the course, I had to decide how to present the contemporary Arab City to a large and diverse audience within the span of a few weeks. This diversity of geography within the Arab world was paired with a diversity in background. Those 5,700 students represented a tremendous variety in terms of educational, professional, social, and cultural experience, and also in terms of age. In more traditional classroom settings, such variety is far less pronounced and a somewhat more homogeneous student body prevails, not only in terms of the students' backgrounds but also in terms of their expectations. Among other things, this means that the course participants did not share a general understanding of the city in terms of its physical components and its population. They did not identify the same factors that shape the built environment, nor did they have a set of generally agreed upon textual and visual sources to describe and analyze the city.

This pedagogical context raises questions: What is the city? And what it can be for the multiplicity of people who live in urban areas? One needs to consider that those who live in Arab cities define the lived reality of that space, and envision aspirations for what it can be, in different ways. Through this course, I encountered a range of differences and similarities in the understandings of the contemporary Arab city.

My assessment of this issue is based on the questions students posed online and on the three short reports they were required to submit. Participants were asked to select a city that they knew relatively well, preferably one they lived in, and to discuss its evolution over the past thirty years from three perspectives. The first report was about the demographic and geographic evolution of that city. The second report focused on its cultural heritage and contemporary cultural production as presented through cultural institutions and activities. The third and final report considered the city's political and administrative evolution over that period, concentrating on its political significance on the national, regional, and international levels; its administrative systems and institutions; and its infrastructure networks.

Many of the students emphasized a particular concern about or quality relating to the city they selected. Some expressed interest in issues relating to environmental sustainability. There were those who were concerned with the city as an object designed through a master plan rather than one that organically grows with time. Others reduced the city to iconic monuments, both historical and contemporary. For some, the city wasn't too interesting from the physical point of view. They instead viewed it primarily as a container for the memories of a glorious past, one usually connected to specific historical periods, events, figures, and dynasties. Some viewed it through a romanticized lens and discussed its unique, personal qualities. One student even mentioned that people can always distinguish the special taste of his city's water.

The marginalization of residents in the processes of city making is a problem that besets the Arab world. While many are aware of it, now is the time to think collaboratively and rigorously about how to change it. New forms of pedagogy, ones that bring together students across a range of social backgrounds and geographic locations, enable new modalities in seeing the city both as it is and as it could be.

1   Mohammad al-Asad and Sandra
Hiari, "City Management in Jordan:
Challenges Awaiting Solutions," translated from Arabic by Mohammad
al-Asad, Farah Tell, and Tooma Zaghloul
(Amman: Center for the Study of the
Built Environment, 2013), http://www.
csbe.org/activities/diwan-al-mimar/
city-management-in-jordan-challenges-
awaiting-solutions-report-english.

The Shekels of
Sheik Shakbut

Exporting the UAE: National Pavilions and the Manufacturing of Identity

YASSER ELSHESHTAWY

Kanat "hadithan" aktar min kauniha "hadatha"
("It was more of an accident than modernity"; a play on the
word "modernity" [*hadatha*], which in its verbal form can also
mean "event" or "incident" [*hadithan*])
—Noura Al Sayeh, 2014

In a 1963 article on Abu Dhabi and its newly discovered oil riches, *Life* magazine prominently displayed the emirate's ruler, Sheikh Shakhbut. Preceding the text is a full-page portrait of the sheikh standing on a Persian carpet holding a falcon. Next to him is a "a solid-gold model, worth $36,400, of an offshore oil derrick, gift of a grateful Anglo-French oil consortium."[1] In the back looms his seat of power, the White Fort, described in the same article as "made to measure for a movie about the French Foreign Legion." It is

Staged scenery for Sheikh Shakhbut's portrait.

the quintessential image of Arabia. Yet panning away from this portrait and looking at how this image was constructed we see a carefully staged tableau. Shakhbut is standing in the middle of the desert, with his props placed next to

Sheikh Shakhbut in a *Life* magazine pictorial standing in front of the White Fort, 1963.

him. The photographer is in control, observed by a curious group of onlookers; further in the back are the ruler's devoted citizens, observing the entire scene with curiosity.

Thus, an image is manufactured to communicate to outsiders a particular view of Arabia, instigated by Westerners and with the tacit approval of the ruler and his citizens. And it exposes the inherent contradictions in heritage and identity discourse and their implications in architectural representation. On the surface, the photograph aims to establish a sense of independence vis-à-vis a dominating expatriate population; at a regional level, Gulf countries seek to assert their presence in the midst of the traditional and established centers of culture. Yet in many cases it is more about a branding strategy. Images of exotic wealth were intended to attract investment and tourists through the adoption of generic cultural symbols. Such conflicting objectives are still evident in the construction of national pavilions in world expos and biennial exhibitions.

The United Arab Emirates has been at the forefront of such events since its participation as a still-not-formed nation in the 1970 World Expo in Osaka, where its pavilion was constructed in the shape of a traditional fort. Recognizing that there was no substantive built patrimony or a clear architectural heritage from which to draw references, a fort was the only model available. At more recent exhibitions, UAE pavilions have employed a seemingly more sophisticated imagery, relying on landscape references and indirect allusions to tradition and history. Such depictions are framed through the notion of modernity in the form of exhibits and displays that demonstrate progress. These pavilions are conceptualized, constructed, built, and curated by outsiders. This raises the question of whose identity is being represented. Who are the various stakeholders involved in portraying the nation's cultural achievements to the world? What right do those living outside those countries have in selecting what constitutes components of local culture?

Taking these questions as a starting point, this essay discusses my own involvement with the UAE National Pavilion at the 2014 Venice Architecture Biennale. My role entailed supplying the organizers with material for display (graphic representations) as well as taking part in a series of filmed interviews and public talks. I was thus able to observe, and participate in, the process that led to the final product. The various meetings, discussions, and collaborations of multiple transnational teams with local players reveal a complex mosaic of interactions whereby heritage, identity, and cultural representation are manipulated to cater to a global, multicultural audience.

Much has been written about world's fairs and the extent to which they have shaped the imaginary of Western audiences in the nineteenth century, bringing to their doorsteps carefully staged simulations of exotic places.[2] Such depictions were typically cast through a framework of cultural representation, with emphasizing the inherent dominance and hegemony in the fair. Zeynep Çelik has observed that "world's fairs were idealized platforms where cultures could be encapsulated visually." In her analysis she pays particular attention to the role of architecture in evoking certain representations, which in many instances led to a "redefinition" of local cultures. Thus, "cultural characteristics of the represented culture were determined by the colonizing culture; the outcome was to empower the latter."[3]

In order to facilitate such visions, pavilions were designed to replicate certain features from their countries. The Egyptian pavilion in the 1889 Paris Exposition Universelle, for example, included a Cairene traditional street, carefully reconstructed in all its details, complete with animals and actors dressed as ordinary Egyptians. The effect sometimes exceeded that of the original, with some visitors lamenting that what they had seen in Egypt did not match up to the "reality" they had seen in Paris.

In using the Cairo display as a case study, Çelik (alongside other scholars like Timothy Mitchell) replicates the Orientalist tendency to a certain degree by viewing these events primarily through the lens of colonial domination and the outside manipulation of cultural symbols. In a similar manner, Tim Winter observed of the Shanghai Expo that "one of the defining characteristics of imperialist fairs in Europe and the United States was the attribution of the self as enlightened modern through the presentation of others as primitive, exotic, or less than civilized."[4] Yet aside from these cultural considerations, the commercial factor was, and continues to be, one of the main driving forces behind these events. From the first world's fair, for which London's famed Crystal Palace was designed, trade governed both the logic and content of the exhibition. As Mitchell notes, the fairs were "sites of pilgrimage to the commodity fetish."[5] The question then becomes, how does the specific design of pavilions respond to this desire to promote and to sell (i.e., brand) a country? In the nineteenth century, the answer was, by copying features of a country's past or by evoking certain lost traditions. The pavilion thus was a site of nostalgia, through which a country asserted its place on the world stage. Yet from the twentieth century onward, modernity, and by extension technology, dominated the visual lexicon of the fairs, now jockeying grounds for industrial prominence. Not all exhibitions made this shift from nostalgia to modernity. Arab nations in particular did not escape the constraints of heritage, and the perpetuation of cultural stereotypes.

Arab nations, to a large degree, have focused their pavilions on purely representational matters. They were (and remain) a visualization of Orientalist fantasies, composed of arches and structures evoking the deserts of Arabia. In a fascinating 1970 article titled "The Arabs at Osaka," the writer Paul Hoye

Pavilions of Arab nations at Expo '70. Clockwise from top left: Kuwait, Saudi Arabia, Abu Dhabi, Algeria.

described some of these pavilions. His depiction relates how many of these structures were designed by Westerners, who, having little knowledge of the respective countries, resorted to recycling stereotypes. For instance, the Saudi pavilion was designed by two Japanese firms that—recognizing their lack

Exporting the UAE

of historical and cultural knowledge—"dispatched two teams of researchers to Saudi Arabia to ground themselves in Islamic thinking, compile data and accumulate the materials they would need to capture, in a meager 4,800 square feet, the flavor of a country in which dynamic social changes and an ancient religious code go hand in hand." The results were not as exciting, according to Hoye, who observed that "the Saudi pavilion with chaste white arches, green domes and pale golden panels, seems inappropriately austere." The Kuwaiti pavilion, designed by an Egyptian architect was composed of a "a low, square structure with 82 fiber glass domes painted gold, 10 tiled panels in green and gold depicting life in Kuwait, and a pool in which floats a model of a pearling dhow." Inside the pavilion, "hostesses in pale orange miniskirts and capes guide the crowds through a one-story series of exhibits." The only exception to this historical approach was the Paris-designed Algerian pavilion, fashioned "in handsome, free-form stucco, and including a cool, chic French restaurant and a swift escalator that lifts the visitors from the ground floor to a theater."[6]

Such a focus on historicity, a perpetuation of clichéd images, was particularly prevalent among the newly emerging nations of the Gulf. Lacking a substantive urban heritage to draw from, they had to engage in a process of cultural invention. This of course was not uniformly the case. For instance, the Kuwaiti pavilion in the 1992 Seville Expo was designed by the architect and structural engineer Santiago Calatrava, and comprises abstract moving elements enveloping an exhibition space.

REPRESENTING THE UAE

The United Arab Emirates' involvement in world's fairs began in Osaka at Expo '70. Unlike other participants, however, the UAE was not yet formally recognized as a country (that would happen a year later). Its participation at the expo was under the flag of Abu Dhabi. The pavilion's architect was Abdul Rahman Makhlouf, an Egyptian, Abu Dhabi–based architect and city planner. His pavilion resembled a fortress, drawing on the square crenelated parapets and tall cylindrical towers associated with Arabian Gulf mud-brick forts.[7]

The commissioner general pronounced the pavilion a "symbol of the bright future awaiting Islam and the Arab world."[8] Yet the display had nothing to do with the future. Historical photographs obtained from the Aramco archive reveal the glaring contrast between the high-tech displays, pavilions, and monorails and the representation of an ancient structure surrounded by sand and palm trees.

One of the participants in this event, Rashid Abdullah al-Nuaimi, provided an in-depth account. He noted that Sheikh Zayed had to convince the British, who were formerly in control of the emirate, to allow Abu Dhabi's participation. His reminiscences were particularly poignant as they highlighted the limited development in Abu Dhabi: "They had developments, history, sciences—we barely had rudimentary primary schools." He explained the concept behind the pavilion: "We kept thinking of something that is an example of our culture and development but again we only had forts and, at the time, we had just come out with a new concept, the *barajils* (wind towers)." Ultimately, they settled on Al Ain's Al Jahili fort.[9] Archival photographs show a pristine, sanitized image of a fort, roughly modeled on its original counterpart.

Abu Dhabi in the late 1960s and early 1970s was in the midst of a massive construction boom that transformed a small settlement into a modern city. Up until 1966 it remained in a remarkable state of underdevelopment, even though oil had been discovered in 1962. With the ascension of Sheikh Zayed as ruler in 1966, development began in earnest. A satellite image from the late 1960s shows roads being dug, an expanded waterfront, and remnants of older settlements. In 1970, the city was still in a state of rapid change, with all traces of its past on their way to being wiped out—with the exception of the fort. The pavilion was thus an apt reflection of the state of affairs at the time. A tradition and a culture were still being developed to be more in line with modern and contemporary expectations.

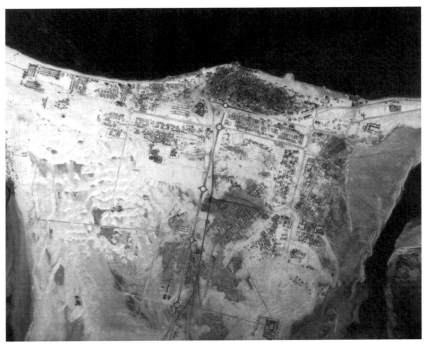

Satellite image of Abu Dhabi, 1969.

Exporting the UAE

The UAE's engagement with expos continued beyond Osaka, with the image of the fort used extensively. In the Hannover 2000 Expo, for example, whose main theme was "sustainability," many of the participating countries designed their pavilions accordingly. Yet the UAE recycled the fort image again, this time larger in size and an amalgamation of a variety of forts, including Al Jahili. The architect was Alain Durand-Henriot, a UAE-based consultancy in Abu Dhabi, in collaboration with the German firm Obermeyer Planen & Beraten. For the 2010 Shanghai Expo, a different formal approach was used. The pavilion, designed by Foster + Partners was—seemingly—a radical departure from previous incarnations. Dominated by a sweeping curvilinear roof structure, the form drew inspiration from "vast rolling sand dunes." The changing light and colors of the desert were further evoked in the building's reflective "skin of gold-coloured stainless steel," according to the architects.[10]

The following expo took place in Milan in 2015, and one would perhaps have expected a different conceptual approach. However, Foster + Partners were selected again for the design of pavilion. Their approach this time was inspired by such elements as a traditional desert city, courtyards, the textures of sand dunes, and irrigation aqueducts (or *falajs*). This inspiration was turned into a contemporary expression. Their response to the expo theme, "feeding the planet," was to integrate a variety of dining options exploring modern Emirati food. So we have, on the face of it, a different approach, one based loosely on the natural landscape of the UAE. But does this approach represent a changing paradigm, or does it continue to summarize a culture and a people through a few select symbols? It used to be the fort; now it is the desert.

Moreover, the architectural design is not the only element used in marketing and displaying the pavilion. In fact, there are several multinational consultancies involved that are responsible for theming and packaging both the structure and the event. This entails producing slick promotional videos, populated by stand-in Arabs and others, as well as curating the exhibition. Rather than representing some sort of authentic vision or evoking certain universal values, such approaches aim at packaging a country. Using a few select symbols, as well as crafting an imagined identity, the objective is to cater to tourists and the business community. The involvement of multinational players further disengages such displays from their home country. In that sense they are no different from the Disneyesque copying of a fort to represent Arabia or the *Life* magazine photographer staging a scene.

Overall, though, there clearly has been a change in the concept of the pavilion designs, particularly in the last two expos. And placed within the larger context of such world events, and given the UAE's late participation, the change is quite remarkable.

The UAE Pavilion at the Venice Architecture Biennale, 2014.

CASE STUDY: VENICE BIENNALE

In 2014, the UAE was invited for the first time to participate in the Venice Architecture Biennale. The country was allotted a space inside the Arsenale—a long hall once used for shipbuilding—to construct a national pavilion. Like expos past, the Biennale offered an opportunity to represent the UAE, and the curatorial decisions that governed the exhibit reflect a notion of identity comparable to those twentieth-century world's fairs. The story of that pavilion speaks to varying notions of identity, the construction of traditions, and persistence of certain thematic articulations present in earlier expos and fairs.

The pavilion was commissioned by the Abu Dhabi–based Salama bint Hamdan Al Nahyan Foundation, a philanthropic organization engaged in "initiatives in the areas of education; arts, culture, heritage; and health."[11] A UAE-based curatorial team was tasked with overseeing the content to be displayed, as well the exhibition design, which was done in collaboration with Milk Train, an Italian consultancy composed of architects, historians, and urban designers. The project team claimed not to "believe in any constraints or limitations given by cultural ideologies or aesthetics."[12] Previous projects by this collaborative group include an exhibition design for "Made in Italy" taking place at the lavish Emirates Palace Hotel in Abu Dhabi.

The design of the pavilion or display space evokes elements of traditional architecture: courtyards, screens, veils, and *arish* (a traditional material made of woven palm leaves). Indeed, early residences along the Gulf coast display some of these elements. According to the curator, "The installation design allows entry behind privacy screens and boundary walls into an inner space evocative of a courtyard, yet functioning as an archive. The play of shadows that trace back to woven patterns of *arish* resonates with the ephemerality of memory. The exhibition encourages audience participation through opening the drawers of the archive."[13]

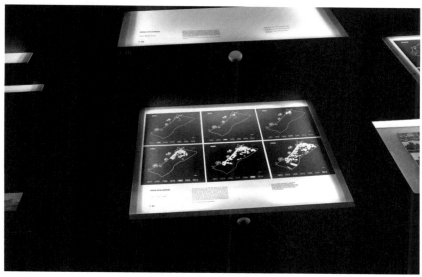

Archive drawers at the UAE pavilion.

The exhibit content is diverse—including drawings, photographs, graphics, models, personal photographs, postcards, and physical mementos—and focuses on the period of the 1970s–80s, the entry of the newly formed UAE into the modern age. Architecture from the 1970s receives particular attention, given its partial (and continuous) dismantlement due to rapid urbanization. All these are displayed in drawers that can be opened by visitors, building on the archive metaphor. Permeating the entire pavilion is a sense of nostalgia and loss. Much has been said about the event itself, critically dealing with the notion of modernity as articulated by the curator and responding to national pavilions that engaged in a kind of subversive treatment of the subject. The UAE pavilion was generally well received, although some criticized the lack of "critical engagement" with the subject. According to Farah al-Nakib, one of the contributors to the Kuwaiti pavilion, the UAE entry "is an archival display of the United Arab Emirates' architectural and urban development, with little critical assessment of this development."[14] By physically expressing the idea of an archive, consisting of drawers that can be opened and closed, the exhibit aims first and foremost at documenting existing and vanished buildings. Given the relatively young age of the UAE and the complete absence of any previous efforts at documenting the region's urban and architectural heritage, such an approach is understandable, yet it may lead to nostalgia and a fetishization of displayed objects.

Bahrain Pavilion at the Venice Architecture Biennale, 2014.

My own involvement came in two forms. First, I was asked to prepare figure-ground diagrams, which showed the urban growth of the UAE's main urban centers: Abu Dhabi, Dubai, and Sharjah. Second, I participated in a filmed conversation with an urban planner, a long-time resident and civil engineer, and an architect. The discussion centered on the role of infrastructure, the impact of political leadership, and other issues on the urbanization of Dubai and Abu Dhabi.

From the outset it was clear that the curatorial team was interested in engaging a wide segment of UAE society. Thus, numerous universities were involved, and the participation of students was particularly encouraged. The focus was on documenting, taking stock, and archiving. Clearly there were many other issues and considerations—such as lighting and material—that drove the concept, and indeed no decision was ever taken and finalized without getting back to the Sheikha Salama Foundation and its chairperson. Significantly though, the installation, unlike the Kuwaiti pavilion, for example, which had a much more participatory feel, was treated as a precious object that needed to remain true to an "initial vision." Any ad hoc elements that may have made the exhibit more dynamic and engaging were thus promptly dismissed (the Korean pavilion, which won the Golden Lion award, was a perfect example for the sheer sense of exuberance used in their display). The end product is elegant in its form and purity, but there remained a lack of spatial articulation, an inadequately developed experience that could have expressed the UAE's engagement with modernity.

This becomes particularly evident if one looks at the Kuwait and Bahrain pavilions, located in close proximity to the UAE's installation, both of which moved beyond the more celebratory depiction of the UAE. (The Arab world was also represented by Egypt, but despite having its own dedicated building, the Egyptian entry was comparatively incoherent.)[15] Bahrain's entry was designed and curated by two leading Lebanese architects and academics, Bernard Khoury and George Arbid. Rather than simply representing Bahrain, it aimed at larger themes—a "polyphonic history of pan-Arab modernism," in the words of one critic.[16] Spatially, it is perhaps the most interesting of all Arab contributions. A circular enclosure is dominated by a table, on which one can find a map of the Arab world with markers depicting modernist buildings from the twentieth century. Looking up, one sees a continuous video loop of a narrator who recites slogans that evoke nationalism. The surrounding bookshelves contain copies of a book in which these buildings are meticulously catalogued according to country (in the case of the Gulf, they are all lumped together, with the exception of Bahrain).[17] The book features photographs and drawings from the Beirut-based Arab Center for Architecture. The entry is curious, given that Bahrain won the Golden Lion in the previous Biennale. For that pavilion, an entire fisherman's hut was transported to Venice, to communicate displacement, alienation, and the loss of a traditional way of life. It was a truly local theme that stands in contradiction to the pan-Arab orientation of its more recent entry. In its 2014 entry, the pervasive sentiment seems to be loss, or "forgotten histories," a popular notion in the Arab world.

Kuwait Pavilion at the Venice Architecture Biennale, 2014.

The Kuwaiti pavilion was based on a restaging of the opening of the Kuwait National Museum, a building designed by the French architect Michel Ecochard in 1983. Mostly composed of large photographs displayed on walls and oversized detailing of roofs and columns, there is not much else. As Farah al-Nakib, a historian and contributor to the pavilion, points out, it is "a pleasantly serene space," but "a minimalistic approach can certainly be effective, but not to the point of emptiness." Moreover, "the pavilion recreated the spectacle of Kuwait's modernity without really saying much about it."[18] What truly distinguishes the Kuwaiti pavilion, according to al-Nakib, is the team responsible for its design and execution, a "hybrid team, consisting of twenty-three Kuwaitis and non-Kuwaitis of mixed backgrounds, reflecting the cosmopolitanism that the country's modern era was so famous for." The pavilion catalogue has the feel of a research report, documenting opinions and viewpoints and displaying archival images and drawings. The Bahraini pamphlet takes a similar approach. In terms of production, they stand in stark contrast to the UAE book, which is of a highly polished quality (designed by a local graphic design team known for the production of slick architectural magazines) but does not have that imperfect sense of incompleteness.

Avinash Rajagopal provides a thoughtful critique of the 2014 Biennale and the extent to which national pavilions have subverted Rem Koolhaas's thesis that "architectures that were once specific and local have become interchangeable and global." He thus questions the sort of thinking that has permeated architectural history, namely the North gifting modernism to the South. Drawing a distinction contrasting "Modernism, an architectural style, with modernity, a way of life," he points out the various ways specific countries have aimed to show that their particular versions of modernity contradict modernism. In his telling, the whole notion of the loss of local architecture is a kind of Western-induced concept, smacking of a form of "hipster joy" that is perhaps motivated by "the desire of European and American architects to continue to build mega projects on other continents."[19] Sarah Goldhagen expressed similar views in the *New Republic*, arguing that "modernism was never a style. It was a cultural, political, and social practice: the practice of making buildings suited to certain exigencies of life in a rapidly changing and developing world."[20]

Indeed, making a distinction between the stylistic components of modernism and the extent to which it also absorbed a social and cultural project forms a significant component of both the Kuwaiti and Bahraini pavilions. Thus, the loss of this social agenda in favor of pastiche approaches are decried by the avant-garde Lebanese architect Bernard Khoury, one of the curators of the Bahraini pavilion. He argues that "the exhaustion of the modernist project in the Arab world, [voided] it out from its initial agenda…bringing forward ostentatious images of a blindly imported and sometimes baseless modernity." His cocurator George Arbid highlights the fact that tradition is more or less a "compilation of modernisms over time."[21]

Noura Al Sayeh, a Bahraini cultural representative for the pavilion, provides a fascinating historical context in a highly provocative essay titled "Modernity, Miniskirts, and Cladding in Manama." Recalling "a fleeting moment of apparent and extroverted modernity" where women wearing miniskirts were posing in front of a modernist building, designed in a style that was modern but "responded to the climatic specificities of its location." Yet the moment passed, and that apparent conflation between lifestyle and modernity disappeared. Thus, modernity became more about skyscrapers marking the city's skyline. Significantly, modernism "was mostly assimilated as a stylistic movement rather than as a political project; never completely absorbed and only partially consumed." The Arabic translation of this last statement is telling: "Kanat 'hadithan' aktar min kauniha 'hadatha'": "it was more of an accident [*hadithan*] than modernity [*hadatha*]"; the terms are similar phonetically.[22] Farah Al Nakib, from the Kuwaiti pavilion, constructs a similar narrative. She also notes how Kuwait's encounter with modernity led it to have one of the best education systems in the region, along with a progressive, creative culture in which "women were burning their abayas to demand equality, when local arts, music, and theater were thriving, and when Kuwait's democratic institutions were established." Also, making a distinction between formal consideration of buildings and their social role, she argues, is not "about the actual spaces, nor about fetishizing the past as we do with heritage sites. It is about remembering what those spaces once stood for, and what they signify about us as a society."[23]

It is this last point, fetishizing the past, that is important in assessing the UAE pavilion. Unlike its counterparts, it did not engage in a critical assessment with its modernist past. Nor was it coupled with a social project, showing how modernism changed people's lives. Rather, it was about celebrating achievements, listing iconic buildings and structures. The theme of loss permeates every component of the exhibition. This may not be surprising. It is, after all, the country's first participation in such an event; its encounter with modernity came at a much later stage than Kuwait and Bahrain, and as such it was mostly about taking stock of what exists. A valuable effort in and of itself, given that a few years ago modernist buildings were not considered worthy of preservation or even discussion. Now, however, such efforts abound: Abu Dhabi Tourism & Culture Authority (TCA)'s database of modernist buildings; the Abu Dhabi architectural guide, produced by Pascal Menoret and his students at NYU Abu Dhabi; and, of course, curator of the UAE pavilion Michelle Bambling's initiative "Lest We Forget," developed with her students at Zayed University. In a similar manner, I have developed the UAE Modern initiative, which looks at modernist architecture in cities beyond Abu Dhabi and Dubai. These initiatives respond to a growing awareness about the importance of memory in the country, yet the discourses that gave rise to them may lead to undesired results.

THE PITFALLS OF NOSTALGIA

> We turn to memory for comfort. But what comfort is to be had
> from memories of the twentieth century?
> —Andreas Huyssen, *Present Pasts: Urban Palimpsests and the
> Politics of Memory*, 2003

My argument about the UAE's self-representation in the international sites of world's fairs, expos, and biennials has centered on the notion that by evoking traditional symbols, landscape features, and perceived or imagined heritage, these interventions have played into a sense of loss, a pervasive sentiment in the Arab world.[24] That idea of a sense of loss is based on a perception that due to rapid urbanization, traditions and history are "lost." It thus is the duty of the country's "enlightened"—both outsiders and insiders—to safeguard these treasures and ensure that their memory is preserved or that the few remaining traces are protected from demolition.

Such a pervasive sense of loss is a popular sentiment in many parts of the world. Indeed, postmodern theorist Andreas Huyssen notes that there has been an "explosion of memory discourses at the end of the twentieth century."[25] Others argue that this is a form of "invention of tradition," a psychological device through which some aspects of the past are rejected to "validate the new, but sometimes also [to retain] the past as 'other' as a continuing proof of the superiority of the new."[26] Thus, a deep dissatisfaction with the present prompts a kind of collective effort to reminisce about the past. Yet there is a danger that this can lead to fetishization, as noted above—exaggerating the significance of the fort, mythologizing the desert landscape, or celebrating the gimmicky application of an irrigation system.

Another important dimension here is the complicit role of experts—such as historians and conservationists—in furthering this vision. Huyssen observes how historiography can serve as a tool of domination and perpetuate ideologies. The historian establishes a form of authorship through listing, indexing, documenting, and archiving—laying claim, for instance, to the body of modernist architecture produced in a certain timeframe. Architectural experts invoke their knowledge of architectural history to freely plunder forms and details from the region's past and reconstitute them in a different context.

In the case of cities, memories and temporality are beginning to invade the spaces of neutral modernism. Yet there is a danger here, as Huyssen correctly points out, that we may not be able to distinguish between a mythic past (one that we are imagining) and a real past (what was actually there): "The strong marks of present space merge in the imaginary with traces of the past, erasures, losses, and heterotopias."[27] For longtime residents in the transient cities of the Gulf, evoking such nostalgic recollections may act as a form of resistance to obsolescence and disappearance. Clinging to any kind of remnant of the past becomes an all-pervasive effort. It is thus significant that one should distinguish between "usable pasts and disposable pasts." And as Huyssen reminds us, it "is time to remember the future, rather than simply to worry about the future of memory."[28] If such advice is not heeded, cities run the danger of becoming a fossilized version of their past, their citizenry disengaged from their own spaces, leading to alienation, dissatisfaction, and exclusion.

1   Timothy Green, "'O Long of Life' Drinks Camel Link and Runs on Oil," *Life,* vol. 54, no. 8 (May 1963): 49–61.

2   Joy Hendry, *The Orient Strikes Back: A Global View of Cultural Display* (Oxford, England: Berg, 2000); Allan Pred, "Spectacular Articulations of Modernity: The Stockholm Exhibition of 1897," *Geografiska Annaler,* Series B: Human Geography vol. 73, no. 1 (1991): 45–84; Robert W. Rydell, *World of Fairs: The Century-of-Progress Expositions* (Chicago: University of Chicago Press, 1993); Robert W. Rydell, Nancy E. Gwinn, and James Burkhart Gilbert, *Fair Representations: World's Fairs and the Modern World,* (Amsterdam: VU University Press, 1994).

3   Zeynep Çelik, *Displaying the Orient: Architecture of Islam at Nineteenth-Century World's Fairs* (Berkeley: University of California Press, 1992), 190.

4   Tim Winter, "Cultural Diplomacy, Cosmopolitanism and Global Hierarchy at the Shanghai Expo," *Space and Culture,* vol.18, no. 1 (February 2015): 41.

5   Timothy Mitchell, "The World as Exhibition," *Comparative Studies in Society and History,* vol. 31, no. 2 (April 1988): 18.

6   Paul F. Hoye, "The Arabs at Osaka," *Saudi Aramco World,* vol. 2, no.4 (July-August 1970): 32. The two Japanese firms involved in the Saudi pavilion were Kawashima Architectural Design Office and Dai Nippon Printing, a decorating firm.

7   Hoye, "The Arabs at Osaka," 32.

8   Hoye, "The Arabs at Osaka," 34.

9   Shireena Al Nowais, "A Look Back at the UAE's First Foreign Pavilion at Expo '70 in Japan," *National,* April 27, 2014.

10   "UAE Pavilion Shanghai Expo 2010," Foster + Partners website, http://www.fosterandpartners.com/projects/uae-pavilion-shanghai-expo-2010.

11   Salama bint Hamdan Al Nahyan Foundation, http://www.shf.ae/en. Its founder and patron is Salama bint Hamdan Al Nahyan, a member of Abu Dhabi's royal family, whose aim is "supporting emerging Emirati and Arab artists from the earliest stages of their development and providing them with the support and opportunities that will enable them to fulfill their potential." Participation in the Biennale was further supported by the Ministry of Culture, Youth, and Community Development. The curator tasked with developing the vision and overseeing the exhibition design was Michelle Bambling, an American expatriate resident of the UAE and an art historian. Assisting her was a curatorial team, which included architects Marco Sosa from El Salvador and Adina Hempel from Germany. Milk Train, an Italian consultancy specializing in the design of display spaces, translated the "curatorial vision into the exhibition design."

12   "About," Milk Train website, milktrain.eu/pages/about.html.

13   Michelle Bambling, "Lest We Forget: Structures of Memory in the UAE," in *National Pavilion of the UAE, Catalogue* (Abu Dhabi: Salama bint Hamdan Al Nahyan Foundation, 2014), 22.

14   Farah al-Nakib, "Understanding Modernity: A Review of the Kuwait Pavilion at the Venice Biennale," *Jadaliyya,* September 17, 2014, www.jadaliyya.com/pages/index/19265/understanding-modernity_a-review-of-the-kuwait-pavn.

15   Egypt's display was a winning entry in a competition that had some initial promise, but, due to lack of funds, inexperience of the designers, and the general turmoil following the January 2011 revolution, resulted in a space that appears remarkably undeveloped. The installation comprised two darkened corridors separated by a wall. Buildings from the twentieth century are projected on one side; the other displays Cairo's "chaos."

16   Avinash Rajagopal, "The Conflict between the Global North and South at the 2014 Venice Biennale," *ArchDaily,* August 31, 2014, www.archdaily.com/542644/the-conflict-between-the-global-north-and-south-at-the-2014-venice-biennale.

17   Most commissioned articles for the Bahrain catalogue were of high quality, with the exception of the Gulf piece, which contained generalized and generic statements, utterly ignoring any local differences and instead perpetuating outdated stereotypes and imagery. For example, it noted that street widths in "Islamic" cities were determined to allow passage of a donkey. This was actually written in reference to cities in the Gulf.

18   Al-Nakib, "Understanding Modernity."

19   Rajagopal, "The Conflict between the Global North and South at the 2014 Venice Biennale."

20   Sarah Williams Goldhagen, "The Great Architect Rebellion of 2014," *New Republic*, August 29, 2014, www.newrepublic.com/article/119202/architectures-rebellion-2014-venice-biennale.

21   George Arbid ed., *Fundamentalists and Other Arab Modernisms* (Manama, Bahrain: Ministry of Culture, 2014).

22   Noura Al Sayeh, "Modernity, Miniskirts and Cladding in Manama," in Arbid, *Fundamentalists and Other Arab Modernisms*.

23   Al-Nakib, "Understanding Modernity."

24   Yasser Elsheshtawy, "The Middle East City: Moving Beyond the Narrative of Loss," in *Planning Middle Eastern Cities: An Urban Kaleidoscope in a Globalizing World*, ed. Yasser Elsheshtawy (London: Routledge, 2004), 1–21.

25   Andreas Huyssen, *Present Pasts: Urban Palimpsests and the Politics of Memory* (Palo Alto, CA: Stanford University Press, 2003).

26   Richard Dennis, *Cities in Modernity: Representations and Productions of Metropolitan Space*, 1840–1930, Cambridge Studies in Historical Geography (Cambridge, England: Cambridge University Press, 2008).

27   Huyssen, *Present Pasts*, 7.

28   Huyssen, *Present Pasts*, 29.

Architects as Migrants

GWENDOLYN WRIGHT

Let me begin with Edward Said, who spoke of scholars as migrants. First, let's ask how architects are like scholars and how we're different. (We could also think more broadly about urban designers and historic preservationists.) Second, let's explore more fully the positive and negative implications of the recurring references to architects as transient "migrants" or "nomads," peripatetic as they go from place to place for a job, a visit, or other reasons. Do we move about like Bedouins, who know a great deal about the terrain, or like foreigners, who must learn about a place and its culture?

The term "peripatetic" derives from *peripatētikos*, referring to Aristotle's practice of continually walking to and fro while teaching. Travel is still valued as a way to learn from new sites and experiences, breaking out of old habits and ways of thinking. Strangers may notice qualities that locals don't see, whether because of overfamiliarity or simply being bogged down in the myriad details of specialized knowledge.

At the same time, like other outside observers, architects who come from elsewhere can miss truths that are conspicuous to local people. All too often they presume that the locals are unsophisticated, unable to comprehend the world at a distance or even the complexity of what is around them. This attitude looks back to the colonial era. When French and British scholars formulated a unified notion of the Arab City in the 1920s, they eschewed any input from indigenous scholars, architects, and artists. In much the same way, colonial architects of the era, intrigued by the idea of "hybrid" forms that were simultaneously modern and situated in a locale, insisted that only they had the ability to cross-breed.

Prejudice continued after World War II despite the demise of colonialism and the rise of global modernism in economics, social life, political policy, and architecture. Architects considered modernism to be a "gift" they would bestow on the rest of the world. Even quite recently, those who studied architecture at local schools were chided for merely "imitating" Western ideas or copying traditional designs, derivative and thus incapable of innovation.

Fortunately these attitudes are changing. We recognize that both world travelers and local architects, including those in Arab cities, can be innovate, yet both can also fall prey to a set of ubiquitous generic images—which includes the very idea of the Arab City. The Arab world remains diverse and often contentious. Radically different human experiences based on class, gender, urban or rural upbringing, or one's confessional group or secular convictions, as well as many other factors, affect every individual. If I am wary of idealizing pan-Arabism, I'll take up a patently neocolonial example: Skidmore, Owings & Merrill (SOM)'s 1978 pamphlet "Urban Design Middle East: A Primer for Development." Echoing colonial-era publications, it brazenly contended there had been no significant advances in Arab design for over two and a half centuries. This assertion in turn allowed SOM's architects to establish a set of formal typologies drawn from the entire Islamic world, from Isfahan to Seville to Mughal India, combining formal elements as they wished, even from far disparate places.

Both Western and Arab architects have long been immigrants, settling in new places. They carry with them certain memories and imaginaries about their past that inevitably affect what they see in the present and how they imagine new projects. Their lives may be defined by neighborhoods as much as by particular cities or nations. Unlike migrants, immigrants will always be between places, and likewise between the past and the present, seeking continuities that will give them some reassurance. The issues we're exploring here focus on yet extend beyond Arab cities. The first concerns the clients who invite or hire an architect. The richest and most conspicuous of these want architecture that captures specific assets and ineluctable qualities: wealth, cosmopolitan taste, political power, and stable social relations in their cities and enclaves. Although architects often talk about progressive social change, and they certainly encourage aesthetic innovation, clients in Arab cities tend to be hostile about any break in the established social order. While this attitude typically correlates with traditional architectural forms, modernism can also fit the bill, especially if it involves grandiose projects by well-known foreign designers, projects that reinforce the status quo and the power of the elite.

Even so, the trajectories have often been ambiguous rather than simply oppositional. The end of colonial domination saw major Western architects invited to the Middle East (as to other parts of the Third World) for expensive, extravagant architectural projects meant to embody independence and excitement about the future. There were other influences as well, including major commissions by Japanese architects, notably Kenzō Tange, who designed buildings and entire urban plans in Islamic countries from Saudi Arabia to Pakistan, and later Nigeria.

These issues of representation raise several questions addressed in this publication. The first looks at how architects analyze a place and generate the gist of a design. Let's start by asking who might take an architect around a city, helping him or her get a sense of the place. This guide will typically be either a local architect or some kind of official employed by the client. We should heed anthropologists who warn that every informant only gives a partial truth and may even tell lies. In any case, architects tend to take in a place quickly, visually and intuitively, usually without much close study. Some design without so much as visiting a site, or at most spending a day or even just an afternoon there. They believe in their distinctive and immediate ability to intuit how a particular place works, how the people interact, the meanings of history and possibilities for the future. Such intuition doesn't need confirmation, and it's rarely investigated, much less questioned.

For an alternative, let's turn to John Dewey, the pragmatist philosopher and professor of education at Columbia University. In 1916, Dewey presented his idea of "the constituted community" as an ongoing and expanding forum for debate. Acknowledging that there is usually some cohesion within a group, including architects, who can talk among themselves about ideas they share, Dewey encouraged professionals and public officials to keep expanding not just the particular individuals but also the kinds of people gathered at the table and the issues they would take up. This constituency would intentionally disrupt presumptions that everyone agreed on and engage difficult but important issues. Dewey's approach questions familiar rhetorical tropes such as "the public" or "the city." It is essential to engage diversity and acknowledge tensions, rather than focusing on facile commonalities.

This approach, and its acknowledgment of difference, takes us to a difficult topic for Arab cities—urban destruction. Middle Eastern cities have suffered from recurring waves of foreign invaders, including colonial military forces and internal civil wars. The past several years have witnessed a new scourge caused by other Arabs. Tens of thousands of residents of Sana'a, Homs, and especially Aleppo have had to flee. The destruction of buildings is often carried out in the name of a puritanical Islamic approach to culture. The so-called Islamic State, the Taliban, and Wahabism seek to obliterate anything built before Muhammad, as well as buildings that serve other faiths. We cannot talk about the Arab City without asking how to address this destruction, including efforts to help refugees.

Yet if we must talk about destruction we must discuss construction too. We can also ask who builds the architecture of Arab cities, not simply listing the architect but asking who actually does the construction, whether for permanent or temporary buildings, from foreign or local sponsors. We should consider those who build the exhibition halls and other highly visible representations of Arab nations, such as major museums. The workers are typically brought in from elsewhere, notably South Asian nations like Nepal. It seems more acceptable to pay them poorly and treat them badly, especially if they're not other Muslims. Critics have focused their ire on Frank Gehry and Zaha Hadid, but the questions expand more broadly. Every architect has some responsibility for construction workers on the job site, especially in the harsh physical conditions of the Gulf. Both skilled craftsmen and relatively unskilled workers are necessary, even for the buildings that are going up today. What are their working conditions? How are they paid? How are they treated? This affects architecture, cities, and human lives. If architects are to operate as migrants, then it is their responsibility to see the city with the eyes of a newcomer—and to seek to understand what constitutes its urban fabric and its urban community, and how that community might be represented.

ری الدكتور سيد كريم أن تنشأ فوق النيل مجموعة من الكبارى مقيما متعدد الطبقات أبى بطالب العصر ومواصلاته

بقلم الدكتور سيد كريم

نشط المهندسون العالميون فى وضع مشاريع تعمير العواصم التى دمرتها الحرب .. فلو تيسير لنا هدم القاهرة وإعادة بنائها .. فأين نبدأ ؟وكيف تنتهى ؟ هنا ما يجيب عنه الدكتور سيد كريم الأستاذ بكلية الهندسة الملكية

لو هدمت القاهرة!

— ٨٢ —

Cairo After the Second World War and the Rise of Arab Engineering Professionals

MOHAMED ELSHAHED

Arab cities underwent immense transformations in the decade following World War II. During this period, architecture and engineering became increasingly popular professions as developmentalist discourses accompanied heightened nationalist politics across the region. As Clement Henry Moore noted in his study of Egyptian engineers during the years Gamal Abdel Nasser ruled the country, "Egyptian engineers were organized as a corporate body several years before the Free Officers seized power... Modern university schools of engineering were almost fully Egyptianized by the end of the Second World War. Already in 1920 a fully Egyptianized professional society was launched, and a professional syndicate achieved recognition in 1946."[1] Architects and engineers faced the challenge of maintaining professional autonomy in the face of shifting national politics. At the same time, professional associations across the region, particularly in Egypt, Lebanon, Syria, and Iraq, became entangled in national politics as architects and engineers sought patronage from the ruling elites and aimed to advance their careers by engaging with international debates about planning, urbanization, and development. While recent studies and exhibitions have focused on the work of European and American architects in the region, it was local professionals who drew plans for future urban expansion as well as various interventions in existing cities that rapidly transformed urban life in the Middle East between 1945 and the end of the 1950s, and it was local capital that funded them.[2] This decade-and-a-half of the region's urban history was characterized by cautious optimism, as reflected in the discourses of architects in professional conferences and in a variety of publications.

Egypt's revolutions and coups d'état between the world wars produced many images and texts that were debated within professional circles as well as consumed by the general public. Hygiene, materialization of capital, political control, and population growth, in addition to architects' search for patronage, motivated the production of the plans and visions in places such as Cairo during a time of sociopolitical transformations and modernization. How differently would our understanding of the region's postwar architecture and urbanism be if that history was written through the events, experiences, and discourses of Arab professionals deeply involved in a rapidly transforming Middle East?[3] In this essay I consider the convergence of the rise of professional corporatism in the Middle East and Arab politics of independence and developmentalism. The Arabization, or in the case of Egypt the Egyptianization, of engineering and architectural professions coincided with the crystallization of nationalist movements across the Middle East after World War I. In the interwar period, mounting urban problems coincided with the rise across the region in numbers of university-educated engineering professionals who sought to play a prominent role in solving such problems. What did this convergence of events and developments mean for the Arab City and for Arab architects and engineers?

THE DESIRE TO BUILD ANEW

In 1945, architect Sayed Karim published an article in *al-Ithnayn wa-l-Dunya*, one of Egypt's most popular magazines, titled "If Cairo Were Destroyed?" The article was accompanied by an illustration showing an imagined bridge crossing from the Garden City district in central Cairo and over the northern tip of Roda Island toward the still agricultural west bank of the Nile. The multilevel bridge passes through a series of building blocks rising over the river. In the accompanying text, Karim laments Cairo's survival during World War II: "Alas, Cairo was not damaged by war."[4] According to the aspiring architect, large-scale destruction would have presented Cairenes with the opportunity to rebuild their city based on the latest planning principles. "World architects are busy designing the reconstruction of cities destroyed in the war," Karim writes. "If we had the opportunity to destroy Cairo and rebuild it, where would we begin and what would we do?" European modernists in the postwar years shared Karim's confidence. For example, Noel Annan wrote about British architects of the period: "Perhaps no profession faced the future [after World War II] with such confidence as did the architects. The destruction of wartime bombing gave them their chance... The modernists captured one after the other the university architectural schools...the Oxbridge colleges became their patrons."[5]

Patronage was precisely what Karim was seeking as a modernist architect in Egypt in 1945. However, without great destruction in Cairo there was little opportunity for a large-scale modernist reshaping of the city. That did not stop Karim from publicly seeking patronage from the highest echelons of the ruling elite through his open letters, articles, and lectures. According to him, peacetime had resulted in slow but widespread damage to Egyptian cities and had delayed a process of rapid modernization similar to what had commenced in Europe with the mass destruction of its cities during the war. In this instance, Karim fits within Marshall Berman's definition of what it is to be modern: "To be modern is to find ourselves in an environment that promises us adventure, power, joy, growth, transformation of ourselves and the world—and at the same time, that threatens to destroy everything we have, everything we know, everything we are."[6] Karim's pursuit of a better urban future in Cairo necessitated its destruction.

Since Cairo was not destroyed and a new city could not be planned ex nihilo, Karim modified his aspirations for Cairo's modern urban future. In the 1945 article, he proposes eight urban interventions to modernize the city. On the pages of one of the country's most read magazines, Karim presented broad ideas for what he would have done to improve the city: redesign the riverfronts, implement a forestation program in Cairo's urban periphery, "cleanse" unhealthy districts, flatten hills to allow for the building of new districts, replace tram systems with underground trains, remove military barracks and other state buildings from urban areas, and implement a program of *tajmeel al-madina* (urban beautification). A project on such a scale as the one Karim schematically presented required the patronage of the state or the king.[7] Karim's vision was modestly future-oriented, but its spirit was of his time. It was a modernist's response to pressing urban needs combined with an aspiration to realize architecture and planning at an unprecedented scale in the Egyptian context.

Karim's article was part of a critical convergence between Egyptian modernist and nationalist aspirations. Throughout the late 1940s popular Egyptian magazines such as the weekly *al-Musawwar* were inundated with articles, infographics, and rudimentary proposals for reimagining Cairo's urbanity and particular spaces within it. For example, Karim's concern for the future of the city, and for his career, manifested in another article, published in January 1950 in another variety magazine, *al-Hilal*. Anticipating what Cairo might look like five decades into the future, "Cairo in the Year 2000" optimistically imagines an industrial capital that reflects "enormous advances in science, technology, and economy."[8] Karim's futurist vision showcases his synergetic design practice, incorporating elements from various utopian and futurist plans such as General Motors's Futurama as displayed at the 1939 New York World's Fair, Ebenezer Howard's Garden City (1898), Le Corbusier's City of Tomorrow (1929), and Frank Lloyd Wright's Broadacre City (a concept that first appeared in his 1932 book *The Disappearing City*). Despite the variety of references, Karim's vision was grounded in Cairo with particular attention paid to various parts of the city in need of restructuring.

Between 1948 and 1952 *al-Musawwar* featured a series of centerfolds combining images, graphs, texts, and maps. Each of these centerfolds sheds light on a pressing urban issue such as the lack of green space, the lack of a plan for future growth, or the major interventions needed to sustain urban functionality. For example, in 1948 the headline warned "Cairo is suffocating; let her breathe!" The writer argued that modern cities need to dedicate 10 percent of their territory to squares and green spaces while in Cairo only 1 percent of

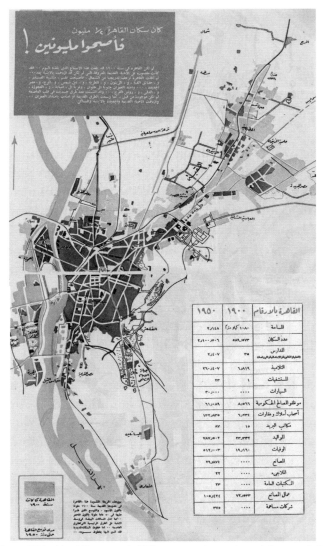

An illustration published in *al-Musawwar* in 1950 conveys urban and population growth (areas colored pink were urbanized after 1900) with a chart comparing population totals by district in 1900 and 1950.

the city was being used for those purposes. This series of journalistic interventions regarding urban issues and the visual language they used to communicate those issues to the general public illustrates how the editors of *al-Musawwar* believed that urban affairs are (or should be) a popular concern, not something only for experts or politicians to discuss. In a dysfunctional urban context such as Cairo during the late 1940s, creating public awareness through images and information about the city was a powerful act, transgressing the limitations of who should have a say in these affairs.

In 1952, only months before the coup d'état and seven years after his 1945 article and the first Arab Engineering Conference held in Alexandria, at which he attempted to appeal to King Farouk as a patron of architecture and urbanism,

A session at the Third Arab Engineering Conference held in Damascus in 1947.

Engineering professionals onboard a bus during one of the excursions of the
1947 Arab Engineering Conference.

A group photo of participating architects and engineers at the end of the
1947 Arab Engineering Conference.

Sayed Karim grew frustrated. That year he published an article in *al-Musawwar* alarmingly titled "Cairo Is Diseased, Very Diseased."[9] The city, as dissected by Karim, was composed of cells, lungs, and circulation, each represented by a diagram paired with a photograph. A diagram of a cluster of biological cells was paired with an aerial view of the city showing multiple neighborhoods; a diagram of lungs was paired with a photograph of a park; and the diagram of the body's circulation system was paired with an image of a highway interchange. This mediated call for action to improve the city reflects Karim's shift in focus from appealing to heads of state and government institutions as potential patrons to generating public demand for urban improvement.

Before having the opportunity to practice urban planning in Egypt, Karim drew plans for the expansion of Baghdad (1946), Jeddah (1949), Riyadh (1950), Mecca and Medina (1952), Amman (1954), and Aqaba (1958).[10] A decade later, in the mid-1950s, architects were competing to attract the attention of a new regime set to transform Egypt, including its cities. In the immediate aftermath of the 1952 political transition, the emerging military regime attempted to respond to Egypt's urban challenges in publications and speeches. However, the military officers leading Egypt's transition lacked the vision and expertise to produce effective plans for the future of Egyptian cities.[11] The formation of Egyptian engineering professional associations were directly linked to nationalist discourse following the 1919 revolution, and in the aftermath of 1952 architects such as Sayed Karim built on this link to provide plans and visions for reshaping the physicality of Egyptian space. The relationship between architects and engineers on one side and military officers on the other was mutually beneficial. While officers presented themselves as developers of a better future and patrons of industrial, planning, and architectural projects, architects and engineers, abundant in numbers but with few commissions, were given opportunities to build their careers.

BUILDING A NETWORK OF PROFESSIONALS

One way to better understand Sayed Karim's vision for Cairo in 1945 is to consider it within a regional historical context, particularly in relation to the evolution of a regional professional community of architects and engineers.[12] The formation of an Egyptian professional engineering culture in modern times has always been linked to the ruling elite, in most cases the rule of a strong man, such as Muhammad Ali. Moore notes that "half a century before the British occupation of 1882 a nucleus of Egyptian engineers was being trained aboard and then training others at home and acquiring experience managing the Nile."[13] Muhammad Ali's vision for an industrialized Egypt and his patronage of urban and industrial construction projects in and out of Cairo led to an early professionalization of engineering. Similarly, Khedive Isma'il sought to transform the physical shape of Egyptian cities and industries, with patronage of engineering projects also central to his rule (1863–79). It is in this particular historical context that a twentieth-century Egyptian architect such as Sayed Karim is embedded. By the 1940s engineering professions were nearly fully Egyptianized, but the patronage of a strongman ruler had waned and Egyptian architects and engineers were in search of projects to exercise their expertise.

In the aftermath of World War II, as aspirations toward nation-building and Arab solidarity grew, Egyptian architects and engineers sought to expand their influence.[14] With the establishment of the Arab League in 1945, the first Arab Engineers Conference was organized and hosted in Alexandria.[15] In a published handwritten open letter, architect Mustafa Fahmy praised the conference for bringing together professionals from across the region and for focusing on research. Fahmy believed that research had the potential to benefit the international community in general but Egypt and Arab countries in particular.[16] Fahmy, who was Egypt's head architect for royal palaces and head of the Tanzim administration, led the conference panel on reinforced concrete. The panel presenters shared their research on matters as diverse as the deterioration of concrete in coastal structures, the uses of concrete in paving and concrete foundations. The presented research, Fahmy writes, should be shared regionally and internationally for the advancement of engineering practices. The conference's opening address was delivered by Sayed Karim, who proclaimed that such meetings were part of a national (*watani*) engineering project, which "will produce new knowledge that will be reflected in new projects in the region and beyond." Fahmy's letter concludes by thanking King Farouk, an honorary architect, for his support for science and the arts.

The conference was the first attempt after the end of World War II to energize the academic and professional society of engineers, including architects, who had been affected in the previous years due to the uncertainty caused by the raging war. For example, Egypt's leading professional architectural journal, *al-'Imara*, founded in 1939 by Sayed Karim, interrupted its publication in 1943 and 1944 due to paper shortages. Additionally, during the same period, shortages of building supplies raised prices of construction and led to a slowing down of the industry altogether. At the same time, Egyptian cities began to expand as rural-to-urban migration increased. This population shift presented engineers with new problems, as the need for industrial development increased and training and housing the new urban population became a necessity.[17] The conference organizers also sought to bring together Egyptian and Arab engineers in a multidisciplinary pan-Arab setting to build a network of professionals across the region and across various disciplines associated with engineering.

In his keynote address, Sayed Karim referred to the 1945 conference as the second of its kind.[18] The first such meeting of professionals, according to him, was three thousand years before, during the reign of Pharaoh Akhnaten. That ruler had brought together the scientists and artists of the time to eventually produce some of ancient Egypt's most highly regarded art and architecture (called the Amarna period). Karim added that like that ancient meeting of artists and scientists, the 1945 conference was taking place in the era of the young and enlightened King Farouk. Karim's opening address, titled "Postwar Projects," highlighted the problems with development projects before the war and argued for the need for large-scale projects in the postwar period. Prewar projects lacked vision and proper planning, Karim argued. He stressed that the damage done to Egyptian cities by the slow decay of peacetime was perhaps more dangerous than the damage European cities had experienced during the war. Only a comprehensive national building and development program implemented in five-year stages could guarantee Egypt's sustained growth.[19] Karim called for the conference to lead to a comprehensive development project, an expansion plan for Cairo in honor of the king and named after him, following the tradition of previous rulers. Each major expansion in the city's modern history was associated with a monarch with a vision, and Karim proposed that Farouk's Cairo would be the city of the future and the site where the outcomes of the latest urban research and design would be implemented.

Karim presented Farouk's Cairo as a vision rather than a specific proposal. It was not yet designed, but conceptually it was meant to be a vehicle for the architect to respond to a series of pressing urban problems. Karim outlined nineteen areas he anticipated to dominate professional practice and discourse for the following years: "The entire east needs to develop the idea of a village university," he suggested; bringing education and culture from the urban centers to villages across the region was an essential component of a comprehensive development project; increased industrialization must be accompanied by the development of workers housing in addition to the development of agriculture to feed these populations. Karim's final recommendations were in the category of public health, calling for the implementation of a hospital-building program that would guarantee access of health services to all sectors of society. Other areas highlighted in Karim's statement included: sports facilities for the masses, cultural institutions accessible to the population, redevelopment of poor districts, university housing and campuses, roads and transport networks, tourism development, development of the Nile banks for recreation and other uses, and conservation of historic and ancient sites. It should be noted that Karim's approach to city planning appears to be in conversation with contemporary debates among members of Congrès internationaux d'architecture moderne (CIAM), particularly in regard to the concept of the Functional City, the result of a series of meetings and collaborations lasting a decade from 1933 to 1943 and resulting in the Athens Charter.[20] However, there is no documented evidence of any interaction between Karim and other leading members of Arab engineering circles with members of the renowned European group of architects in CIAM. The functional zones within Karim's vision of the modern city were discussed in the various panels at the Arab Engineering Conference in Alexandria in 1945.

The conference met again the following year in Cairo, and in 1947 the meeting was held in Damascus and was hosted by the Syrian president.[21] The Damascus conference was the largest of the three meetings, and it had the widest range of panels and professionals, and thus a wider representation of the region. The conference was heralded as "the greatest display of national solidarity (*qawmiyya*) in Damascus' history" with pan-Arabism and Arab unity as the rallying themes. The Damascus conference coincided with the Arab Cultural Forum (Mu'atamar al-Thaqafa al-'Arabi), which was held in Beirut. The first Arab archaeology conference was also held in Syria that year. It was an active moment for Arab professionals in an effort to undertake a pan-Arab renaissance across the cultural register. Tawfiq 'Abd al-Gawwad, representative of the Egyptian architects delegation at the Damascus engineering conference, presented the great advances resulting from such professional meetings as a reflection of the political transformation Arab society had been experiencing. Together these conferences comprise significant momentum not only in the region's homegrown professional class but also in their collective assertion of national and regional development in the face of lingering colonialism.

Indeed, there was a direct relationship between these professional meetings and the political elite in the host counties. While the first engineering conference was hosted by King Farouk, not only did the Syrian president host the third conference when it was held in his country, but also the Syrian defense minister was its president. The ruling elite had a vested interest in supporting the engineers' society, as issues such as energy generation, housing, and town planning were seen as essential to the survival of the political orders. The conference's 440 engineers, including women, from Egypt, Syria, Lebanon, Palestine, Iraq, and Transjordan presented research and projects that fit into two main categories: hydroelectric infrastructure and modern villages (*al-qarya al-haditha*). The official motto of the conference was "the third engineering conference for Arab lands." By its third cycle, participants at these engineering professional gatherings saw their contributions to the conferences within the aims of the League of Arab States. In his statement at the opening of the conference, the Syrian president stressed that the future of modern Arab nations depended on the contributions of artists and scientists and that "the league of Arab states unifies our goals and consolidates our scientific efforts." These efforts, he added, were for the good of humanity.[22]

Not only was this regional gathering of architects and engineers an opportunity to acquaint architects from various Arab countries with each other, but it also facilitated the formation of a professional community familiar with the region's complex histories and present advances. The conference was followed by a series of visits to various locations in the Greater Syria region, organized by the Syrian Engineers Society (Jam'iyat al-Muhandisin al-Suriyyin). The tour took the architects to ancient sites in Baalbek, followed by Zahle in Lebanon, then to Homs to inspect the latest irrigation system there. On their stop in Aleppo, the group inspected archaeological digs, the historic city center, and the latest textile factories. The tour ended in Beirut after a visit to Latakia's historic sites as well as a stone quarry and an asphalt plant. Following the itinerary of these tours, their stops at ancient and heritage sites as well as modern factories, suggests that conference organizers and participating architects and engineers foresaw the future of the modern Arab city built on both heritage and industry, not one over the other.

The housing panel's ten recommendations were based on the presented papers and projects, and on subsequent discussions. The panel recommended that governments invest in planning new residential quarters and provide incentives for businesses and industries to build housing for their workers. It also advised drafting laws that would encourage individuals to become members of housing cooperatives that should enjoy no or low taxes, plus access to affordable land for development, and to public transport and facilities. The profits of construction companies, the panel advised, must be limited to a certain percentage, and the governments of the region should closely monitor the prices of building materials, their production, and distribution to "guarantee the equal rights of producers and consumers of these essential materials."

A list of recommendations by each of the conference's three main panels (healthy affordable housing, water resources management, general) was published in al-'Imara. While some of the recommendations had clear professional and scientific implications, others were overtly political, recommending, for example, that Arab governments invest in research and development of the management of water resources and hydroelectricity. There was also a concern raised by the panel regarding Zionist projects affecting Palestine's water resources. Finally, the panel commented on the situation in the Maghreb and how the colonizers had monopolized water resources. These and other recommendations were sent to the recently established League of Arab Nations "to take the necessary steps to protect the rights of the people of these lands."[23]

The 1947 Damascus congress was hailed as a great success. The professional community emerging from it and the two previous conferences had become invested in national and regional politics. Moreover, participants were developing a clear political position vis-à-vis colonizing powers, a position in which the development of national engineering professions was seen as vital not only for the defense of national interests and the modernization of the region but ultimately for the achievement of independence.

A fourth conference was planned to meet in Egypt in 1949, but it was postponed due to the outbreak of the Arab-Israeli War in 1948. The fourth congress was relocated and convened in July 1950 in Beirut.[24] It took place in the UNESCO Palace, built in 1948 to host the Third International Congress of UNESCO. Noticeably absent from *al-ʿImara's* report on the Beirut meeting is any mention of the Arab-Israeli conflict that had caused the meeting's delay. Instead there seems to have been a focus on technical matters such as irrigation and road and electricity networks, all in a rather depoliticized fashion. Did engineering professionals retreat from politics in light of Egypt's humiliating defeat to the Israelis? The Beirut congress, with 950 attendees, also marked a shift away from architecture and the decline of Egypt's influence over the field. In fact, Egypt's delegation filed a complaint regarding the underrepresentation of the practice of architecture during the meeting.[25] Egypt would host the congress again in 1954, 1963, and a final time in 1972.[26]

In 1946 the Egyptian Engineering Syndicate was established and included architecture as only one among a wider field of engineering professions.[27] The purpose of the Arab engineering conferences, as highlighted in Sayed Karim's opening address at the first meeting in 1945, was to create a community of Arab engineering professionals. Such a professional community was "entangled in politics from the very beginning."[28] In the postwar political context and after the initial conferences, architecture was quickly marginalized and overshadowed by other fields of engineering regarded as far more vital for the development of the region. The reasons for architecture's decline in prominence within these professional meetings are possibly related to the region's transforming political environment. From the start, heads of state were the official conference hosts, regardless of which country the meeting was held in. Political establishments in host countries were interested in accessing the knowhow and homegrown expertise that could provide blueprints for national development projects and infrastructure. After World War II, "processes of decolonization and development" began to replace the "fiscally conservative, export-oriented colonial structures" of economic and political systems.[29] The need for governments to build dams, electricity networks, road infrastructures, and sewage systems overshadowed the need for architects to provide plans and designs for individual buildings. In this emerging developmental nationalism, architects came second, after civil, electrical, agricultural, and mechanical engineers.[30] Eventually, the presence of engineers as ministers in the region's many nationalist autocratic governments provided such regimes with a veneer of legitimacy.

CONCLUSION

At the moment the Arab League was established, Arab cities were experiencing immense physical as well as political change, but what did an Arab city circa 1950 look like, and who was to decide the fate of its future? In Cairo in 1945, Sayed Karim had attempted to reshape that city's transformation by utilizing popular media outlets, such as magazines, to circulate provocative ideas imagining a modern Cairo for the future. At the same time, Karim was active in another arena; he participated in the formation of a regional professional network of architects and engineers. Despite the potential for the development of a vibrant Arab national and regional professional community during the initial years of the Arab engineering conferences, turbulent political events such as the Arab-Israeli War and later events on the national front, such as Egypt's coup d'état of 1952, greatly affected the ways in which professionals such as Karim practiced.

In Cairo, and in other Arab capitals, modernist architecture and the professionals capable of producing it were mobilized by the new nationalist regimes that laid claim on independence, anticolonialism, and developmentalism. Such architecture was deployed around the world by vastly different political entities with diverse and even conflicting aims and aspirations.[31] Arab engineers and architects presented themselves to the Arab public and state elites in the immediate aftermath of World War II as integral to national progress.[32] Cultivating local technical knowhow, including the knowledge of how to build modern cities and housing, as practiced by Arab architects and engineers, presented revolutionary governments with the opportunity to realize what James C. Scott calls "high modernism": "a strong, one might even say muscle-bound, version of the self-confidence about scientific and technical progress."[33] When it comes to architecture in Egypt, Scott's "high modernism" manifested in terms of the contentious relationship developed by an architect such as Sayed Karim and the regime that followed the July coup. Ultimately, Karim managed to secure large-scale government commissions that finally allowed him to graft his modernist vision on the landscape of Egypt's cities under the patronage of the "revolutionary" government. The outcomes were designs for public buildings and some housing schemes, rarely built as designed by the architect due to budgetary restraints or practical difficulties, as well as the urban expansion plan of Nasr City in Cairo. Such projects, urban and architectural, reflect the level of maturity, and shortcomings, of Arab engineering professions at the time. But they also reflect the mutually beneficial relationship between architects and the state in the immediate aftermath of independence and the subsequent attempts at reshaping the built environment.

1   Clement Henry Moore, *Images of Development: Egyptian Engineers in Search of Industry* (Cairo: American University in Cairo Press, 1994), 11.

2   Sandy Isenstadt and Kishwar Rizvi, eds., *Modernism and the Middle East: Architecture and Politics in the Twentieth Century* (Seattle: University of Washington Press, 2008). The exhibition "City of Mirages: Baghdad, 1952-1982" focused on the work of renowned European and American architects and discounted, willingly or not, the presence of local and regional engineers and architects. As a counter example, the exhibition and accompanying book curated by the Arab Center for Architecture for the Bahrain Pavilion in the 2014 Venice Architecture Biennale shifts the focus on the work of Arab architects in Arab cities.

3   This question is deeply embedded within the scholarship on histories of modernism from the "margins" of the historiography. See William S. W. Lim and Jiat-Hwee Chang, *Non West Modernist Past: On Architecture and Modernities* (Singapore: World Scientific Publishing, 2012).

4   Sayed Karim, "If Cairo Were Destroyed," *al-Ithnayn wa-l-Dunya* 586 (1945): 12–13.

5   Noel Annan, *Our Age* (London: Weidenfeld & Nicolson, 1990), 291.

6   Marshall Berman, *All That Is Solid Melts into Air: The Experience of Modernity* (London: Verso, 1985), 15.

7   Karim's search for the patronage of the king or the state in order to implement large-scale urban projects is reminiscent of the gratitude expressed by planners and architects toward absolute rulers in other political contexts from colonial North Africa to fascist Italy.

8   Here, Karim deploys a discourse about modernization and progress that has been commonly used in a variety of locations, including Egypt, since the nineteenth century. Sayed Karim, "Cairo in the Year 2000," *al-Hilal* (January 1950), 110.

9   Sayed Karim, "Cairo Is Diseased," *al-Musawwar*, May 15, 1952.

10   Mercedes Volait, *L'architecture moderne en Egypte et la revue al-'Imara (1939–1959)* (Cairo: CEDEJ, 1988), 55.

11   Moore, *Images of Development*, 1.

12   Mercedes Volait, "Town Planning Schemes for Cairo Conceived by Egyptian Planners in the 'Liberal Experiment' Period," in *Middle Eastern Cities, 1900–1950: Public Places and Public Spheres in Transformation*, ed. Hans Chr. Nielsen and Jakob Skovgaard-Petersen (Aarhus: Aarhus University Press, 2001), 44.

13   Moore, *Images of Development*, 24.

14   The Arab League was established in March 1945, and as Israel Gershoni and James Jankowski note, "Egypt was the unquestioned leader in the involved inter-Arab diplomatic negotiations resulting in the formation of the Arab League." It is in this context of Egypt's expanding political ambition that the Arab engineering conferences commencing in 1945 should be understood. Israel Gershoni and James P. Jankowski, *Redefining the Egyptian Nation 1930–1945* (Cambridge, England: Cambridge University Press, 1995), 192.

15   The First Arab Engineering Conference was held in Alexandria on March 15–19, 1945. The faculty of engineering in Alexandria's Farouk University was established in 1941.

16   Mustafa Fahmy, *al-'Imara*, vol. 5, no. 2–3 (June 1945): 6.

17   According to the one of the conference's keynote addresses by Farouk University professor and the conference secretary general Sayed Mortada, *al-'Imara*, 7.

18   Sayed Karim, *al-'Imara*, 9.

19   It is possible that Karim was inspired by the Soviet five-year plans. Beyond the Soviet states, such plans were established in places such as Turkey and China. However, Egypt's first formal five-year plan was not until 1960/61–1964/65. Albert Gray Jr., "Egypt's Ten Year Economic Plan, 1973–1982," *Middle East Journal*, vol. 30, no. 1 (Winter 1976): 36.

20   John Gold, "Creating the Charter of Athens: CIAM and the Functional City, 1933–43," *Town Planning Review*, vol. 69, no. 3 (July 1998): 225–47.

21   Tawfiq Ahmad 'Abd al-Gawwad, "The Third Arab Engineering Congress," *al-'Imara*, vol. 7, no. 5–6 (September 1947): 4.

22   Ahmad 'Abd al-Gawwad, "The Third Arab Engineering Congress," 6.

23   Ahmad 'Abd al-Gawwad, "The Third Arab Engineering Congress," 12.

24   Tawfiq Ahmad 'Abd al-Gawwad, "Fourth Arab Engineering Congress," *al-'Imara*, vol. 10, no. 6–7 (October 1950): 5–23.

25   Ahmad 'Abd al-GawwadAbd al-Gawwad, "Fourth Arab Engineering Congress," 5.

26   The Arab engineering conferences have continued to meet irregularly. The last such conference was held in Jeddah, Saudi Arabia, in 2012.

27   Donald M. Reid, "The Rise of Professional Organizations in Modern Egypt," *Comparative Studies in Society and History*, vol. 16, no. 1 (Spring 1974): 52.

28   Reid, "The Rise of Professional Organizations," 52.

29   Martin Bunton, "From Developmental Nationalism to the End of Nation-state in Iraq?" *Third World Quarterly*, vol. 29, no. 3 (April 2008): 633.

30   Roger Owen and Sevket Pamuk, *A History of Middle East Economies in the Twentieth Century* (Cambridge, MA: Harvard University Press, 1999).

31   Vladimir Kulic, "Modernism and the State: Introduction," in *Sanctioning Modernism: Architecture and the Making of Postwar Identities*, ed. Vladimir Kulic, Timothy Parker, and Monica Penick (Austin: University of Texas Press, 2014), 8.

32   Architects have done so in other political contexts during this period. See Mark Swenarton, Tom Avermaete, and Dirk van den Heuvel, eds., *Architecture and the Welfare State* (New York: Routledge, 2015).

33   James C. Scott, *Seeing Like a State: How Certain Schemes to Improve the Human Condition Have Failed* (New Haven, CT: Yale University Press, 1999), 4.

Mohamed Elshahed

Ideology

From the Nation-State to the Failed-State: The Question of Architectural Representation

ZIAD JAMALEDDINE

In July 2014, the so-called Islamic State of Iraq and Syria (or ISIS) announced itself as a new Islamist "caliphate" while unilaterally declaring statehood across vast territories of the Middle East. The day after their announcement, its members proceeded to demolish religious shrines and mosques of other Islamic sects, seeing them as a threat to their orthodox religious views. Their brutal and ruthless propaganda videos are usually set either against a background of a bare, empty desert (an appeal to the Arabian landscape of the prophet Muhammad's era) or in a religious setting—in front of the Grand Mosque of Mosul, for example. The Grand Mosque and other backdrops like it were obviously not built by ISIS, but in them they found a properly religious representation. In short, everything is wrong with this picture. What we witness here is what the theologian Mohammad Arkoun has described as the religious ideological confusions of the modern time, where nihilistic (extremist) groups, driven by distorted nostalgia of an identity from distant past, are filling the void created by failed secular nation-states. The architecture of this mosque is, critically, part of this construct.

NATION-STATE

By the mid-twentieth century, the newly liberated and formed states of the Middle East had witnessed a surge in architectural production that was deeply rooted in modernist ideology. Architecture at the time, in the eyes of the State, was meant to construct a national identity for these young nations, with the aim of providing identifiable forms and building types associated with a supposedly unifying and a modernizing society. The nation-states that were carved out of former colonial territories embarked on a political journey, stitching together (within newly established borders) communities and ethnic groups that had loosely coexisted under the decentralized and relatively stable Ottoman Empire. Almost a century later, this project of nation-building has proved to be faulty at best. Far from being a smooth continuum, the process of modernization and secularization of the region was deeply fragmented and incomplete.

In 1928, in Beirut, the Place de l'Etoile became an allegory of this encounter with modernism. As described by the sociologist Samir Khalaf, the radial star

Holiday Inn in Beirut designed by Andre Wongenscky and Maurice Hindie, 1975.

95

was the most visible instance of grandiose French urban planning superimposed on the old city. The parliament building was located in the square, projecting its legitimacy and instilling a sense of civic identity. However, the star-shaped French urbanism, which was in tension with the religious reality of Lebanon, was amputated at birth. The two eastern arms were obstructed by the presence of three prominent historical religious buildings: a Greek Orthodox Church, a Greek Catholic church, and a historic Islamic shrine. The religious plurality of the newly formed nation, and its architectural representation, stood in the face of the singular, didactic, colonial form of the star.

Almost a century later, the dysfunction of the Lebanese government is mirrored by the political decline of countries throughout the region. Internal conflicts and Western interventionism have instigated failure in civic institutions in many Arab states, undermining the legitimacy of their governments in the eyes of their citizens. The architectural history of this new period remains to be written. With this in mind, the long-standing aspiration for architecture and urbanism to represent a place or a single identity becomes ever more problematic. Yet in the midst of this upheaval, international and local architects in the Arab world continue to be obsessed with the question of identity while simultaneously producing a self-effacing architecture. Typically, the *mashrabiya* screen and other regional architectural clichés are employed as an expedient and convenient represention of what is in fact a complex and dynamic culture. The façade articulation of Jean Nouvel's L'Institut du monde arabe in Paris was perhaps one of the earliest example of this attitude, fixing an Orientalized signifier—the screen, now mechanized and modernized—to a whole culture.

In Lebanon, the reconstruction of downtown Beirut after the end of the civil war in 1990, along with other, similar, large-scale urban developments in the region (namely in the Arab Gulf), exacerbated this condition. For instance, Nouvel's proposed residential tower, with what looks like simulated shrapnel holes scarring its façades (with the random fenestration composition), reinvigorates the cliché image of destroyed buildings during the war. It invokes a catastrophic time all too familiar and mundane to Beirutis. Nearby is the heavily damaged but still-standing Holiday Inn building, a never-occupied modernist slab structure designed by Andre Wongenscky and Maurice Hindie, built in 1975 when the war started. A real relic of the Lebanese war, the building is within walking distance of Nouvel's tower.

The proximity and uncanny visual resemblance between the two structures belies the extreme disparity in what they signify. While one stands as a ghostly carcass of the wonder and potential of the city of Beirut, the other will represent the sure future of the city under a neoliberal, all-exclusive urban agenda dressed to blend in with a still war-riddled context.

Although Nouvel's project is still unrealized, this kind of symbolically charged aesthetics is adopted in the design approach of local architects. The Université Saint-Joseph campus (designed by Youssef Tohme and 109architectes) is located in another area that witnessed fierce battles during the Lebanese war, the Al Mathaf intersection. The project itself has many urban merits in the way it carves out a public space within the campus and organizes the different schools around that void. This, however, became overshadowed by the buildings' obsessive façades' fenestration and fragmentation (supposedly meant to represent the schizophrenic psyche of the Lebanese people in the time of war).

The project that may best epitomize the problematic of contemporary architectural practices in Lebanon in the last decade is Giancarlo de Carlo's residential complex, currently under construction in Beirut. Here, the architect, who seems to have overcompensated for Modernism's percieved anonymity, started his design by sampling and selectively collecting and combining façade elements from Beirut's architectural "heritage." This neoclassical visual bricolage of the façade features of the French Mandate building typology is peculiarly assumed to best represent the diverse communities of the nation today. This typology mushroomed across the city under the French influence of the 1930s, housing the emerging elite class that was installed by the colonizer and long benefited from its domination over the rest of the population.

In all these examples, we see the craving for contemporary practice either to fetishize the recent past through the lens of the supposed permanent trauma of the war or to ignore it altogether in favor of the idealized glory of colonial Lebanon. Both attitudes gloss over the relevance of the modern period, when architecture was believed to carry an agenda of social change and betterment for a state still in the making.

FAILED-STATE

In the 1950s, Lebanon witnessed a boom in well-regulated construction and modernist architectural sensibilities. From the 1960s until the outbreak of civil war in 1975, several canonic modernist buildings were added to the Beirut skyline. The period's modernist optimism is exemplified by the EDL (Electricité du Liban) headquarters by the architect Pierre Nema and CETA, built in the mid-1960s. Towering above a sunken courtyard, the architecture affirmed the political will of the central state to supply power to the nation far into its rural territory. Today, the dilapidated façade, its rundown service systems, and archaic office spaces embody the woeful inadequacies of the electric sector in Lebanon, where power shortages are the norm. Instead, an informal economy of private generators is growing around the city to compensate for power rationing.

Electricité du Liban, CETA, 1962.

Makeshift balcony enclosures on the Yacoubian Building in Beirut.

From the Nation–State to the Failed–State

The weakened central state was supplanted by community-based spatial practices over the years, each responding to specific needs at specific moments. Filling voids in power and governance, these community groups continuously transformed the generic modernist slab building. The face of the city clearly demonstrates this evolution. Water tanks have been added atop apartment buildings (fed by private water trucks, compensating for city water shortages), and balconies have been enclosed with makeshift walls, accommodating the transforming needs of families. With each of these episodes, the state tried to catch up. Futilely, the government has attempted to regulate informal construction, producing unintended negative consequences with a new patchwork of laws. In an attempt to regulate balcony enclosures, for instance, an amendment to the building code in 2004 finally legalized this practice, with the use of one specific folding-glass system. Apartment blocks today, if designed carefully, plan a balcony that is ready to receive the installation of that glass system and internalize forever that outdoor space. The once organic and enriching transformation of the city's façades, made by the initiatives of individuals based on their needs, became an orderly erasure of the city balconies conceived by policy makers and carried out by architects. Now, one of the last remaining semi-public zones in the city may be regulated out of existence.

Left alone, these spatial practices generate a more complex picture (failed-state architecture?), a representation that does not flatten the concept of identity or freeze it in time; instead, they tell the story of the rise and decline of the city of Beirut and the resilience and resourcefulness of its residents during times of war. While contemporary architects continue to fetishize identity (is it Islamic, Arabian, French, Middle-Eastern, Mediterranean, Phoenician?), the city of Beirut (as well as other Arab cities with precarious governments), driven by the lived reality of its spaces, is writing an alternative urban tale, one that perhaps does not ask the question of representation but almost always answers it.

BEIRUT EXHIBITION CENTER

How does one negotiate this environment? How does the architect build in a context in which representation is so overdetermined and the space of the city so wracked with politics? These are questions that, as architects, we have thought much about and have tried to resolve in our office work in Beirut. The civil war created a fracture in Lebanese society between two very different political visions. One territory, however, remained common and shared in use between the two. The trash mountain—a pile of rubble created by both sides at the border of their territories—was located in the sea by the no-man's-land of downtown Beirut, an area that witnessed the fiercest battles. With the end

Beirut Exhibition Center, L.E.FT, 2014.

of the conflicts in 1990s, the (premodern-era) buildings of supposed historical importance in downtown Beirut were preserved; the rest was destroyed and dumped into the sea, creating a landfill and expanding the growth of the city into the water. The trash-and-rubble island became not only a prime piece of real estate but also a common metaphor among the Lebanese. The destruction of the war literally became the foundation for the new city. Its development, like all development in the city center after the war, was administered by the real estate company Solidere.

A few years ago, Solidere approached our office to design a temporary exhibition center on the landfill. We hoped that there, on this settling rubble pile, we could create architecture in an ever-dynamic state; architecture that would reflect the constantly shifting context at the urban scale, creating a new skyline for the city and housing constantly shifting exhibitions on the inside. In response, we designed a hangar structure wrapped with a custom corrugated mirror aluminum skin. As a reflection, the building becomes the index for the growth of the city in the making around it.

The exhibition center suspends judgment and becomes a placeholder that derives its identity from the broken image of the ever-changing urban context and environment. The mirror cladding refuses shadows in order to accentuate the placeless nature of the building. Working with the topography, the building sits in a pool of water that reflects both building and context into an immaterial state, just like the city that will "become" but "is" not yet.

Fallen Cities:
Architecture and Reconstruction
ADRIAN LAHOUD

The nature of contemporary power is architectural and
impersonal, not personal and representative
—The Invisible Committee, *To Our Friends*

THE SITUATION

In Arabic conversations, "the situation" (الوضع) is used to indicate prevailing
political, social, and economic uncertainty.[1] Those who use the phrase rarely
specify what situation they are referring to. *Has there only ever been one situation?*
The multiplicity implied in its nonspecificity binds one speaker to another in
an implied assumption that is both intimate and collective. A former Baathist,
Phalangist, Communist, or Pan-Arab Nationalist no longer. Not yet a martyr.
Just a shared hesitation to speak the language of parties, names, and events.
In their place, an empty term that stands for all possible parties, all possible
names, and all possible events: "the situation." Like an incantation, if you repeat
it enough times, a million tiny acts of solidarity will add up to a collective perception. Curiously, this affective precision is secured by the complete absence of
content in the statement. "The situation" can literally refer to anything. Its task,
however, is not to convey information but rather to forge agreement that the
predicament is so self-evident as to require no further explanation—"it's bad,"
"we" are "in it," "together."

This "we" is its work. Perhaps nothing forges solidarity like a shared sense of
malaise. Perhaps it all depends on whether this shared sense is exhausted by its
capture *as malaise*. In any case, whatever it lacks in specifics the term more than
makes up for in scope. Indeed, the seeming inescapability of the situation colors
every question and every judgment on the Arab City. Like the "Arab street," a
foreign policy term now used as shorthand to describe popular Arab sentiment,
the "Arab City" appears perpetually aggrieved and inflamed. Undoubtedly, the
fact that Arab identity, Arab cities, and Arab streets are constituted as certain
kinds of problems, ones that command public interest, invite debate, and are
worthy of discussion, cannot be separated from the multifarious geopolitical
investments in the region. After all it is *Arab* identity, not some other identity,

Northern edge of the Rachid Karame Fair and Exposition entry plaza, showing
rows of unadorned flagpoles. The plaza datum directs visitors toward an inclined
ramp and the entry pavilion.

that is at stake here, and not only for Arabs, since the question has for some time merited discussions of a broader and certainly more pernicious nature within colonial states with respect to their former empires. The streets and cities of other communities are mainly matters of interest for those communities, as well as those whose job it is to be interested in such things; they are simply not burdened in the same way or by the same fears. To enter into this particular debate then, even as a strenuous critic, risks accepting its frame and reactivating the habit of posing questions according to these terms.

How to proceed then? One might take "the situation" and the commonality of its use in everyday speech as a sign of caution and equivocation, a reluctance to betray positions or enter into public dispute out of fear of recrimination. But why insist on seeing this expression as a lack rather than an act of everyday resistance? Its compulsive repetition is evidence of an attempt to suspend representation long enough to allow mutual sympathies to form. If the statement is not framed as lack, failure, or disavowal—and the suggestive ambiguities it offers are pursued—then another entry point into questions about the Arab City can become possible. This other entry point would not presuppose either of the two terms that guard its entrance, either "Arab" or "city," let alone the colonial legacies that mark the significance of their conjunction beyond the Arab world. So instead of starting with its refusal to specify, let us try to start with its function, which is to forge a collective sentiment. These sentiments, as articulated through the countless expressions of popular sovereignty that have been heard in the last few years, suggest a nuanced understanding and sensitivity to the relations between implicit and explicit registers, as well as to the tension between affect and its capture through systems of representation.

After all, the implicit affective solidarity produced by

الوضع / الحالة al-wad'a [the situation]

can suddenly crystallize into a perfectly explicit revolutionary demand:

شعب al sha'ab [the people]
يريد yurīd [want to]
إسقاط isqāṭ [bring down]
النظام an-niẓām [the regime].

I would like to examine the way that new collective sentiments are expressed, formed, and made explicit within contexts of social transformation. Architecture has a fundamental role to play in these processes, and the examples cited above provide new insights into how we might understand the political function of architecture. Beyond an attention to the intrinsic precarity of these utterances is their urgent need to acquire a life beyond their performance in everyday conversation, to take forms that survive moments of "popular jubilation," as Jonathan Littell recently put it.[2] When the chorus of voices falls silent, it is urgent to seize possession of all the passions of resistance, the investments, the sympathies, and the sentiments, and to finally discover what structures best secure their fate. It's a question of desire: how to produce it, how to satisfy the demands that flow from it, how to secure this satisfaction into the future?

Architecture has a fundamental role to play because it is able to contribute something essential to the durability of new social diagrams—an impersonal form. By stating that "the nature of contemporary power is architectural and impersonal, not personal and representative," the anonymous collective the Invisible Committee point to something that is growing clearer in leftist thought—the need for a constructive political architectural project.[3] This is not to say that personality has nothing to do with politics, or that we are done with the significance of the face, or manners of speech, or charismatic leaders, but rather to indicate the way that contemporary forms of power cannot be understood without a serious examination of our imbrication in material and technical worlds and the subtle yet persistent solicitations these worlds make on life.

To make this proposition more concrete, I want to draw on a moment in Lebanese history that was as unlikely as it was decisive. Commissioned by a proto-state, named after a *zaim* (leader), and designed by a part-time communist and full-time Carioca, the Rachid Karame Fair and Exposition project in Lebanon by Oscar Niemeyer is an object lesson in architecture and the problem of nation-building. The project depended on the model of the state that gave birth to it, one that conceived of the nation as something plastic, one that reserved the right to intervene in that plasticity in order to shape it. But already by the 1970s, when an aggressive return to laissez-faire markets and the civil war interrupted the nascent movement toward a social welfare state, Lebanon's political leadership was no longer willing or able to secure the conditions in which the project was supposed to operate.

For many, the sense that individual projects fail to produce social transformation is troubling, if familiar. Maybe because it mirrors the secret presupposition that individual works effect social transformation in the first place. At the very least, it raises the question of architecture's contribution to social transformation. In the case of the project in Tripoli, the failure to build a new Lebanese state, legitimate institutions, and a workable idea of citizenship makes broader questions regarding the instrumentality of architecture and its contingency within social movements more explicit rather than less. Still, this judgment of failure can only be made from the perspective of the 1960s *Nahda*, or renaissance, and its commitment to socialist, nationalistic, and pan-Arab programs.[4] A contrary position could be taken, that the inability to take a monolithic form in a country without a hegemon was what lent Lebanon its peculiar ability to endlessly absorb regional pressures: not quite a state in any real sense, not even a peace—more a permanent, uneasy truce.

In either case, nation-building is an impossible burden for a work of architecture to carry when extracted from the political, financial, and institutional context that commissioned it, lent it sense, and struggled to sustain it. More useful than any appeal to Arab-ness, then, is to examine the concrete processes of experimentation in which social diagrams are produced and how the instruments of modernity are taken up and modified, reactivating and mobilizing archaic structures like feudalism. By social diagram, I refer to implicit norms and explicit spatial and institutional forms that work together to produce, stabilize, and secure specific relations of power, including the production of national identity. In doing so, a more consistent, if transversal, genealogy can be cut through different claims for social change regardless of their periodization or their supposed regional or linguistic commonality. By way of Niemeyer's intervention in Tripoli, I propose that the diagram is what secures the operation of the work. It is what sustains the drive for transformation, what allows it to persist.

Finally, I suggest that this work sets out to manufacture a certain kind of subject. The era of nation-building projects was directed toward an imagined subject to come, one whose natural affinity to family and community had to be reoriented toward the promise of citizenship and national belonging. In this process, one kind of collective sentiment had to be replaced by another: familial, communal bonds would need to dissolve and national ones would need to emerge to take their place. However, there was a challenge. The nation did not exist. It would need to be invented. In the case of Lebanon, the reformist nature of this project meant that this transformation would take on an inherently pedagogical nature. The state would draw heavily on urban, infrastructural, and architectural projects to dissolve filiations at a communal scale in order to better establish it at the scale of the state. Exactly how this was supposed to be accomplished is a matter of importance not only because the era was such a crucial juncture in Lebanese history, one that belies the catastrophic upheaval soon to follow, but also because it raises questions of a broader disciplinary nature.

THE DOME IN THE PARK

Returning to social transformation via this refrain, "the situation" requires that we distinguish between two different aspects: an interpretation that signifies some lack on one side (the inability to specify) and a direct intervention in the field of subjectivity between the speakers on the other (implying a common perception). One could say that architecture is still far too indebted to the first at the complete expense of the latter. In order to explain this and justify why it is relevant to a discussion on architecture, a digression through theory is necessary, primarily to differentiate between signifying and a-signifying operations of signs. This distinction, which comes from the work of Félix Guattari, refers to those signs or aspects of how signs work that are independent of what they mean. Guattari uses the concept to break the dominance of structuralist linguistics and psychoanalysis on our understanding of the unconscious. With respect to the statement "the situation," it *works* to mobilize certain kinds of passions prior to the allocation of positions or the articulation of identities. In fact, we could say these substrata of affect become a kind of raw material for the subsequent formalization of linguistic statements. The difference is crucial: the absence of the referent with respect to the meaning of "the situation" *produces* the conditions under which a new referent (solidarity) can emerge. The condition that is being produced by the statement is nothing less than a small but precise intervention in the formation of subjectivity itself. The concept of the a-signifying operation of a sign invites us to attend to processes of subjective transformation that exist prior to or alongside understanding—that is to say, prior to or alongside of the recognition of meaning in signs.

Acknowledging both the operational and semantic character of signs through this spoken example offers a way of thinking about architecture, especially the idea that "intelligibility" should be the dominant mode of reception. Consider the example of the dome, a paradigmatic element within Christian and Islamic architectural traditions. It's an enduring form whose resistance to transformation makes it particularly qualified to reflect the immutability of sacred and profane images of the cosmos. Think not only of churches and mosques but also of observatories and planetariums. Responding to historians Rudolf Wittkower and Heinrich Wolfflin—who argued that dome of central-plan church was the ideal embodiment of Renaissance thought—the architectural critic Robin Evans suggests that, within the Christian tradition, these structures and the frescoes painted on their inside were evidence of nothing less than an architectural and artistic struggle to reconcile contradictory theological concepts of heaven and earth.[5] After all, the heavens were composed of orbiting celestial bodies arranged in concentric spheres around the earth, yet all power—including divine power—radiated out from a central point. The dispute, as Evans puts it, was between envelopment and emanation. Each position embodied distinct and sometimes antagonistic social, theological, and political claims about the location of God with respect to man. According to Evans, the achievements of Brunelleschi or Raphael lay in their ability to literally give form to the contours of this dispute by bringing these differences into proximity and holding them in a space of coexistence. Somewhat perversely, when it comes to domes, the very recalcitrance of their geometries has only encouraged rather than limited

Dome for experimental theater and music, Oscar Niemeyer, 1975.

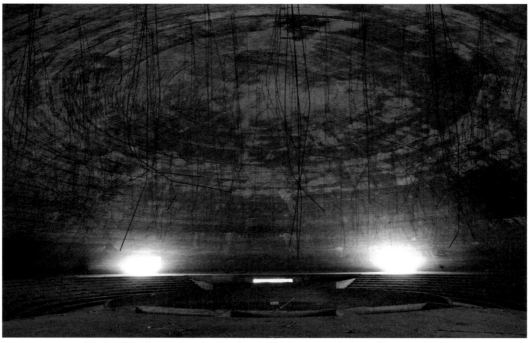

Interior of the theater dome for experimental theater and music, Oscar Niemeyer, 1975.

this kind of interpretation and speculation. For Wittkower and Wolfflin, the dome embodied perfection, while for Evans it embodied dispute. Yet all agreed that the dome must be interpreted. What was at stake was never signification as such, only what was signified.

Indeed Wittkower, Wolfflin, and Evans might well be justified in framing this problem in terms of codings and decodings of meaning insofar as such framing describes how the work was often reasoned by its authors and received by its audiences. The legacy of this question and its hold over contemporary accounts of architecture is of more concern. The issue of Arab identity and its architectural representation is a case in point, since it is still posed in terms of tropes and their representational adequacy. So the debate around domes or even the problem of appropriate and inappropriate orders now persists in the *mashrabiya*, geometric tiling, pointed arches, and vaulting that are deployed to signify "Islam" or "Arabness" along a spectrum ranging from very subtle and discreet (good) to vulgar and kitschy (bad). Consider the Lebanese Pavilion in the Rachid Karame Fair and Exposition site: a square-plan, open auditorium framed by a colonnade using a pointed arch. Most will recognize that this particular form refers to Ottoman traditions, of which there are many examples in the area. Some will not grasp the allusion, however, since the sign's legibility is dependent on the observer's prior knowledge. I happen to like the arches; others will find them unadorned, and most will probably pay them little attention. In any case, the form is supposed to signify cultural belonging and history.[6]

Architecture works on us and through us regardless of whether we "get" it, regardless of its intelligibility, and regardless of our capacity to appreciate its tropes or derive pleasure from their modification. This is an important political point; at stake is nothing less than a claim about what architecture does outside of architectural discourse—what it does to nonarchitects. Buildings are primarily nondiscursive objects even if they are always ensnared in discourses of every kind. This is why the concept of the diagram is so relevant here. It allows us to place the nondiscursive, a-signifying aspects of architecture into relation with the discursive, signifying aspects—architecture's instrumentality is always bound to the nonarchitectural. Diagrams are not manifested literally as specific tropes, or even as systems of organization. Neither the pilotis, the free plan, the New York frame, nor the Dom-ino is diagrammatic in and of itself, nor can they be ever considered in purely architectural terms, whatever that might mean. They only act on the social body as intended when they are secured by a constellation of cultural attitudes, laws, customs, regulations, and other requirements. The discursive and nondiscursive elements work together within any diagram. The panopticon would simply be a damp, round building with a tower in the middle without the transformation of penal codes, prison reform movements, the judiciary, and a police force. The modern domestic unit would just be an odd way of strategically segregating and bringing together bodies without the "charitable" incentives of philanthropic organizations, the regular assessments of housing inspectors, or instruction manuals for poor families. Do prisoners or members of a nuclear family need to *recognize* these histories in the disposition of rooms and arrangement of functions? Will the disposition of rooms and arrangement of functions cease to act on their habits, pattern their socialization, or structure their gender roles if these histories are unintelligible? In other words, absent an *understanding* of its sociopolitical motive, will the prison cease to shape them as certain kinds of human subjects?

To answer this, consider another dome. In the northern Lebanese city of Tripoli, in the park-like Rachid Karame Fair and Exposition site, there is a dome that wears its dereliction a little better than the buildings around it. Some 62 meters wide, its slightly squat, not quite hemispherical shape gives little away. Only the acoustics and the sunken orchestra pit inside betray its uniqueness. The dome was supposed to be a venue for experimental theater and music, a program that makes it possible to calibrate the precise distance between the present situation in Lebanon and the past situation in Lebanon.

Back when it was still called the Syrian army and not yet "the regime," thousands of soldiers were stationed in temporary barracks alongside the dome. These days, because of the situation, only the especially curious venture in. A one-hour drive from Tripoli will take you to the top of the Lebanese ranges, where you can look out to what used to be Syria and listen to the sounds of shelling from the Qalamoun Mountains across the Bekaa Valley. From either vantage point, the sense of resignation is hard to shake. Nevertheless, these lost modernities deserve closer scrutiny. If a system of subjectification was built into the fair and exposition, it is worth asking exactly what kind of techniques would be addressed to the bodies and characters of those meant to populate the project? What was specific about architecture's contribution to the project of nation-building during this period? Is it possible to account for the imagined instrumentality of the project without relying exclusively on a semantic interpretation of its tropes?

TECHNOLOGIES OF NATIONHOOD

The exposition type played a critical role within nation-building projects throughout the nineteenth and twentieth century, exemplifying concepts of citizenship and cultural belonging. The Rachid Karame Fair and Exposition site draws on this history, especially its appropriation during the postcolonial era. Surrounded by a four-lane road and nestled in the elbow of a freeway connecting Tripoli to Beirut, the 1.1 kilometer long elliptical site might passfor the world's largest roundabout were it not for the occasionally beguiling structure poking past the canopy of trees. The exposition and fair facilities occupy maybe one-third of the site, with the rest set aside as an imagined parkland for the metropolis that never materialized around it. The 750 meter long expo hall is the most dominant element. To its east lie pavilions set in gardens, most of which were intended for some form of ongoing cultural production.

Commissioned in 1962, the project depended on the brief appearance of something resembling a social welfare state, in which large-scale public works were seen as integral to perceptions of political legitimacy and therefore to nation-building. By the 1970s, however, pan-Arabism, which first came to prominence with Nasser's regime in Egypt and Gaddafi's proposal for a Federation of Arab Republics, was on the decline. This indicated a regional shift away from secular and socialist principles toward sectarian political alignments. Military defeats and economic stagnation contributed to widespread discontent in the Arabic-speaking world. In Lebanon, the contraction of the state, the withdrawal of government from social services, and an inability to implement electoral reforms or build stable institutions coincided with the extreme regional destabilizations occurring as a result of the conflict between Israel and the Palestine Liberation Organization (PLO), now operating from Lebanese bases.

Most exposition histories focus on the organization of the exhibitions and the strategies used to order, represent, and juxtapose different cultures. At times, scholars will turn to the technical innovations used in the construction of the exposition hall or within the exhibits themselves. Niemeyer's proposal for Tripoli is different from the prototypical world's fair or international exposition in that it combines an exhibition hall with buildings dedicated to cultural production within a landscaped urban complex that was intended to be used as a model for structuring the growth of a city. These four elements—the exposition hall, the cultural pavilions, the park, and the urban plan—should be understood as complementary components within a nationalistic, pedagogical project.

There are two main forms of movement through the site corresponding to the linear organization of the exposition hall and the placement of the pavilions. Niemeyer constructed a series of ramps and elevated vantage points that encourage visitors to continually withdraw from the mass and survey the crowd before returning back down to the ground. Here, the crowd could see itself seeing and being seen. Outside of protests and demonstrations, organized public gatherings of this scale were unprecedented, and the effect of finding oneself caught in this reciprocal spectacle would have been quite powerful. Being shaped here was not just architecture; that architecture forged an audience that could, in the vastness of its own spectacle, become self-aware.

As Lebanon urbanized during the colonial period, *asabiyyah* (an Arabic term referring to social cohesion within a community group) and feudal familial ties that had traditionally structured sectarian belonging persisted in response to a highly competitive capitalist environment and the insecurity such an environment produced. Old networks of patronage remained important in the absence of a legitimate state able to insure the poor against the difficulties of urban life. In Lebanon, metropolitan anonymity did not dissolve feudal or familial bonds; it reterritorialized them and made them stronger. For a brief decade between the mid-1950s and 1960s, however, a concerted attempt was made to dissolve these links in order to establish them on new and different terms. The project in Tripoli is part of this history. Its organization manifests an attempt to orchestrate a set of affects and feelings of belonging that, when inscribed in dominant narratives of nationhood, would become untethered from their communal histories.

One can see the project as a machine designed to produce new relationships between the crowd and the individual, and therefore the nation—a mass orchestration of affect. However, the surplus of affect produced by the spectacle of the crowd that Niemeyer orchestrated through the ramps and vantage points would as yet remain undifferentiated, little more than a mass gripped by various existential intensities and feelings. This unformed set of affects therefore had to be captured and assigned a proper location within the social order. The crowd recently decoded must be recoded, classified, and naturalized within a national narrative. The exposition hall and the display of "characteristic" elements from the various nations assembled would inform the normalization and stabilization of a new Lebanese identity. Visitors would learn to distinguish themselves as citizens by acquiring new rules of public conduct, especially the consumption and appreciation of cultural artifacts.

Ordering the world into an image, as Timothy Mitchell puts it in his description of the Paris Exposition Universelle of 1889, produces two effects: first, a representation of national difference and, second, the extension of a colonial system of representation into the world itself.[7] In Tripoli, the mass public organization of the crowd and the relation of the individual's vantage point within it draw on the typological history of the international exposition and its curatorial organization. Through arranging encounters with artifacts, the fairground would have attempted to recode this undifferentiated population in order to define Lebanon's newly won place among other nations. In addition to exposition planning and exhibition design, Niemeyer introduces a third element: the pavilions for cultural production and performance. These pavilions locate the citizen in a position of imagined ownership over the products of cultural activity.

We might imagine the components of the fair working together to achieve the following ends: The subjects' communal bonds are confronted by something new—an *orderly* mass public spectacle, in which the subject undulates into and out of the mass producing a charge of affect that is not yet formalized. The consumption of the artifacts within the exhibition positions them in the world through a national narrative, until finally they are led to see themselves as the imagined producers of this national narrative. This is what the architectural machine accomplishes within the social diagram. The first component of the machine operates using a-signifying signs. The ramps and changes in height are not symbols to be interpreted; they intervene directly in the subjective field. Only later do the elements collaborate to produce signs whose meaning must be read. However, the precondition of meaning in the sign is the visceral charge produced within the subject. This representation of nationhood can only operate insofar as it can recode and formalize this substratum of affects and passions the spatial qualities of the project produce. However, this a-signification was only the architectural aspect of the diagram. The larger pedagogical ambition depended on more than the designs buildings have on human nature. They depended on a state that was willing to see itself as the architect of this national narrative, one in which these kinds of large-scale infrastructure projects were secured and oriented to specific ends through forms of cultural administration, curatorial strategies, exhibition programs, and the media. The weakness of the state meant that the pedagogical diagram and its technologies of nationhood did not stabilize before the onset of civil war in 1975.

AFTER THE REGIMES

> Those who refuse to wean themselves off an enthusiasm for
> politics project insurrections without end, powers constituent
> but never constituted, interruptions that are never the prelude
> to less abject continuities.
> —The Invisible Committee, *To Our Friends*

Of the many outcomes of "the situation," perhaps the most accepted is the conflation of destruction and reconstruction. Revenue from luxury apartments will shower down upon those who broker peace. In war, land speculation makes a joke of military calculus. Soon enough, the rhetoric of imminent futures promised in renderings of a new Aleppo or a new Damascus will double, albeit in an architectural register, the present legacy of violence through systematic destitution and dispossession. Before these images of cities to come have acquired their final touches, however, the future they depict will have been engineered into existence through land expropriation and models of real estate speculation, through promissory notes based on calculations of future revenue according to reliable standards and estimates of return. Untethered from the realities of existing land tenures, undisciplined labor markets, and unpredictable steel prices, they will reach purely speculative heights. Like the images of many urban futures, those destined for the "Arab world" will need to become standardized before they can be bankable—the recent images from a design for a city of seven million people between the Suez Canal and the shores of the Nile being a case in point. Like a bushel of wheat or a barrel of oil, the urban future has become a standard measure. Its consistency, its ubiquity, and its reliability are what allow it to circulate. It is not surprising that promised cities act like commodities: in one sense, that is increasingly what they are. The future has to learn how to flow. Its promise has to become liquid before it can become solid. As with grain and oil, too many inconsistencies leads to friction.

Rendering of masterplan for Capital Cairo, Skidmore, Owings & Merrill, 2015.

Despite the inherent conservatism of real estate markets and the dispiriting reliability of these propositions, their colonization of imaginations is far from complete. There is no lack of discontent toward—or critique of—these propositions within architectural discourse, and certainly no lack of emotional investment in alternative futures for Arab cities and Arab streets. In Aleppo, in Amman, in Beirut, in Cairo, in Damascus, in Gaza, and in Jerusalem, there are the most startling signs of political experimentation, social movements, activism, and institution building. There are, in other words, signs of survival, resistance, and invention to be found everywhere. From experimental coalitions on human and natural rights in Lebanon to proposals for democratic federalism in Southeastern Anatolia, from feminist movements in Kurdish communities to autonomous neighborhood assemblies in beleaguered Syrian cities, we see brave and vital attempts to reimagine social ties and forms of political organization. But without access to the equivalent of what Timothy Mitchell describes as the future's "engineering works," it is difficult to imagine how these precious experiments of alternative social orders can be sustained.[8] Discontent, critique, and desire alone will not be enough to turn aspirations into reality, because the various systems of calculation and capitalization that drive real estate development have a particular kind of durability.

The aversion toward "social engineering" within architecture or urban design has not resulted in societies that lack "engineering," let alone societies that are more perfectly ordered. On the contrary, the result is simply societies whose *order* and *engineering* have been dictated by those who have access to the future's infrastructure, leaving the rest condemned to precarity. The persistence and dominance of these conditions is often described as "neoliberalism," but this term fails to capture the specificity or diversity of the many socioeconomic diagrams that it is said to encompass. Moreover, it misses the fact that it is precisely these different socioeconomic structures that normalize processes of subjectification. The stability of the links forged between foreign capital, real estate speculation, and the domestic unit, for instance, works to ensure the reproduction of social and political power in urban space. The elements that compose these diagrams—their links, their ability to persist in time, repeat in space, and shape forms of subjectivity—cannot be reduced to matters of representation and interpretation. Financial calculation, debt, and living and working arrangements secure their own reproduction because they appear as sets of norms, material constraints, and habits that function regardless of the meanings or interpretations that critics assign to them.

Dome for experimental theater and music, and Lebanese National Pavilion, Oscar Niemeyer, 1975.

Adrian Lahoud

115

Perhaps the people that were supposed to inhabit the fair site in Tripoli ended up materializing fifty years later in the streets and squares of other cities? These crowds, recently gathered and too quickly dispersed by brutal counter-revolutions, insist that we question assumptions about the durability and stabilization of new social orders. The contingency of architecture with respect to these orders suggests a more careful examination of histories of sub-jectification as a pedagogical project. Such an inquiry would not simply entail escaping from signification but rather describing the feelings, codings, and struc-tures in which signifying and a-signifying elements cooperate within a political project. The institutionalization of social movements might be one place to start, and architecture's impersonal form might have much to contribute. After all, when regimes are brought down and after the people have expressed their demands, new kinds of structures to support new habits of life are needed if legacies of social transformation are to be kept alive.

1   Important parts of this essay evolved as a response to Timothy Mitchell's keynote address at "Architecture and Representation: The Arab City," Columbia Graduate School of Architecture, Planning and Preservation, New York, November 21, 2014, included in this volume as "The Capital City" (page 258), and as a result of an ongoing con-versation with Nora Akawi, beginning in Palestine on March 20, 2015, on the func-tion and understanding on "the situation."

2   Jonathan Littell, *Syrian Notebooks: Inside the Homs Uprising, January 16–February 2, 2012* (New York: Verso, 2015).

3   The Invisible Committee, *To Our Friends* (South Pasadena, CA: Semiotext(e); Cambridge, MA: MIT Press, 2015), 83.

4   The exemplary account of this period and its regional effect is Samir Kassir, *Being Arab* (London: Verso, 2006).

5   Rudolf Wittkower, *Architectural Prin-ciples in the Age of Humanism* (New York: Norton, 1971); Heinrich Wölfflin, *Classic Art: An Introduction to the Italian Renaissance* (1899; New York: Phaidon, 1952); Robin Evans, *The Projective Cast: Architecture and Its Three Geometries* (Cambridge, MA: MIT Press, 1995).

6   Writing a decade after Evans, Jeffery Kipnis makes the following comment regarding Villa Savoye: "It works for me and on me, but I can understand why others just see a nice looking house." Jeffery Kipnis, "Re-originating Diagrams," in *Peter Eisenman: Feints*, ed. Silvio Cassarà (Milan: Skira, 2006, 194). The comment comes in the context of an attempt to explain the role of the diagram in architecture and its potential political instrumentality. Yet in every example cited in the text, from D. H. Lawrence's appreciation of Cezanne's apples to the author's own appreciation of Bee-thoven's Ninth Symphony, intelligibility is tied to recognition, especially the recogni-tion of signs. As he suggests, "only some are sensitive to architectural effects in the full political dimension" (194). The cultivation of "sensitivity" notwithstanding, and regard-less of whether one reads this as a claim for prior acculturation or just personal taste, these signs are always things that are conveyed through formal tropes, in this case Le Corbusier's Five Points. Architecture may or may not have specificity as a medium, as Kipnis claims, but the model for how the medium works is stubbornly linguistic.

7   Timothy Mitchell, "The World as Exhibition," *Comparative Studies in Society and History*, vol. 31, no. 2 (April 1989): 217–36.

8   Mitchell, "The Capital City."

Reading the Modern Narrative of Amman: Between the Nation and the National

SABA INNAB

The formation of Amman as the capital of the "modern state" of Jordan was a gradual process beginning in the 1950s and lasting through the 1980s, a period punctuated with over fifty proposed master plans within the capital and across the country as a whole. In a city that was being constructed within the framework of nation-building, those attempts were tools of negotiation and even reclamation of spaces by the state, where the "nation" and the "national" were always contested. However, it was not until the 1980s that signifiers of the modern state started to become evident in the cityscape: the master plan, the plaza, and the monument.

This symptom of a belated modernity cannot be read outside of the ways that Amman was experiencing successive separations from Palestine, from *naksa* (the setback) in 1967 to the disengagement of the West Bank and Jordan in 1987. Those "separations" varied in their intensity but were all inscribed in the cityscape, leading to schisms in the city's structure. In the official discourse, a new phase for Amman as a modern city—in a postmodern time—was announced during the 1980s, introducing a new kind of monumentality that emphasized those schisms.

The growth of Amman has come in response to regional upheavals and to shifts in Jordan's economic and political conditions, reflected in the morphology of its formative years. The influx of refugees called for fast and often arbitrary solutions that caused confusion in the city structure, a confusion only exacerbated by later efforts at remediation of such confusion. The city was thus shaped by these reciprocal actions, creating a multicentered urban geography. Yet it was precisely those things that were unspoken, lost, and avoided in the process of nation-building that formed an alternate image of the city over the years. This loss created a systemic denial of historic memory that caused a disjunction not only in the official history and collective narrative of the city but also in its spatiality. Amman is a city that portrays itself as in a state of permanent temporariness, a metropolis on the cusp of emerging.

The episodes that follow index moments in which pivotal events of Amman's modern history were inscribed in its built environment. This text builds around two ceremonial events and their spatial inscriptions in the city. Those ceremonies may be read as an official narrative produced by the state in the process of

A service driver looking through the fence of Raghadan bus terminal construction site in 2003. The reonovation of the terminal is the most recent episode in a history of state-generated urban transformations to the site.

nation-building. In order to understand the spatial and social dimension of such events, we have to map history onto places and understand the genesis, shifts, abandonments, and resurgences that occurred there. Those patterns explain or chart the relationship between political ruling power, on the one hand, and spaces—their representations, and identifications—on the other. Superimposing spatial analysis, records, and walks on top of this process of mapping helps create a timeline of the city's recent history.

This nonlinear timeline is a record of a process of trial and error, or of erasure, whereby the state, in its process of reclamation, seems to be constantly building a "ruin" that soon will be abandoned and replaced by another in an endless process of building the "national." Jumps across time reveal the operative quality of the state's official narrative. This exercise of moving back and forth as a method of excavation creates a necessary tension between the current situation and the past. Scenes in different periods of times are portrayed as "evidence," constructing a framework that connects the experience of a given space with the different narratives that fashioned that space.

SCENE I:
AL-SAHA AL-HASHEMIYEH (HASHEMITE PLAZA), WINTER 2002

A pastiche of landmarks surround the Al-Saha Al-Hashemiyeh plaza, each vying for attention. Standing amid what seems an endless stretch of pavement, one faces the Citadel—a palimpsest of ancient ruins—and the mountain where the royal palaces have been built since the 1920s. The Roman amphitheater is to the left. On the right is the Raghadan bus terminal, which links downtown to other areas of the capital, the surrounding mountains, and nearby cities. Three public spaces align on one axis, each defining and representing a different "public." The first thing one notices is the competing monumentalities. Here the spatial inscription of the relationship between the "ruling" powers and public space takes two forms—the Roman temple and the Agora; the royal palaces and Hashemite Plaza.

As part of the "Amman downtown tourist zone" project funded by JICA (the Japanese International Cooperation Agency) and governed by the Municipality of Greater Amman, Raghadan bus terminal has been temporarily relocated to the city's eastern end, al-Mahatta. The project aims to promote tourism in downtown Amman through small-scale interventions, like pedestrian trails linking significant historical sites or the upgrading of main streets, but its primary focus is the redesign of the bus terminal as a tourist transportation hub. Walking by the construction site of the terminal, al-Saha al-Hashemiyeh seems dysfunctional, obsolete, and empty—a sinking plaza on downtown's eastern fringe.

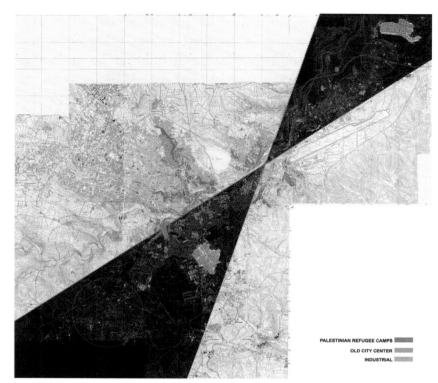

Map showing the concentration of industrial areas and factories around the Palestinian refugee camps.

PALESTINIAN REFUGEE CAMPS
OLD CITY CENTER
INDUSTRIAL

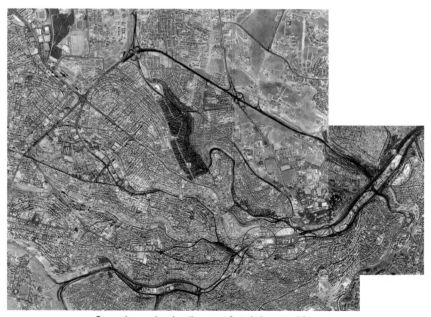

General map showing the area of study in central Amman.
1. Hashemite Plaza   2. Roman Ampitheater   3. Raghadan Bus Terminal   4. Citadel   5. Royal Palaces Mountain
6. Temporary Bus Terminal   7. Mahatta Camp   8. Al Salt Street   9. Al Abdali Bus Terminal   10. Al Abdali Regeneration Project
11. Al Hussein Camp   12. City Hall Compound, Ras al Ain   13. Saqf al Seil Street   14. Al Husseini Mosque

Saba Innab

121

Climbing the mountains, paralleling the highway—but 40 meters higher—passageways cut through clusters of concrete homes, taking one gradually to the city's edge where the road terminates at another point in flux: the al-Mahatta (station, in Arabic) area, named after the old Hejaz train station. The temporary terminal is located between two highways, next to the Modern Flour Mills and Macaroni Factory Co. (known as the Gazelle factory), and a few workshops and warehouses facing al-Mahatta refugee camp.[1]

The periphery is the space where authority is most starkly revealed. In Amman, the edge condition is where contestation over representation plays out and structures of power become vivid. Cities tend to push the "unwanted" to the edge—thousands of houses overlooking the stream of cars and the industrial areas that rely on cheap labor. Meanwhile, the new city waves back from the horizon. This is a scene of what the city cast aside. It is a center that was forced to become an edge.

Cities grow in accordance with shifts in capital accumulation and patterns of consumption. Those patterns show the city as a field of opportunities supported by a free market, liberated from the state, and generating a fully commoditized form of social life through large-scale development practices and regeneration projects. Gradually, the city is transformed into an "image" that triggers marginalization, gentrification, and dislocation, increasing spatial and social segregation. The purpose here is not to criticize such projects and the impacts of gentrification and displacement; these are natural consequences of capital accumulation everywhere. In the case of Amman, however, a purposeful political act runs through these practices: targeted gentrification is a way of reclaiming place, particularly public spaces, after their abandonment.

Consider, for instance, a triangle whose points are al-Saha al-Hashemiyeh and the Raghadan bus terminal at the eastern end of downtown, the city hall building in Ras el Ain at the western end of downtown, and al-Abdali bus terminal at the end of Salt Street. This triangle, which has come to define, or confine, the downtown area, represents the revival or reclamation of these centers by political power in a way that denies other stories and representations of the recent history of Amman. This "return" is constructed through three development projects and large-scale urban regeneration projects that focus on the idea of "heritage" as a frozen material image and avoid dealing with the space as a social product. With such conscious control of not only the city's patterns of use but also of its image, one ought to ask, for whom is the city being planned?

CEREMONY I:
AL–SAHA AL–HASHEMIYEH, 1986

In November 1986, the Hashemite Plaza was unveiled as a birthday gift to King Hussein. It was the first plaza in Amman to be built as a political plaza. Overlooking it are the royal palaces, making the space an apt venue for military parades and marches. At its corner, the renovated Roman amphitheater hosts a small museum of traditional crafts and objects. The plaza seems to take shape from the amphitheater's semicircular form.

Well sited between Damascus and Medina, Amman grew into a major hub of the Ottoman Hejaz railway in the early twentieth century. By 1908 the railway was in operation, giving the city unprecedented strategic importance. The first municipal council was formed in 1909. After the declaration of the Emirate of Trans-Jordan in 1921, Prince Abdullah turned what was already becoming a city center, the area around the amphitheater, into a government square and, in 1924, designated the mountain overlooking the amphitheater as the location for the royal palaces.

Abdullah's decision built atop existing urban growth and past exercises of power. In the late nineteenth century, Ottoman rulers had encouraged Circassian troops to settle in the lands connecting Bilad al-Sham to the Arabian Peninsula, thereby extending and solidifying the Ottoman presence in the territory. The first troops settled around the amphitheater, its ruins and caves, its

The old city of Amman at the beginning of the twentieth century, showing the Husseini Mosque and the Nymphaeum.

surrounding hills, and the stream of water known as al-Seil. As more Circassian troops arrived and settled along al-Seil, the urban fabric began to grow organically around the area. The nearby Omari Mosque (renovated in 1923 as the Great Husseini Mosque) and its square, located on the Cardo, or main Roman road, served as another nexus of growth. The mosque was already a gathering spot and the stream behind it a useful resource, a logical site for a flourishing trade economy. The mosque and its square gained additional importance by being situated on the major regional thoroughfare, linking the train station and the ancient town of Salt to other neighborhoods and cities.

In 1948, one year after independence and the establishment of the Hashemite kingdom of Jordan, the country's demographics were redefined when incoming waves of Palestinian refugees nearly doubled the population. In 1950, the Jordanian parliament voted for the political unity of the West and the East Banks, which redefined the physical boundary of the nation-state. Several months later, the government decided to grant Amman the title of *amaneh* (municipality), which was a political gesture that created a new hierarchy: Amman, not Jerusalem, became the administrative and a political capital in the newly united banks.[2]

By 1952, the census showed that 29 percent of Amman's population lived in tents and 8 percent in caves.[3] Therefore, in 1953, as part of a UN technical assistance program, Max Lock (a British urban planner working for the United Nations) and Gerald King were commissioned to develop a master plan to address the urgent needs of housing and infrastructure, as well as to propose a new vision for the city.[4] In place of downtown's patchwork-built environment, Lock envisaged a verdant central park anchored by museums, cafes, and theaters, spanning between the Great Husseini Mosque and the Bath Bridge (the same zone of intervention of the JICA project in the 2000s). Lock's plan also saw the historic Citadel transformed. Crowning the mountain beside the palaces, the ancient site was to become the government center and a clear symbol of state power. His vision reflected recent theories of British town planning, drawing particularly on Ebenezer Howard and the Garden City; it also demonstrated a modern understanding of heritage and preservation, stultifying the active commerce of a mixed residential district by designating it an administrative and cultural zone.[5]

However, as Lock drew up his plans, a quite different type of growth was occurring in the city center. Two Palestinian camps were built in the beginning of the 1950s, interrupting any possibility for a citywide master plan. With pan-Arabism on the rise by the mid-1950s, Lock's proposals were seen as an unwelcome Western intervention by the Jordanian nationalist movement, which held the majority in parliament.[6]

In 1957, a royal palace was built west of downtown, in Zahran, establishing a new administrative center. In this shift, one can identify an urban evolution pattern: every ruler comes with a new palace location, a mosque named after the late king, a public plaza, and even a museum. The most recent shift, in the early 2000s, saw the seat of power relocated to the far west of Amman, in Hummar, effectively turning its back on the whole city.

Losing Jerusalem after 1967 was actually a capital gain for Amman. Juxtaposing a 1953 aerial photo and a map from the early 1970s shows the expansion of Palestinian refugee camps toward the city center. In the meantime, there was

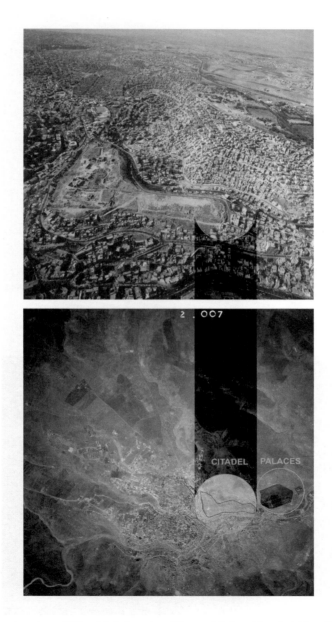

A diagram based on a 1953 aerial photo and an oblique aerial view of the citadel from the 1990s, showing Lock's proposal for the city center.

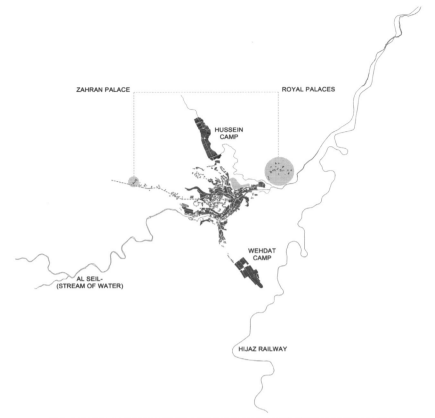

Map based on an aerial photo from 1953 showing the shift of the royal palaces from
Raghadan to Zahran in 1957 in relation to the city center and the refugee camps.

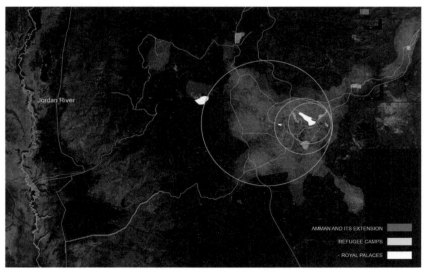

Map based an an aerial image showing the shifts of the royal palaces toward
the west, away from the city.

Reading the Modern Narrative of Amman

significant lower- and lower-middle-class settlement in the voids between the camps, the center, and the royal palaces. The upper middle class of the West Bank settled toward the northwest spine of the city, close to the new center around the new palace, creating another urban enclave.

In the 1960s, King Hussein's Palestinian policy could at best be described as contradictory. He opposed any form of Palestinian organization that could compete with the exclusive "right" of the Jordanian throne to represent the Palestinians, such as the General Palestine Government, set up in Gaza in 1949, or the Higher Palestine Organization based in Cairo and Damascus.[7] Yet he decided, hesitantly, to support the Arab decision to establish the Palestine Liberation Organization (PLO) in 1964, as the PLO did not claim at the time to be the sole representative of the Palestinian people and made no claims of sovereignty over the West Bank.[8] The loss to Israel in the 1967 war was a turning point for the Palestinian-Jordanian dynamic. The complete loss of Palestine to Israeli occupation reinforced Jordan as a political entity. It was also the time when Palestinians were starting "to take matters into their own hands."[9] Although Palestinian *Fida'iyyin* groups from different factions had been forming since the late 1950s, they were now able to improve their organization and mobilize many among the population of Palestinian refugees, especially in Jordan.[10, 11]

These factions sought "the liberation of all Palestine through a Palestinian armed struggle" (*al-Kifah al-Musallah*). They established themselves as a paramilitary institutionalized resistance movement and developed their own culture through educational programs, research centers, and youth associations, along with vivid visual and artistic language, with the PLO as unifying framework. They used Jordan as a frontier for their operations in the occupied West Bank, which led to an inevitable power struggle between the throne and *al-Fida'iyyin*, especially when they formed an alternative political identification and allegiance for Palestinians in the kingdom. The visible presence of *al-fida'i* in the streets of Amman, and the proximity of their bases to downtown—along with the proximity of the two major Palestinian camps (al-Hussein and al-Wehdat) to the center of town and the royal palaces—established a zone of influence and popularity in the city.

In 1968, al-Karameh, a small Jordanian town on the East Bank in the Jordan valley, and the site of a Palestinian refugee camp where many *Fida'iyyin* were stationed, became a target for an Israeli operation.[12] The Jordanian army and the *Fida'iyyin* were able to force the Israelis to withdraw.[13] The general public celebrated the Palestinian *Fida'iyyin* as the battle's victors while in no way acknowledging the role played by the Jordanian army in the fighting.[14] The lack of recognition aggrieved the Jordanian government, so it staged a celebration—held in front of the royal palaces, in what would later be Hashemite Plaza—to mark the Jordanian army's triumph in the Karameh battle. Clashes and confrontations between the army and the *Fida'iyyin* escalated, leading to September 1970, when King Hussein finally ordered his troops to strike and eliminate the *Fida'iyyin* network in Jordan. Thousands of Palestinians were killed in the initial battle, which came to be known as Black September, and vast tracts of Jordanian cities were destroyed.[15] After the Palestinian resistance left Amman and Jordan entirely in 1971, the political void was filled by the rise of the Hashemite throne as the sole political representative of Palestinians in Jordan.

SCENE II:
THE DISAPPEARANCE OF AL-SEIL, LATE 1970S–EARLY 1980S

During the 1960s, under the aegis of "welfare capitalism," King Hussein employed urbanism as a tool for promoting the Westernization of Amman.[16] Development was driven through economic and social ideology delineated in comprehensive plans.[17] Most of the planning efforts at the time focused on building public facilities, such as the Jordan University (1962) and Hussein Sport City (1964) at the eastern edge of the city, and linking major cities, as with the Amman-Jerusalem road, constructed in the late 1950s.[18]

Victor Lorenz, a Czech regional planner, again working through a United Nations technical assistance program, was assigned the task of establishing an administrative and technical framework for planning in Jordan through creating a master plan spanning from 1967 to '81.[19] The Jordanian economy had suffered after the Israeli occupation of the West Bank in 1967, which had "stripped Jordan of 90 percent of its tourism assets." The Jordanian government changed its tourism policy toward attracting shorter-term "stop-over" tourists and began promoting Jordan as a gateway to the Middle East.[20] In this framework, and in coordination with Lorenz's proposals, the idea of a national visitor's center was being developed. The Jordan park planning team and Robert F. Gibbs developed a plan for a central business district that extended from the Husseini Mosque to the royal palaces, with a national library, museum, and plaza at the gate of Raghadan Palace.[21] The proposal resonates with Lock's plan in 1950s in the staging approach of symbols of power; however, here it was targeting another audience: the tourist.[22]

Lorenz's plan for the city, meanwhile, focused on relieving traffic by adding two ring roads and widening the radial ones passing through central areas. These improvements would lead to the covering of the main stream that historically threaded through the middle of the town, known as the Seil of Amman.[23] Those two shifts—catering to a tourist rather than local audience, and covering the stream—changed the spatial logic of the city.

In Arabic, Saqf al-Seil means "the roof of the water stream." It is an informal name given to Quraish Street, built atop the stream. The name implies another space and time, a palimpsest that still haunts the site. In his novel *A Tale of a City*, Abdel Rahman Munif describes the old city as an organic tissue unfolding around the small winding river starting from Ras el Ain (the current location of the city hall) west of downtown and going east and joining with Seil al-Zarqa. Al-Seil unfolded into markets, mills, forests, and ponds that were sometimes used as swimming pools. One faced the Nymphaeum; another faced the Roman amphitheater.[24] While some functions persisted after the disappearance of al-Seil—the open vegetable market, the second-hand shops on both "banks" that exist in sunken levels—many others vanished.

Saqf al-Seil separates the valley of downtown Amman from the surrounding mountains. It marks a different tempo in the movement of the city, a different structure of division. The disappearance of al-Seil was gradual, though it followed the sudden growth of Amman's population, in 1948 and again in 1967. The final disappearance of al-Seil was around two decades after '67; an entire street level was "buried" and new floors built atop it. Monotonous linear arcades were constructed along the stream's former contours, creating a monolithic divide between the mountains and downtown. These were hasty responses, a simplistic accommodation of specific social needs filling the empty space caused by the covering of al-Seil.[25]

The city built a roadway atop the former creek bed, and al-Seil was replaced by a stream of cars. One ought to ask, what becomes of a place when an element of its formative years vanishes?

CEREMONY II:
MARTYR'S MEMORIAL, 1977

In 1977, amid the celebrations of Jordan's Independence Day, King Hussein unveiled a memorial on the anniversary of the Great Arab Revolt.[26] Jordan's independence was not connected to any heroic battles; there were no momentous days or canonical heroes to rally a national psyche around. But at the time it was crucial to create one.

In the aftermath of Black September, there was an urgent need for the Jordanian state to rewrite its narrative. One response was erasure, for example the destruction of the Tomb of the Unknown Martyr in 1971, which the PLO had erected in Jabal al-Ashrafiyyah on October 21, 1970. Another response was the new monumentality imposed on the city, a monumentality that widened the schisms between east and west, between the domestic and the urban. The National Assembly, the Ministry of Defense, the Secret Police Building, and the

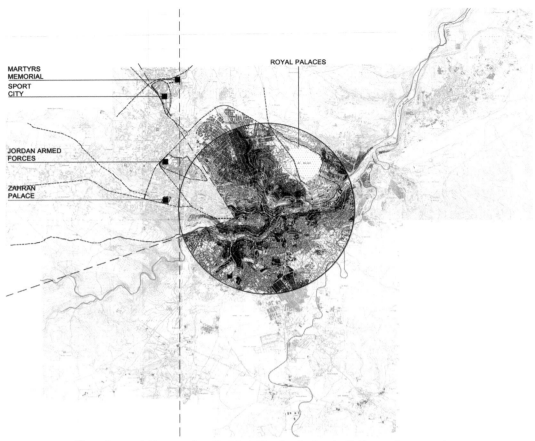

Illustration overlaid on map from the late 1970s, showing how institutions and monuments are gathered around one axis between the city center and the new extension toward west.

Acropolis, Ka'ba, Martyr's Memorial.

Reading the Modern Narrative of Amman

King Abdulla (I) Mosque were built on the main axis between east and west Amman. But the most crucial building to constructing this narrative was the Martyr's Memorial (Sarh Al-Shahid).

Designed by the Jordanian architect Victor Bisharat with the help of the Armed Forces, the memorial draws on two visual references—al-Ka'ba and the Acropolis. Wrapped in a Qur'anic band, the memorial rests on a podium overlooking the city's new expansion. The building emphasizes two pillars of the national narrative: religion and the military. The memorial is composed of a mass within a mass, and a spiral ramp that wraps around a black stone rising to a roof garden that finally celebrates the "purity" of all martyrs. Vitrines are located along the ramp, showcasing objects, arms, and dioramas representing the battles, starting from the Arab revolt to the last confrontation with Israel in 1975 (a confrontation that has been to a great degree excluded from the popular narrative). When built, the narrative seemed complete, suggesting that there would be no new martyrs and no new wars. In 1999, a new vitrine was added, devoted to the late King Hussein. It includes his personal possessions, such as a formal suit, gun, lighter, and Qur'an, adding another layer to this "finished" narrative and a new definition to the term "martyr."

This building, as many others built in the same period, hovers in the background of the widely stretched cityscape. The memorial is another piece of constructed evidence of the unspoken, the lost, and the avoided in the process of Jordanian nation-building, a systemic denial causing a disjunction not only in the official history and the collective narrative but also in the spatiality of the city. This disjunction feeds into the permanent temporariness of Amman, where notions of the "nation" and the "national" are always in tension.

SCENE III:
RAGHADAN AND ABDALI, 2015

Raghadan bus terminal and the Hashemite Plaza have been given a modern makeover. Renovations and a more contextual site plan have streamlined the structures and integrated the Roman amphitheater with the plaza. However, the bus terminal remains empty and unused. Despite the municipality's stated intent to relocate the bus terminal only temporarily to Mahatta, it remains there to this day. At Raghadan, inaccessible pedestrian bridges link the terminal with the facing mountain, and the newly renovated plaza remains vacant, except during special events and on holidays.[27]

Approaching the once-temporary Mahatta terminal, the site seems near unraveling under the strain of constant influx. People, vendors, cars, and buses converge in one wide street; above, the palaces rise like a phantom of power.

Close-up of the transformation of the Hashemite plaza, from the bottom; aerial photograph 1978, 1990s, and 2015.

Here one finds the slums, camps, buses, warehouses, and workshops composing an unspoken narrative of spatial violence.

In the early 1970s, this downtown area became increasingly disconnected from the rest of the city, following spatial and socioeconomic segregation between the city center and east Amman on the one side and fragmented growth toward the west of the city on the other. From a physical point of view, this segregation resulted from uneven patterns of growth, abandonment, and sprawl, as well as gaps in the urban fabric due to the city's multinodal nature. This was aggravated by the different patterns of movement and the distribution of public transportation between east and west Amman.

Users of the old Raghadan and al-Abdali bus terminals were, and will continue to be, spatially excluded and pushed farther away from the centers, to al-Mahatta bus terminal and to Tabarboor, the new location of al-Abdali terminal, creating huge detours for locals and residents of downtown's adjacent mountains. While Amman's working classes are made to travel the perimeter of the city, its center is opened up as a site for the meandering tourist to consume.

Al-Abdali Regeneration Project, previously the site of the General Jordan Armed Forces Headquarters (built as a military base during the British mandate in the 1930s, overlooking the Abdali bus terminal), is a new development with over 1.7 million square meters of apartments, offices, retail, hotels, and entertainment facilities. Its towers and architectural language suggest a new monumentality in harmony with an existing one: the National Assembly, Supreme Court, and Abdullah I Mosque. It is a real estate project that is embraced by governmental monumentality. The new commercial monumentality is replacing another one carved in the memory of the surrounding streets and neighborhoods. This is a site that witnessed contestation between the armed forces and the *Fida'iyyin* in the surrounding mountains in the late 1960s, where the infamous Secret Police headquarters once stood. But the Secret Police Building has been replaced by the "new way of life" towers, echoing the slogan of the project along with "new city center." That phrase may ring familiar, resurrected from King Hussein's definition of welfare capitalism fifty years ago.

By the mid-1980s, many major projects Jordanian nation-state building in Amman were finally implemented or under way, sites such as the National Assembly, the king Abdullah I Mosque, the Hashemite Plaza, and most importantly, the first comprehensive master plan for greater Amman.[28] Simultaneously, on the other bank, the Palestinian uprising was not only resisting the Israeli occupation but also rejecting the Jordanianness of the West Bank. Since the PLO was increasingly recognized as the only political representative of the Palestinians, Jordan's king "disengaged" from the West Bank.[29] This was a paradigm shift that changed the tone of Jordan's foreign and interior policy but also had a profound impact on the national identity and the spatiality of Amman. For a few years after, state rhetoric mobilized peace with Israel as a means to generate economic opportunity and investment in a time of an economic slowdown. However, the choice for peace was a redefinition of Jordan's national interest and identity; it was a move to embrace the global economy in order to imagine a post-Palestinian Jordan.[30]

In this framework, it is evident that the current regeneration projects are a replacement of symbols of the state, announcing a new era of neoliberal development. When a retail tower or mall replaces the Secret Police Building, it does not end the police state; rather, it masks it, hiding further expanding circles of exclusion and suppression in another form, through banal architecture that impedes mobility, covers up memory, and perpetuates a kind of everyday oppression.

One cannot help but read the current morphology of Amman as a cumulative struggle over places and their representations. That struggle is clearly visible in the withdrawal of power from urban centers or in the reduction of those centers' influence, and it is revealed in the attempts to write atop a specific and usually unspoken history or memory of a place. This struggle is equally evident in the "return" of power to those same abandoned or avoided places within the framework of renewal, which is nothing more than another way to subvert the meaning of particular parts of the city to a dominant narrative.

View of al-Abdali towers and King Abdalla I mosque, 2014.

Reading the Modern Narrative of Amman

1   Al Mahatta Camp is a Palestinian refugee camp that is not registered with the United Nations Relief and Works Agency (UNRWA) and is therefore technically called an "unofficial" camp.

2   Raed al Tal, *Structures of Authority: A Sociopolitical Account of Architectural and Urban Programs in Amman, Jordan (1953-1999)* (Binghamton: State University of New York at Binghamton, 2006), 48.

3   Nabil Abu Dayyeh, "Persisting Vision: Plans for a Modern Arab Capital, Amman, 1955-2002," *Planning Perspectives*, vol. 19, no. 1 (Spring 2004): 86.

4   Abu Dayyeh, "Persisting Vision," 86.

5   Abu Dayyeh, "Persisting Vision," 87.

6   The Jordanian national movement was a political movement that emerged from the same ideological basis as Arab nationalism. In 1956, parliamentary elections brought an Arab nationalist majority into power. A coup attempted by members of the army, led by prime minister al-Nabulsi and supported by General Ali Abu Nowar, failed. Martial law was declared, all political parties were dissolved, and all political expression suppressed. Some scholars highlight this event as "the birth of modern Jordan."

7   Both Jordan and Egypt resisted any proposal that called for a separate Palestinian entity. Due to the split into two major regional/international alliances—Amman/Riyadh/USA versus Cairo/Damascus/USSR—and the increasing popular support for the PLO, the leaders of both countries changed their position in the early 1960s.

8   See Joseph Massad, *Colonial Effects: The Making of National Identity in Jordan*, (New York: Columbia University Press, 2001), 236

9   Massad, *Colonial Effects*, 236.

10   *Fida'i* (vernacular plural, *Fida'iyyin*) translates literally as "one who sacrifices himself (for his country)."

11   Massad, *Colonial Effects*, 239.

12   Massad, *Colonial Effects*, 239.

13   On a tactical level, the battle did end in Israel's favor and the purpose of the mission was achieved, as the town of Karameh was leveled and both *al-Fida'iyyin* and the army suffered heavy damages. However, for the Palestinians it became a mythological victory that established their national claims. Yazid Sayegh, *Al-Kifah al-musallah wa-al-bahth 'an al-dawlah: al-Harakah al wataniyah al Filastiniyah, 1949–1993,* trans. Basim Sirhan (Washington, DC: Institute For Palestine Studies, 2002).

14   Both the Jordanian army and the *Fida'iyyin* minimized the role of the other in the battle.

15   See Massad, *Colonial Effects*.

16   "By the spring of 1957, the Eisenhower doctrine proposed replacing the British aid to Jordan with American, in exchange for Jordanian support of against communism." Ranjit Singh, "Liberalisation or Democratisation? The Limits of Political Reform and Civil Society in Jordan," in *Jordan in Transition, 1900-2000*, ed. George Joffe (London: Hurst & Company, 2002), 73. For more on welfare capitalism in Amman see al Tal, *Structures of Authority,* 58.

17   These plans included the Five-Year Program for Economic and Social Development, 1962–67, which was interrupted and later replaced by the Seven-Year Program of 1964–1970, which was followed by the five-year plan from 1976 to 1981. Abu Dayyeh, "Persisting Vision," 90.

18   Sir Charles Johnston, *Al-Urdon 'Ala-al Haffah*, trans. Fahmy Shamma (Amman: Ministry of Culture in Jordan), 145.

19   Abu Dayyeh, "Persisting Vision," 90.

20   Matthew Gray, "Development Strategies and the Political Economy of Tourism in Contemporary Jordan," in *Jordan in Transition, 1900-2000,* 310.

21   Abu Dayyeh, "Persisting Vision," 92-93.

22   Abu Dayyeh, "Persisting Vision," 92-93.

23   Abu Dayyeh, "Persisting Vision," 92-93.

24   Abdelrahman Munif, *Seerat Madinah, Amman Fil-arbi'inat* (Beirut: Arab Institute for Research and Publishing, 2006), 220.

25   This development was part of a project by The International Engineering Consultants Association, Japan (IECA) and was published in 1978 as the *Preliminary Study on the City Center Development of Municipality of Amman.* The only proposal from the IECA plan to be implemented, marginal as it was to the plan, was the redesigning of al Seil street (currently Quraish Street) as an arcade with pointed arches, aimed to reflect continuity with a certain vision of the history of Islamic architecture. Abu Dayyeh, "Persisting Vision," 95-98.

26   Elie Podeh, *The Politics of National Celebrations in the Arab Middle East* (Cambridge, England: Cambridge University Press, 2014), 186.

27   "Seven years after a major bus terminal in downtown Amman was renovated and then abandoned due to disputes between traders and the Greater Amman Municipality." Muath Freij, "For Shop Keepers, Raghadan Terminal Relocation Has Lasting Repercussions," *Jordan Times,* May 10, 2012.

28   The 1987 master plan was the first comprehensive plan to be put forth for Amman, and was a joint work of Dar Al-Handasa Consultants and the Municipality of Amman.

29   See Massad, *Colonial Effects*.

30   Waleed Hazbon, "Mapping the Landscape," in *Jordan in Transition*.

Architecture and Nation-Building
FELICITY D. SCOTT

The conference "Architecture and Representation: The Arab City" invited us to participate in the important task of critically rethinking the nexus of architecture and representation. It was an invitation to ask how we might begin to dismantle some longstanding, problematic, and persistent assumptions that have attended this nexus, particularly as they relate to nationalism and nation-building in the Middle East. Within architecture, questions symptomatic of these assumptions have often taken the following forms: How can architecture give identity to a new nation-state? What should an Egyptian architecture look like? How can architecture shore up the image of a new state as modern and democratic? These conventional and limited expectations of architecture's role in a transforming modernity now seem not only inadequate and naïve but also potentially pernicious (in the wrong hands). If not necessarily symptomatic of malevolent tendencies, when appearing in the context of differential power relations and military strengths in the region, such conceptions of architecture harbor the potential to be mobilized to particular ends via the long arm of other (nonregional) players—including the United States, the UN, and multinational corporations—even to participate in or exacerbate ongoing regional conflicts and challenges to sovereignty; hence the explicit or implicit importance of Palestine, of the Palestinian diaspora, and the Israel-Palestine conflict to many of the stories emerging during the conference.

My role was a modest one: moderating a panel that included Mohamed Elshahed, Saba Innab, Ziad Jamaleddine, and Adrian Lahoud. Each helped to complicate our understanding of the ways architecture operates within conditions of conflict, diaspora, rapid transformation, and other instabilities, and in so doing to reformulate the nexus of architecture and representation. Their work helps us ask how, whether as scholars or practitioners, we might rethink architecture's perceived role as always facilitating stabilization or unification, particularly vis-à-vis national identity. Architecture is typically assumed to be successful when it provides some type of clear identity, image, or organizational structure that enables these types of consistencies. Yet architecture can also, as their work demonstrates in different ways, be a powerful marker of ambivalences, discontinuities, and instabilities, and of course (unfortunately), it can be a site of violence. So we might ask whether there remains scope within the discipline not only to reflect on but also to self-consciously offer a post-identitarian and nonessentialist model of representation. Can the lens be shifted in order to think a type of postnationalist figuration of architecture, a paradigm that refuses to collapse into, or even actively contest assumptions informing, exclusivist notions like an Egyptian architecture, a Jordanian architecture, a Lebanese architecture, and so on?

As all too evident in the so-called Arab Cities today, the decoupling of persons from a nation-state or place of origin, or even their integration into new urban and cultural contexts, has important ramifications for traditional modes of understanding the relation of a people to their architecture. This identification of place, and of a coherent identity with and within it, has historically been understood as the basis of authenticity, what allowed earlier generations to speak of Italian architecture, French architecture, the architecture of the Dogon, and so forth. It was this idea of architectural forms developing over generations—handed down through customs and responding to climate, local materials, cultural patterns, etc.—that characterized more traditional ways of understanding what was proper to architecture in a particular place, what gave rise to its identity or consistency. So if forms of life are disrupted, dispersed, violated, incoherent, what status does that sort of architecture continue to have? And how do we, in turn, find adequate terms with which to understand more heterogeneous or complicated relations to place? So I want to ask whether architecture can operate otherwise on this playing field, in a manner that does not congeal into forms of representation that can be mobilized for regressive or violent ends. (George Arbid, for instance, spoke at the conference to some of the destructive effects of what he terms the Lebanonization of post-civil-war work.) These questions quickly entail others: Could the state sponsor alternative types of work? Could states remain clients for a post-identitarian paradigm, whether commissioning government buildings, public infrastructure, or projects for expos, trade fairs, and other key sites of nationalistic representation? Beyond buildings and urban plans, how would other dimensions of the discipline and discourse of architecture enter this picture? How might architecture's many other discursive and institutional registers, its many media and formats of dissemination—from exhibitions and new research paradigms to publications and pedagogy—contribute to a more complex reading of this conjunction of architecture and representation in a condition of territorial insecurity?

Saba Innab highlights the "multiple inner schisms" found in the fabric of the city of Amman, schisms born, as she puts it, of successive separations from Palestine. For her, this process led to the emergence of a new kind of monumentality, one not taking the form of representing the state as such but speaking to or embodying those schisms. It is an important provocation, one calling on us to ask why, or in what role, architecture might retain the figure of monumentality, and to what ends. What other roles can a schismatic monumentality play, for example in Amman's Monument to the Unknown Soldier, wherein the

137

monument is not a national monument within the context in which it stands but speaks to events elsewhere? What can an older term like monumentality continue to offer? What does retaining and refunctioning it do to our conception of architecture?

In a distinct manner, Mohamed Elshahed identifies the necessarily fragmented, noncohesive, and nonstatic images of the city of Cairo and its many possible futures as they emerged within popular images and proposals for the city. In so doing he suggests that the multiple frameworks of media, including the magazine and its tactical modes of intervention, can implicitly undermine any type of essentialist or centralist claims to Cairo's identity. It is a strong call not only for other voices but also for other media and modes of dissemination to assume a strategic function in emergent models of identity-in-formation and to offer ideas for other roles that architects might bring to the table within a politically unstable condition. Adrian Lahoud takes us in a different direction, complicating stories of architectural production and representation (the once-favored terrain of architectural scholarship) by reminding us of architecture's imbrication within the violence of war and occupation. He tells a remarkable story in which a canonical figure, Oscar Niemeyer, and his late modern formalism find themselves situated in an intense discursive proximity to the destruction of Syria and the death of its citizens. So again we find that the very platform for asking questions about architecture shifts in a manner that demands further questions. Not unlike the way monumentality persisted in a different guise, here we find the persistence of a canonical figure, but one whose work speaks to different stories. Ziad Jamaleddine in turn suggests that one might seek to identify in Beirut not national representation as such but rather traces of forms of life within the lived reality of urban spaces in the city. He invokes the figure of an alternative urban tale, indicating that narrative forms might be key. But, in a Foucauldian sense, we could also refract this type of practice back to questions of power and ask whether we could read such forms of life to manifest emergent techniques of power and the ability of contemporary subjects or of architects to counter them, to forge practices that cut across those forms of rationality to other ends.

I asked each of the speakers to further identify what was at stake in moments within their research when new openings in older narratives of architecture's contribution to nation-building took place, moments when new types of political space or new voices began to emerge as part of a discourse, or when unexpected tropes regarding architecture and its relation to the state came to the surface. I asked this not out of a naïve desire for optimism but to underscore points of potential transformation, even points of interruption of more tired conceptions of the nexus of architecture and representation. At stake was certainly the suggestion that architecture can be (or can continue to be) a medium or practice through which one widens the field of social and political struggles, that architecture's discursive tools, including its disciplinary expertise and forms of knowledge, can bring new material to the table. For as the projects here make evident, such research and practice tell us much about the constant, even permanent, need to reinvent a conception of democratic politics and the ways in which it might manifest—whether through semantic and representational logics or through strategic engagement of program, organization, and so on—and that such a reconception or re-valencing can be formulated through architectural and urban questions. Not necessarily always through design, but also through documentary, critical, and interrogative roles.

Interview with Suad Amiry

AMALE ANDRAOS and CAITLIN BLANCHFIELD

AMALE ANDRAOS   Suad, as the Director of the nongovernmental preservation organization Riwaq, you initiated what you call the Riwaq Registry, where you indexed historic buildings in Palestinian villages. From that you developed the 50 Villages Project, in which you selected a network of specific villages to preserve. It is a very interesting preservation strategy: instead of trying to preserve everything, or concentrating in one area, you create this web. It's a beautiful geography, and I wanted you to speak about why you chose this method.

SUAD AMIRY   Before the 50 Villages Project in rural Palestine began, the Riwaq Centre for Architecture worked on compiling, and eventually publishing, a comprehensive architectural survey (*Riwaq's Register of Historic Buildings in Palestine*), in which we documented 50,320 historic buildings (built before 1945) in about 420 villages and 16 towns. Based on the data and maps in this publication, we realized that we didn't have the human and financial resources—nor the time for that matter—to protect every historic building or historic center in what I call "Minor Palestine" (the West Bank, East Jerusalem, and the Gaza Strip). Hence, we had to be selective; otherwise we would end up losing everything. By protecting the most significant fifty villages, we concluded, we would end up protecting 50 percent of cultural heritage in Minor Palestine.

We looked at villages that still had intact or semi-intact architectural fabrics, as well as varied architectural typologies. Of course we tried to cover different geographical areas; we wanted the different communities in the various regions to feel that their cultural heritage was being protected.

The map "A Geography: 50 Villages" was a project by the artist Khalil Rabah that addressed the discontinuity and disconnectivity of Palestine—in other words, the difficulty of moving between these villages.

AA   This map is like a fragmented memory—and a fragmented idea of the past, but also of the future. You mentioned the choice of the rural and the choice to preserve a rural cultural heritage. I wanted to hear your thoughts about that, as well as the relationship of the village to the land.

SA   In Palestine, old cities such as Hebron, Nablus, Jerusalem, and Bethlehem have Rehabilitation Committees and Municipalities that work toward protecting them. That is why Riwaq has dedicated most of its time, energy, and budget to the villages.

CAITLIN BLANCHFIELD   Have you found the nature of public spaces changing in these villages as the economy becomes less agricultural, and does that affect the restoration work that you are doing?

SA   Yes, public space—as well as the historic centers—over the last sixty years have become unused, deserted, and hence dilapidated. In the 1930s and the 1940s, during the British mandate, major economic changes took place that resulted in changes to the landscape and the built environment in villages—basically the shift from farming to wage labor. This transformed villages from autonomous, inward-looking agrarian communities into outward-looking communities integrating into the global economy. While the extended families and clans still formed economic and social networks, the nuclear family became the basis of the labor force. This is reflected in the layout and the spatial organization of the village.

Floor tiling at the Nisf Jbeil women's center.

141

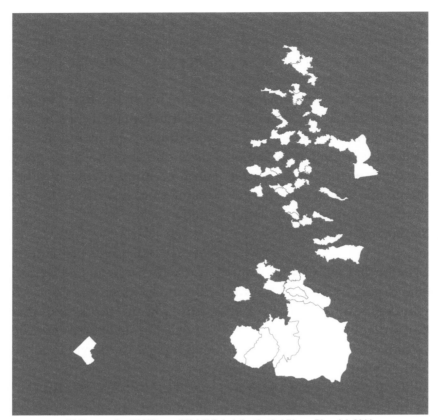

"A Geography: 50 Villages," Kahlil Rabah for the 3rd Riwaq Biennial, 2014.

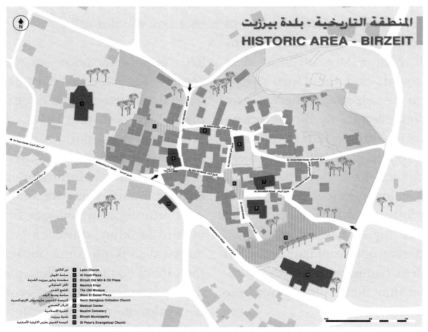

Map of the historic buildings in Birzeit, Palestine.

During the British Mandate, the orange industry around coastal towns of Palestine—places like Jaffa, Asqalan, and Gaza—boomed as exports to Europe rose. Many people went to the coast to work as wage laborers in these orange groves. Around the same time, the Iraq Petroleum Company Pipeline was constructed, connecting the Kirkuk oil fields to Haifa Port, drawing even more labor to the coast. In addition, many peasants left their villages to become schoolteachers, police officers, or civil servants in major cities such as Jerusalem, Nablus, Lod, and Ramllah. It was more profitable to leave one's land and join the market economy. This meant that the traditional historic centers, which were organized to serve the life of an agrarian community, became obsolete. Of course the 1948 war, the creation of the state of Israel, and the expulsion of 90 percent of the Palestinian population radically altered the landscape and its economic and social fabric.

By the 1950s, oil extraction started in the Gulf; hence, many waves of migration from both the rural and urban areas took place. People left their towns and villages in large numbers to go work in rich oil countries such as Kuwait and Saudi Arabia. Then came the 1967 war and the Israeli occupation. From that point on, the Palestinian villagers started working in the Israeli market and earning much more money by being laborers in Israel (sadly and ironically, in the building sector). Now I suspect that agriculture only accounts for 15 percent of people's income in the villages.

AA   In this process of preservation and reconstruction, I know that Riwaq worked with the idea of an integrated economy and bringing back a sense of craft, which is a really interesting, holistic approach to preservation: to preserve the architecture and the land but also the social capital. Have people reinvested in these villages? Have they come back? Or is it more about maintaining them for those who are there now? Or is it about inviting new people to create new kinds of industry or tourism?

SA   Perhaps all of the above! At the beginning, in the mid-nineties, it was difficult because neither we nor the villagers knew what we were doing or what we were up to. We were very academic in our approach. We would go and talk, or rather lecture, to people about the importance of protecting and preserving the cultural heritage in Palestine, addressing issues such as identity, history, and how the Israeli settlements are threatening our homeland. Reflecting on it now, I think that it was only out of politeness, curiosity, or respect that they would attend our lectures. Most would get bored and fall asleep or leave.

We realized that to effectively reach people, we needed to demonstrate the great economic and social potential in these historic centers and buildings. Hence, in the year 2000, we started our job-creation-through-conservation program. This entailed the rehabilitation of single buildings that were then used as community centers, such as women's centers, youth clubs, music centers, or health clinics. In doing so we sought partnerships with village councils and municipalities, as well as many local nongovernmental organizations (NGOs). We never worked alone in a village. The very first step was to connect with the community by explaining what the Riwaq organization was, its aims. The building needed to have historic value and be located in the historic center. Apart from that we left it up to the local community to decide which building had

A newly built playground Abwein, Palestine (above) and the courtyard of the restored al-Kamandatji Music Asssiation building in Ramallah, Palestine (below).

the potential to satisfy their needs. Once we agreed that this was the most suitable building, we would leave it to the NGO to work out the long-term renting agreement with the owners.

Riwaq would raise the necessary funding and also work on the design and alterations of the building; we would prepare the necessary drawings and documents, bills of quantities, and announce in the local newspapers for the contractors to give their offers. The contractor is not allowed to bring workers from outside the community; often this meant training local workers in skills and crafts like plastering or mixing lime. So people started feeling that their community, their young people, were making a decent living out of this. And the owner of the building would be happy to see his property renovated. Once the work was done, the NGO would move into the heart of the historic center, which would begin to bring some life back into these deserted areas.

Seeing the success of this program, we felt the need to work on a larger scale; hence, in 2005, we initiated Riwaq's 50 Village Project. Rather than upgrading a single building, we had to figure out what it would take to bring to life an entire village center. Our first project was in the town of Birzeit. Birzeit had a lot of potential for success because it's a university town (Birzeit University) and because it's close to Ramallah, creating a natural clientele for the small businesses and restaurants we hoped would open.

The first phase of the rehabilitation project was the infrastructure. We had to dig up all the roads, as well as the alleys of the old town, and install new water, sanitation, telephone and electricity lines, and pipes. This was rather complicated because we needed to coordinate the works with the municipality, as well as with all the relevant authorities and companies.

Second came the preventive conservation phase, which entailed cleaning the façades of all the buildings in the town, cleaning and pointing the stonework, fixing the roofs, windows, and doors.

The beautification process not only lengthened the life of buildings but also convinced the residents that we cared about them and about their environment. In addition to rehabilitating a cultural center, we would intervene in public spaces. These interventions worked in unison to improve the urban fabric: Streets were lit and tiled with stone. The benches and the trees planted along the alleys connected the village plaza (*al-saha*) with playgrounds and the community center, all forming an network of public spaces where activities and life were possible. This encouraged private owners and the municipalities to move their offices into newly restored buildings and to invest in the new shops and cafés. It also encouraged the inhabitants of the old town to start renovating and using long-deserted houses.

AA   I mean, it's really interesting also to think about preservation as the preservation of infrastructure and public space first. It's kind of antithetical to how we think about preservation, which is typically is as a process undertaken for an isolated building.

SA   Absolutely, I think upgrading and rehabilitating public spaces is the secret to making people have a strong sense of ownership over their spaces and pride in their community as a whole.

In the past we would look at the empty buildings first, but with twenty-some years of experience, we said, "Wait a minute. There are people still living here, so why don't we give attention and support to those who are

A women's group holds in a restored palace in Eftar Sabastyeh, Palestine.

Women working during a ceiling conservation workshop.

already there?" Consequently, over the last five years, we have started a housing project with a matching fund.

I must say that with the hard work of the last fifteen years, it is difficult sometimes to evaluate the successes or failures of such projects. We looked at the buildings and the public spaces we renovated a few years back, and to our surprise almost 88 percent of the renovated buildings and spaces were being used. When we evaluate our work, we also always examine how many jobs each of those projects created. So, job creation and training for the workers but also jobs for the local architects with whom we work on site. We also try hard to hire women architects if we have a choice, because when it comes to laborers, it's very difficult, almost impossible, to involve women. However, we do involve women when it comes to community organization but also in conservation workshops.

CB   In the same way that you've gone back and seen 88 percent of the buildings still used, have you seen the training and the skills that you created continuing in other architectural projects afterward?

SA   I'll give you an example: the tile floors. In the Mediterranean area there are these hand-made tiles we call carpets or *sijadeh*. They were characteristic of urban houses in Palestine. When we started renovating, we wanted to revive this form of tile making. When we went around to visit the workshops or small factories where they were made, most of them, if not all of them, were closed. We ultimately convinced the son of the owner of the Wazwaz family, in al-Ram near Jerusalem, to reopen his father's factory. We of course helped him to get it set up and running. He started producing these tiles as his father and grandfather once did, and we started buying and using these beautiful tiles in all our projects. This also encouraged another factory in Nablus, so we now have two factories: one for our Nablus projects and the northern area and one in Jerusalem, for our Jerusalem and southern area projects. They were encouraged to reopen basically because they felt—or we assured them—that there would be a market for it. And not only that, the guy in Jerusalem became super rich because the Israelis discovered him and started buying from him, but I must say that he sells to them with double or triple the prices he sells to us.

"Islamic" Architecture, Community Empowerment, and Market-Debt Relations: The Sayyida Zeinab Cultural Park for Children

ASHRAF ABDALLA

In 1983, the Egyptian architect Abdelhalim Ibrahim Abdelhalim won an architectural competition, sponsored by the Egyptian Ministry of Culture, to design a cultural park for children in the traditional quarter of Sayyida Zeinab at the heart of historic Cairo.[1] While the Ministry of Culture intended for the project to host its activities within the park's borders, Abdelhalim sought to extend the park's activities into the neighboring Abu El Dahab community. In so doing, he attempted to revitalize Cairo's traditional alley life, with its artisan workshops, along the park's border facing Abu El Dahab street. In addition, Abdelhalim and local residents formed Abu El Dahab Group (ADG), a nongovernmental organization (NGO) to manage the alley's activities and its workshops. The park opened in 1990, and Abdelhalim's design won the Aga Khan Award for Architecture in 1992, particularly on account of its innovative approach to issues of cultural identity, empowering local communities, and reviving traditional Islamic architectural forms and practices. Ever since, the children's park has had a profound impact on architectural discourse and practices in Egypt and beyond. However, today, the alley's workshops are closed, ADG is dissolved, and the park is largely abandoned. Most scholarly work on the park project has either focused on issues of cultural identity, and their associated architectural forms, or explained the park's current neglect, by both the Egyptian government and the local community, in terms of the conflict between the Egyptian modern state and Abu El Dahab traditional community. Few have examined the relationship between the park's architecture and the political economic forces mobilized in tandem with the project or have addressed how Abdelhalim's attempts to revitalize local traditions may actually have aided the expansion of the neoliberal marketplace and finance capitalism within the poor community, despite his intentions.

THE PARK PROJECT

The children's park is located in Cairo's Sayyida Zeinab area, which is famous for its annual religious ceremony (Mulid El Sayyida Zeinab) and home to

Cultural Park for Children, CDC (Community Design Collaborative) AbdelHalim, 1990.

149

several Islamic monuments from the Mamluk and Ottoman eras (thirteenth to eighteenth century).[2] With its dense urban fabric (which consists mainly of residential blocks, some dating to the late nineteenth century, with retail and workshops on the street level), winding alleys, and mostly working-class residents, Sayyida Zeinab is one of the most populous and oldest traditional *sha'bi* neighborhoods of Cairo.[3]

The Sayyida Zeinab neighborhood, 2013.

Within the boundaries of the park, the Ministry of Culture envisioned a controlled environment in which it could sponsor activities geared toward promoting a sense of cultural identity in the children of Sayyida Zeinab and where they could learn about their national heritage through play and active participation.[4] The site included a library, a children's museum, and an amphitheater.

An aerial photograph of the park site.

The Sayyida Zeinab Cultural Park for Children

Abdelhalim's vision was bolder. He sought to integrate the park with its surrounding community. He did that in three ways. First, he thought of the park's architecture as a reflection of the "essence" of the local community. Accordingly, he not only used Islamic architectural elements of domes, arches, and vaults in the design, but he also extracted spiral geometrical patterns from the area's historical monuments and from the residents' annual religious ritual (El Mulid) as the overall organizing order of the park.[5] Second, Abdelhalim involved local craftsmanship in the *manual* construction of the park's architectural domes, vaults, and arches. In order to revive traditional building practices in the community, he combined modern construction techniques with traditional methods of stone carving and carpentry for the park's construction. To guide the craftsmen, his design team built cardboard mockups for the park's domes, vaults, and arches. He also identified participating craftsmen by name to acknowledge their role in the project.

Spiral patterns visible are clear refrences in the work of Abdelhalim Ibrahim Abdelhalim as shown illustrating his article "A Ceremonial Approach to Community Building."

Finally, to unite the park with its community, Abdelhalim attempted to revitalize the traditional pedestrian alley life of historic Cairo, with its artisan workshops, along the park's border, facing the neighboring community. He turned the adjacent Abu El Dahab street into a pedestrian alley and, in addition to a prayer room and a coffee shop, designed a series of vaults to host stone carving, carpentry, and metalwork workshops. Instead of acting as a barrier between the park and the community, Abdelhalim envisioned the facilities along the park's border and the alley to function as a connecting element between the two domains.

Abu El Dahab alley, CDC AbdelHalim, 1990.

Shortly after the park's opening, in 1990, the government stopped funding the maintenance of Abu El Dahab alley and refused to operate the workshop activities along the park's border. The park authority claimed that these activities jeopardized its firm control on the park's border and allowed some locals to destroy and

Abu El Dahab alley, CDC AbdelHalim, 1990.

The Sayyida Zeinab Cultural Park for Children

loot the Ministry of Culture's properties inside the park. Abdelhalim was undaunted and searched for other ways to support the workshops. Ultimately he relocated the workshops within the Abu El Dahab alley and changed their crafts productions into pottery, weaving, and sewing. He moved his architectural office to one of the houses overlooking the alley to further cement himself within the local community. In 1995, the architect, with the help of members of the local community, established the Abu El Dahab Group (ADG), which was the first NGO of its kind in Egypt. ADG's responsibility was to represent the community and manage the workshops. In its nine-year span, the organization secured funding from global and local organizations such as the Ford Foundation and Save the Children. During the peak periods of its activities, ADG's reach extended beyond Abu El Dahab alley, into the wider area of Sayyida Zeinab and beyond. Only then did the park authority agree to open some of the vaults to host workshop activities.

Today, however, the vaults are closed, and both the alley and the park are largely abandoned. In 2004, Abdelhalim moved his office out of the area and dissolved ADG. Instead of connecting the park to its surrounding community, Abu El Dahab alley became a dead zone for garbage collection and illegal activities (graffiti, vandalism, and drug use). It now seems that Abdelhalim's narrative of a harmonious continuity between the park and its community is challenged by the fate of Abu El Dahab alley.

The park's present condition, 2014.

Most scholarly accounts of the cultural park limit their focus to issues of cultural identity and explain the project's current impasse in terms of the conflict between the *traditional* community of Sayyida Zeinab and the Egyptian *modern* state. These accounts examine Abdelhalim's work and ADG's operations in the area exclusively through the lens of the local mobilization against state authority.[6]

Notwithstanding the real conflict between ADG and the Egyptian state, explaining the story of the park and its alley solely in terms of this opposition misses the point. In order to untangle the complexities of the cultural park and understand its disappointments and potentials, we have to move beyond this deadlock and to identify other forms of power operating within the park project. To do so requires a brief look at the larger political, economic, and cultural context of Egypt during the 1980s and 1990s.

ADG AND MARKET-DEBT RELATIONS

In 1981, the assassination of Egyptian president Anwar el-Sadat at the hands of militant Islamist groups ushered in a decade of turbulent sociopolitical forces and economic decline.[7] In 1987, the World Bank, the International Monetary Fund, and other international financial organizations (IFOs) loaned the government money in the form of structural adjustment programs (SAPs). Aiming at reducing the country's mounting budget deficit, these programs enacted economic reforms that limited the Egyptian government's intervention in the national economy by rolling back the state's welfare services and opened the country to the global market by significantly reducing taxes on foreign investment. The SAPs reinforced Sadat's earlier *infitah* (opening) policies of free market capitalism and an undoing of the welfare state. By the early 1990s, they had resulted in impressive economic growth coupled with unprecedented income inequality. Interestingly, the same IFOs that enforced SAPs on the state level—resulting in increasing poverty for large segments of the population—funded various NGO efforts toward empowering the poor at the community level.

During the same period, a conservative turn in Egypt's cultural climate led to renewed interest, on the part of politicians, intellectuals, and a large segment of society, in defining the national character of the country in terms of its Islamic past. Following Sadat's assassination, the Egyptian state paid close attention to the hitherto neglected poor of the historic and *sha'bi* neighborhoods of Cairo, which were long thought to be the breeding grounds for Islamic fundamentalism. In its appeal to the residents of areas like Sayyida Zeinab, the Egyptian state sought to promote Islamic models that would not only eradicate radical Islamist elements while fostering forms of "moderate" Islam but also rechannel social anger away from political and economic issues, the hallmark of the political left, and toward de-politicized cultural ideals.

Through its Ministry of Culture and expansive media apparatus, the state promoted and idealized the *sha'bi* inhabitant as the quintessential "authentic" Egyptian, who refused to succumb to either the fundamentalist Islamist militancy or the Westernized national elites.[8] Typically, this *sha'bi* figure was an artisan who preserved the tradition and "national heritage" of handicrafts and who lived and worked within the narrow and winding alleys of historic Cairo.[9]

Modern architecture, which stood for progress and prosperity during the country's pseudo-socialist period of the 1950s and 1960s, came to be largely seen as a Western import discordant with local culture. This disillusion with modern architecture's ideals culminated in efforts, on the part of state officials, private clients, and architects, toward using "Islamic" architectural motifs in various urban spaces, including cultural centers, educational facilities, governmental buildings, leisure parks, tourist resorts, and commercial mega-malls.[10]

Within this context, Abdelhalim's attempts to empower the Abu El Dahab community through reviving Cairo's traditional alley life and "Islamic" architectural motifs should be seen not in opposition to but as part of the Egyptian state's larger efforts to shift attention away from political questions and instead focus on depoliticized cultural issues. After all, it was the Ministry of Culture that selected the project's site, in the heart of Sayyida Zeinab, and elected Abdelhalim's "Islamic" design as the winner of the architectural competition.

Abu El Dahab workshops as depicted in CDC AbdelHalim's reports on "Creative Community Design and Rehabilitation in the Context of Abu Dahab Street in Sayedda Zeinab."

Similarly, ADG's activities in Abu El Dahab alley did not challenge the state-capital nexus of power but instead advanced it. ADG's objectives were to revitalize traditional handicraft workshops and their master-apprentice model, where workshops were identified by the masters' names—Am Megahid's workshop for pottery, Usta Hussien's weaving workshop, and so forth. Children and adults from Abu El Dahab community were involved in the production of these handicrafts. As apprentices, they were guided by the workshop masters, and trained by experts and consultants hired by ADG, to produce puppets, pottery, sculptures, carpets, rugs, and bags. Some of these handicrafts were sold within the Abu El Dahab community; most, however, were sold to upper-class neighborhoods outside Sayyida Zeinab.

Nonetheless, what sustained ADG's revitalization efforts on the community level was an extended financial network of global and local actors. Throughout its development phases, ADG secured funding from various IFOs and several international and Egyptian NGOs.[11] These actors funded the workshop activities, extended microloans to small-scale enterprises and entrepreneurial projects in the community, conducted training seminars (about debt management and marketing skills), and offered a limited number of social services (literary classes and aid for those with mental illness and impaired mobility).

Within this network, ADG's role was to act as an intermediary between these global actors and the local community. In addition to managing the workshops and enlisting community participation in the various activities and services offered by the NGOs in the area, ADG conducted screening processes to determine the eligibility of the community's applicants to receive microloans from the NGOs. Applicants were evaluated based on the strength and extent of their social network and hence the ability of ADG to potentially mobilize "natural leaders" within the community in order to guarantee debt repayment.[12] These "natural leaders" were figures of authority specific to the culture of the community, including religious leaders, male masters, and paternal authorities. Thus, ADG naturalized the ongoing social struggles within Abu El Dahab community and perpetuated the vulnerability of the poor to the existing social structure within their community. Empowering the local community, through extending relations of debt, depended on sustaining the structure of disempowerment engulfing the poor within the community.

Marketing was also crucial to ADG's work in the alley and in Sayyida Zeinab. As a 2001 report to the Ford Foundation concluded, "Marketing the products of the workshops is one of the main objectives of this project phase to establish a framework and implement a process of sustainability for the workshops and the community organization of ADG."[13] As the main sources of revenues for Abu El Dahab community, the sales of the workshops' handicrafts and the small enterprises' products were critical for the residents to pay back the microloans and for the expansion of ADG's activities in the area. The nature of workshops' crafts and the type of empowerment activities, and their relevance to the needs of Abu El Dahab community, mattered less than securing the expansion of debt and commodity exchange within the area. ADG helped promote the workshops' products and advertise for the various NGOs' programs by holding street festivals in Abu El Dahab alley and utilizing multiple exhibition spaces and galleries in upper-class areas outside Sayyida Zeinab.

While marketing was essential to sustaining the flow of credit to the community, the sustainability of the market depended on the unique cultural aspects of the community. ADG's marketing strategies for the workshops' handicrafts appealed to their cultural "authenticity" as handmade crafts produced by poor children and artisans living and working in the city's oldest *sha'bi* neighborhood. As such, ADG's community empowerment efforts and the sustainability of the market-debt relations in the area were strongly intertwined and codependent.

ADG's community empowerment efforts cannot be seen as separate from the structural adjustment programs at the state level. The two enabled and reinforced each other. ADG's attempts within the community would not have been possible without the increasing withdrawal of the Egyptian state from its former public role. In turn, the devastating effects of a weakening welfare-state system on the poor had been somewhat mitigated through the work of NGOs. In addition, the same IFOs that enforced these programs funded ADG's empowerment efforts at the local level. Moreover, the Egyptian government supervised the operations and legal standing of NGOs and provided advertising and exhibition space for marketing ventures. Operating symbiotically, *both* ADG and the Egyptian government reinforced the process of market and debt expansion.

ADG's attempts at empowering Abu El Dahab community only served to further subjugate them through what Julia Elyachar has called the "empowerment debt regime."[14] Entangled within the web of market-debt processes, community members were dispossessed of the power to control their own labor, products, and market outlets. However, ADG's efforts did not secure enough outlets for the workshops' crafts, whether within Sayyida Zeinab or beyond (partly due to the unsuitability of these products to the needs of the local residents). This resulted in limited revenues for the community, which, in turn, hindered the sustainability of the microcredit's flow to the area. It is mainly because of this that the workshops were closed and ADG was dissolved. ADG's empowerment efforts depended on debt and market forms that were not only inherently disempowering to Abu El Dhaba community but also conditioned on *traditional* social practices of domination particular to the community. Rather than blaming the authoritarian state, the main antagonistic forces at play in the park project should be located within these contradictions, which are internal to the market-debt relations themselves.

HAND-CRAFTINESS

All the parties involved in the park project (whether the Ministry of Culture, the ADG, or Abdelhalim himself) focused on the artisan or craftsman as the "authentic" Egyptian. However, as we have seen, artisans in the alley's workshops and craftsmen on the park's construction site were incorporated into Abdelhalim's vision and ADG's activities precisely by being deprived of the power to control either the nature or the marketing of their crafts. Instead of the traditional masters and local craftsmen idealized in the narrative of the park, these were perfectly modern workers incorporated within market-debt relations and employed in the service of producing the *image* of authenticity. This is evident in the fact that artisans in Abu El Dahab workshops and craftsmen on the park's site were trained by ADG and other consultants to regain their "lost traditional" skills. Dialectically, the master's name and the artisan's hand stood in for the workers' dispossession of the power to influence the network of production and marketing entangling their own labor. In the hand of the craftsman, the market's invisible hand took form. The handicraft became hand-craftiness, and, as Theodor Adorno would say, it was, "transformed into that which it wants to repudiate: the same lifeless, reified repetition."[15]

The Abu El Dahab workshops were used to illustrate the designer's, and indeed design's, role in preserving tradition and craft as well as state-supported efforts at "community building" as images in promotional materials and handbooks.

More than alluding to elements of "Islamic" architecture, as Abdelhalim contends, the park's architectural language should be examined in relation to Hassan Fathy's distinct vocabulary of handmade domes, arches, and vaults.[16] In his architecture for the poor, Fathy claimed to have devised an authentic Egyptian style in which architect and local peasant worked together to revitalize premodern, handmade, and affordable methods of construction.[17] Fathy's methods had a significant impact on several generations of Egyptian architects, including Abdelhalim. However, instead of critically examining Fathy's interpretation of cultural identity and local traditional forms, many adopted his architectural style as if it were the genuine Egyptian tradition. In the work of these architects, the use of domes, vaults, and arches came to stand not only for the authentic Egyptian architecture but also for hand-craftiness. Indeed, many traditional handicrafts centers in Egypt, usually sponsored by the Ministry of Culture, adopted Fathy's architectural style for this very reason.

The architecture of handicraft as demonstrated in Hassan Fathy's Akil Sami House, Dahshur, Egypt, 1978.

As such, the significance of the cultural park's domes, vaults, and arches does not stem from their handicraft construction but from their visual function as signs of hand-craftiness. These signs branded the park's architecture as a handicraft product itself. Yet, as signs of hand-craftiness, the park's architectural forms were *not* about rooting the community within its traditional handicraft practices or Islamic past. Rather, they constituted the materials of market exchange in the world of commodity circulation. While they could not be literally consumed or exchanged, the park's domes, vaults, and arches occupied the sphere of what Marx identified as the *fetish* character of market's commodities—this "very strange thing, abounding in metaphysical subtleties and theological niceties."[18]

In their capacity as fetishes of hand-craftiness, the park's architectural forms conveyed cultural messages of authenticity, rootedness in the past, national pride in reviving Egyptian handicraft tradition, and good conscience in supporting the poor, which, in turn, acted dialectically with the workshops' products to enhance their market's exchange value. In the dialectic relation between use-value and exchange-value, the park's domes, vaults, and arches were fetishes because they appeared to embody pure use-value—rooting the community within its distinct past—yet that appearance concealed their true function— their pure exchange-value of enabling the sales of the workshops' products and attracting investment and tourism to Abu El Dahab area.

Nonetheless, the story of the park project and the relation of its architecture to the local community cannot simply be reduced to the logic of cultural commodification. After all, Abdelhalim's design for the park and ADG's efforts in the alley created a micro world with all the messiness this entails. Relying on Abdelhalim's own formulations, most scholarly accounts of the children's park have dealt with its architecture as if it were a transparent reflection of the culture of the community. Yet the park's architecture exists in a dialectic relation to its context. Instead of merely *reflecting* the "essences" of the local community, as Abdelhalim argues, the park's architecture should be perceived as also *deflecting* and negating its context.[19]

Examining things from this perspective allows us to take account of the conflict between the park and the community. While Abdelhalim intended for the alley to integrate the park with its community, his architectural configurations for the park's border and the alley undermined this very possibility. The heavy architectural massing at the park's border, the excessive use of cascading steps, and the splitting of the alley into two paths on two different levels all formed barriers that challenged any smooth continuity between Abu El Dahab community and the park. In addition, the exclusive use of the alley for workshop activities made it harder for the local residents to freely use it either as a passageway or as a place for social gatherings.

The contradiction of inclusion and exclusion is apparent in photographs taken for the Aga Khan Award for Archtiecture in 1992.

Moreover, Abdelhalim made a subtle but significant differentiation in the articulation of the arches along the park's border. While he used pointed arches in the spaces administered by the park's authority, like the prayer room and the side gates facing Abu El Dahab alley, he adopted smooth round arches for the workshop doors. In this gesture, Abdelhalim clearly distinguished between what the state owned and what belonged to the community. This contradiction of integration and separation on the architectural level dialectically mirrored the market-debt contradiction of empowerment and disempowerment at the community level.

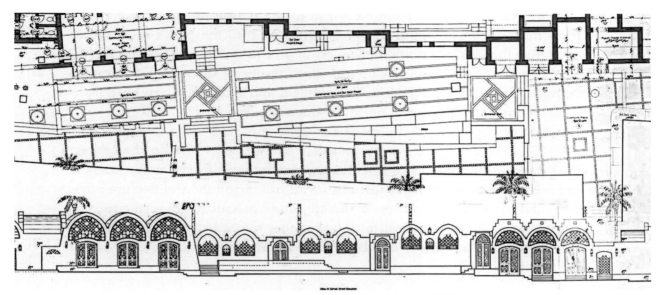

Drawings of Abu El Dahab alleyway, CDC AbdelHalim, 1990.

Contrary to most scholarly interpretation of the park project, Abdelhalim's design for the cultural park for children and ADG's efforts toward community empowerment in Sayyida Zeinab did not pose a challenge to the Egyptian state. Instead, they not only were part of larger governmental efforts toward containing the sociopolitical unrest within the Egyptian society but also contributed to the entanglement of the poor within other forms of power and market-debt relations. As such, ADG's efforts and these market-debt relations were codependent. Similarly, the park's architectural representation of domes, vaults, and arches did not root Abu El Dahab community within its traditional and Islamic past; rather, it formed the very basis on which the market-debt relations could expand. In other words, within the context of the children's park, the question of architectural representation was not separate from the commodification of cultural and artistic forms and their fetishes. Rooting the local community in its tradition was precisely the fetish that placed the architectural forms of domes, vaults, and arches at the heart of capitalist expansion and market-debt relations.

However, the park's architecture not only helped extend these power relations but also resisted them, precisely by making visible their inherent contradictions and conflicts. The park's current impasse is better understood in terms of these contradictions, which are internal to ADG's community-empowerment efforts and the park's architecture and cannot be reduced to the conflict between two coherent and mutually exclusive entities: the state versus the community.

It is precisely within these antagonistic and conflicting forces, on display in the park's architecture and its current ruinous status, that we can unlock the park's potential. These conflicts testify to the refusal of the local community to fully integrate within ADG's activities or into the park's architecture, despite Abdelhalim's intentions. The marks of graffiti on the workshop walls, the broken lanterns, and other acts of vandalism testify to the local community's resentment against not only the state, as Abdelhalim claims, but also to empowerment efforts based primarily on the market-debt regime.

Instead of relying on social models of coherence and unity, as Abdelhalim and ADG tried to do in the park project, a more urgent task, in the context of empowering the poor, is to unearth the antagonistic forces at the heart of every seemingly homogeneous form of social organization. Architecture offers the possibility of rupturing these seemingly homogenous social formations by constructing a site of contestation that engages forces beyond the control of the architect and the various actors involved in the architectural project, as the story of the cultural park shows.

1 Abdelhalim I. Abdelhalim (1941–present) is a renowned Egyptian architect and professor of architecture. He studied architecture in both Egypt and the United States, where he completed his doctoral dissertation under the supervision of Christopher Alexander at the University of California, Berkeley in 1978. Abdelhalim established his practice in Egypt in 1979 under the name Community Design Collaborative (CDC). Over the years, he designed major architectural works for several Arab Gulf states. His most recent project was the new campus for the American University in Cairo (2009). Abdelhalim is the recipient of many architectural awards and currently teaches at Cairo University.

2 The neighborhood is named after the granddaughter of the prophet Muhammad. Her shrine is housed within the historic mosque of Sayyida Zeinab, located to the north of the park's site. The area holds the annual religious festival under the same name in honor of the prophet's granddaughter.

3 *Sha'bi* means "popular" in Arabic, but it can also be translated as "of-the-people." The term has many positive connotations in the Egyptian cultural imaginary.

4 The competition brief was very specific about building a fence around the park to protect it from vandalism. This is the case with most public parks and spaces in Egypt.

5 In his dissertation, Abdelhalim argued that building activities of premodern communities enacted ritual patterns that simultaneously reflected the "essence" of these communities and determined the order of their built environment. See Abdelhalim I. Abdelhalim, "The Building Ceremony" (PhD diss., University of California, Berkeley, 1978). For Abdelhalim, the poor condition of modern-day Sayyida Zeinab is the result of the split between the community's traditional culture and its urban forms. To empower this local community, Abdelhalim thought to reconnect the historical cultural patterns embedded in the community's religious rituals (El Mulid) with historical patterns extracted from the surrounding Islamic monuments. He extracted spiral geometrical patterns from the helix minaret of Ibn Tulun Mosque, which is located to the south of the park's site and is one of Cairo's oldest Islamic monuments. The repetitive and circular rhythms of the participants' bodily rotations in El Mulid ceremonies echoed, for Abdelhalim, the spiral geometry of the minaret. With Alexander's influence,

Abdelhalim translated the traces from the "frozen" historical built environment and the "living" cultural rituals into spiral patterns and geometrical orders that guided the park's organization and forms (spiral pathways, winding steps, domes, and vaults).

6 Exemplary of these accounts is the position adopted by the Egyptian architect Khaled Adham. Adham appreciates Abdelhalim's efforts in Abu El Dahab alley for enacting a site of contestation between two opposing patterns: a top-down order, imposed by the modern institutions of the bureaucratic state, versus a bottom-up culture, spontaneously emerging from the community's local traditions. Adham contends that the lessons learned from the cultural park are that "the urban boundaries of state institutions can become strategic sites for local communities to challenge, contest, resist, or perhaps redirect the dominant cultural forms upheld by the state." Blaming the bureaucratic Egyptian state for the project's fate, Adham maintains that the seeming failure of the park is precisely a testimony to its success. According to him, Abdelhalim's efforts to engage the community in the workshops along the alley were too radical for the government officials to accept and hence they reacted by withdrawing funds and closing the vaults. See Khaled Adham, "The

The Sayyida Zeinab Cultural Park for Children

Building Border: A Hermeneutical Study in the Cultural Politics of Space in Egypt, the Case of El-Houd El-Marsoud Park in Cairo" (PhD diss., Texas A&M University, 1997).

7   Most of the information presented here about ADG and its activities in the area is drawn from a report ADG prepared for the Ford Foundation in October 2001. I obtained a copy of this report thanks to Abdelhalim's son, Nour Abdelhalim. I thank him for all his help in this regard. Abdelhalim I. Abdelhalim, "Creative Community Design and Rehabilitation in the Context of Abu Dahab Street in Sayyida Zeinab, Final Report: Phase II Pilot Project (Oct. 1998–Nov. 2000)," published in 2001.

8   See Lila Abu-Lughod, *Dramas of Nationhood: The Politics of Television in Egypt* (Chicago: University of Chicago Press, 2005).

9   This *sha'bi* figure did not simply represent a revival of the past. He was an idealized construction that nevertheless drew on existing elements from actual living conditions in Cairo's traditional neighborhoods, social reality of contemporary Egypt, and Egyptian cultural traditions. This figure was also an updated version of the idealized "peasant," or *ibn-el-balad*, who was also promoted by the Egyptian culture industry as the "true" Egyptian during the country's modernization and pseudo-socialist period (1950s–1960s). See Abu-Lughod, *Dramas of Nationhood*.

10   This is not to suggest that whereas traditional Islamist aesthetics represented conservative politics, modern buildings reflected progressive policies. It is rather to register the historical transformations within both fields and explore their interrelations.

11   The IFOs included the Ford Foundation and the Near East Fund. NGOs included Save the Children, the Association for Economic Liberation, Coptic Evangelical Organization for Social Services (CEOSS), Centre for Alternative Development Studies, New Woman Research Centre, Association for the Protection of the Environment, and Hope Village for Children.

12   Abdelhalim, "Creative Community Design," 3.

13   Abdelhalim, "Creative Community Design," 37.

14   Julia Elyachar, *Markets of Dispossession: NGOs, Economic Development, and the State in Cairo* (Durham, NC: Duke University Press, 2005).

15   Theodor W. Adorno, "Functionalism Today," *Oppositions* 17 (Summer 1979): 11.

16   Hassan Fathy (1900–1989) was a prominent Egyptian architect whose work has been highly praised by Egyptian and international scholars alike. Fathy pioneered the first vernacular attempts in Egypt to form a national architectural style that was derived from the peasant's tradition and rooted in the rural environment. Fathy's endeavors were directed against architectural modernism with its universal ideals, detached from the local context, and mass-produced monotonous designs. In his housing project for a model village in the New Goura (1945–48), Fathy developed his philosophy of "appropriate technology," which was based on using local materials and native building methods. Instead of mass-produced reinforced concrete and red-brick structures, the common practice for most public housing buildings in Egypt at the time, Fathy utilized the local manual methods of mud-brick making and invited the villagers themselves to participate in the construction of their own houses. Many students and followers of Fathy considered his architectural style of handmade domes and vaults to be the "true" Egyptian architecture.

17   Hassan Fathy, *Architecture for the Poor* (Chicago: University of Chicago Press, 1973).

18   Karl Marx, *Capital*, trans. Ben Fowkes (New York: Vintage, 1977), vol. 1, 163.

19   If we were to take at face value Abdelhalim's claims that his architectural design for the park is but a reflection of the community's essence and culture, then attempts to critically examine the park project and its impact on the local community would be undermined. A supposedly smooth continuity between the Abu El Dahab community and the park's architecture would simultaneously *naturalize* both Abdelhalim's architectural design (as it would be viewed as merely a reflection of the community's culture) and the existing social structure of domination within the community (as they would be reified into the park's architectural patterns).

Qaisumah

Rafha

Arar

Turaif

Saidon

Territories of Oil:
The Trans-Arabian Pipeline

RANIA GHOSN

In a paper delivered to the Royal Geographical Society in 1934, Baron John Cadman, chairman of the Anglo-Persian Oil Company and the Iraq Petroleum Company, addressed the influence of petroleum on the geography of the Middle East. It was *infrastructure*, he noted, that was particularly necessary for the exploitation of oil; light railways, telephone and telegraph lines, and pumping stations and pipes for water supply were essential to the uninterrupted flow of petroleum.[1] It was an obvious assertion. The same year marked the completion of a 12-inch-diameter export crude pipeline that connected the Kirkuk oil fields, located in the former Ottoman *vilayet* of Mosul in northern Iraq, to the Mediterranean terminal ports of Tripoli (Lebanon) and Haifa (Palestine). So significant were these pipelines to the new economy in the land of the Tigris and Euphrates that they were referred to as the country's "third river."[2]

Yet the third river was only the beginning of the global trade of petroleum across the Middle East. In the aftermath of World War II, a few years after large oil reserves were discovered by American companies in Saudi Arabia, the Trans-Arabian Pipeline (Tapline) was constructed to expand the export capacity of the Saudi concession by carrying crude from wells in the Eastern Province across Jordan and Syria to a Mediterranean port in Lebanon. The Trans-Arabian Pipeline Company was chartered in 1945 by the four American oil companies that held shares in the Arabian American Oil Company (Aramco) for the sole function of transporting, at cost, part of the crude produced by the sister company. When completed in 1950, the 1,214 kilometer (754 mile) conduit, with a diameter of 30 inches, was the world's largest oil pipeline system. Conceived to avoid the round-trip tanker voyage around the Arabian Peninsula, as well as the Suez Canal toll, the pipeline was referred to as a "shortcut in steel" and celebrated as an "energy highway." The company's publications featured photographs of the infrastructure as a free-floating pipe that merely overlaid the "far and empty" land and vanished into the horizon.[3] This image of a "modern trade route of steel" spoke of the infrastructural desire to inscribe a space of oil circulation, or to borrow Manuel Castells's term, a *space of flows*, across the Middle East.

Coined by Castells to describe the accelerating conditions of mobility in the global economy, the concept of a "space of flows" captures this intensified

Axonometric drawing of the Trans-Arabian Pipeline, Rania Ghosn, 2014.

165

exchange of resources, money, information, images, and finance.[4] The growth of oil into the largest item in international trade in terms of both value and weight was only made possible by the infrastructure that delivered it from its point of extraction to world markets. Geography, then—or, more accurately, the overcoming of distance—matters greatly. Distance in this respect is not measured in absolute terms but rather as *friction of distance*, quantified economically as the combined effect of the time and costs imposed by transportation. Given that crude is not worth much at the wellhead, the value of oil requires that it be moved in an efficient and timely manner. Such time-space compression involves a multitude of ways of shrinking distance while accelerating velocity. Geographical theory has examined the extent to which it is possible to overcome the friction of distance by improvements and accelerations in infrastructure within the global space of flows. David Harvey, for instance, argues that the development of communications and transport technologies mitigates the difficulties of capital accumulation by expanding markets and annihilating spatial barriers to profit realization.[5]

The concept of a space of flows remains insufficient, however, for theorizing the geographical relations that underpin the system of oil. It borrows from developments in biological sciences during the eighteenth and nineteenth century, notably William Harvey's discovery of blood circulation, to conceptualize the urban process as "flows" of resources through the "arteries and veins" of the geography.[6] Reductive metabolic analogies naturalize the politics of circulation and accumulation and cast circulatory systems as the world's veins and arteries that need to be freed from all possible sources of blockage.[7] The flow has no identifiable agency. It eclipses the territorial fixity and silences the negotiations, contradictions, conflicts, and interruptions in the biography of the infrastructure. Favoring a situation of "moving along," these analogies dismiss friction and violence as the necessary corollaries of circulation. The space of flows is also often used to celebrate the "death of distance" or "end of geography," but distance and geography are hardly immaterial where oil (and any number of other things in circulation) are concerned.

Why does it matter whether geography is abstracted? The erasure of the geographic abstracts technological systems—their materialities, dimensions, and territorialities. It removes from representation the territorial transformations along the conduit, which the inscription of the infrastructure produces, and overlooks the politics of consensus or dissensus necessary to distribute resources.[8] Rather than killing distance and dismissing geography, could we imagine and qualify the spaces of friction within such infrastructural systems? The paramount significance of crude transport within the oil regime could be conceptualized better through the idea of friction within geography. In *Friction: An Ethnography of Global Connection*, Anna Tsing writes that globalization can only be enacted in the sticky materiality of practical encounters, through what she calls "the awkward, unequal, unstable, and creative qualities of interconnection across difference."[9] Tsing suggests that if we imagine the flow as a creek, we would notice not only what the flows are but also the channels that make that movement possible (i.e., the political and social processes that enable or restrict flows). From this perspective, geography is understood as a constitutive dimension of global flows, a tool of government, and a stake of contestation in itself. Space is thus reordered by resource economies rather than eroded by metabolic flows.

Thus, we can reframe the issue of the Arab City through geographies of the Trans-Arabian Pipeline by joining geographical theory and representation to more familiar forms of historical scholarship on energy infrastructure.[10] Three friction-vignettes along the conduit reveal the flows and friction of this carbon commodity: these narratives take place in the water troughs, along the Tapline Road, and in the Sidon Terminal buildings. In attending to these places in time, I heed Timothy Mitchell's call to "closely follow the oil," which he puts forward in his greatly influential work on oil techno-politics in the Middle East. Closely following the oil means "tracing the connections that were made between pipelines and pumping stations, refineries and shipping routes, road systems and automobile cultures, dollar flows and economic knowledge, weapons experts and militarism"—all of which do not respect the boundaries between the material and the ideal, the political and the cultural, the natural and the social.[11] In this framework, one could think of the transnational oil system along the lines of as what Andrew Barry calls a "technical zone," a set of coordinated but widely dispersed regulations, calculative arrangements, infrastructures, and technical procedures that render certain objects or flows governable.[12]

With respect to the Tapline corporation and its pipeline project, the inscription of the flow required exploration trips and mappings of alternate routes, international relations and foreign diplomacy relations, private financing, conventions, procurements of rights-of-way, settling of transit fees, and engineering drawings. The construction of such a large engineering project involved resolving labor availability, training, and expertise, as well as conditions of capital and technology. It meant deciding on the movement of local populations, on procurement of pipes and machinery, on whom to employ to construct and operate the pipeline, and how to secure it. Often operating in regions isolated from central power and unconnected to national and regional networks, the transport operation had to "develop" the frontier by deploying roads, ancillary services, and security posts. Simultaneously, the pipeline was built in public relations, in glossy brochures, colorful photos of communities and landscapes, and promises about positive impacts on people along the route. In its multiple dimensions, the fixation of the circulatory system in space produced a territory—simultaneously epistemological and material—through which international oil companies, transit and petro-states, and populations negotiated their political rationalities.

Four maps illustrate the zones at stake in Tapline's operation. The first represents the Middle East as a space of flows, a continuous background in which state boundaries recede in favor of bold pipelines. The map highlights the desire for a continuous zone of operation in which oil flows *in spite* of boundaries. However, and as the second map suggests, the continuity of operation did not imply that Tapline would annihilate political borders, for the kingdom's northern boundary corresponded with that of the Aramco concession. Tapline was a vertically integrated operation, in which the production and transport sectors operated as sister-companies; the flow of oil in the pipeline therefore depended primarily on the perpetuation of the Aramco concession and the reinforcement of Saudi territoriality. For both the concessionary company and the sovereign state, land—or, more precisely, the land's underground resources—was the new source of value, one that required an enduring order on the surface to secure the subsurface interest.

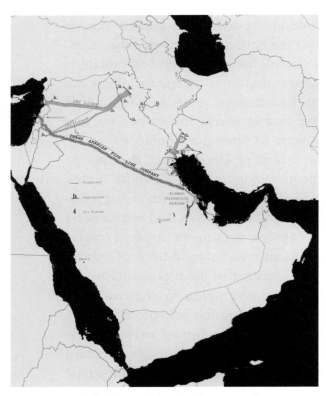

Map illustrating the Middle East as a zone of oil flows crisscrossed by pipelines.

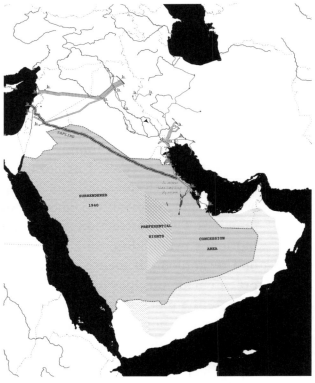

Map illustrating the zones of control by concessionary companies in Saudi Arabia.

Territories of Oil

For Saudi Arabia, the northern boundary represented a double security challenge. The kingdom was keen to guard its northern region against possible external threats from Iraq and Jordan while also reinforcing its rule over the range of Bedouin tribes, particularly those who had seasonally moved back and forth into Iraq in search of water, as shown in the third map. Arabian political boundaries previously had been defined in relation to the territorialities of the tribes, who in turn defined their ranges in relation to access to water. One of the tasks of the Arabian Research Division (AAD), Aramco's in-house research and analysis organization, was to survey the tribes, their geographies, and their water access. The fourth map speaks of such efforts to depict the tribal zones of influence. It roughly represents the tribal ranges, or *diras*, for the principal tribes of Saudi Arabia. A *dira* was not a strictly bounded and exclusively occupied territory but rather a loosely hemmed area of clan control, based around claims to permanent wells. The clear demarcation of the northern boundary was to replace a shifting and negotiated territorial order across northern Arabia. Collectively, the four maps visualize a project of rule with the overlaid territorial claims of the concession, the kingdom, the *diras*, and the secure border zone.

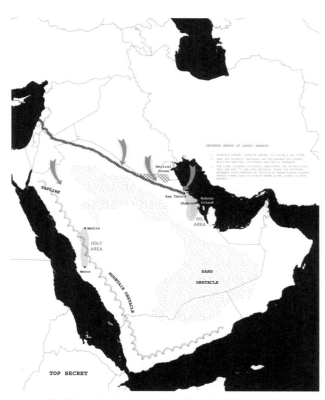

Map illustrating the geography of Saudi Arabian security.

Map illustrating tribal composition of the region.

Tapline thus delineated control in the northern Saudi territory—it inscribed boundaries, settled populations, demanded security, and drove the economy. The Saudi-Tapline Convention exempted the company from an income tax or royalties during its first fifteen years. In exchange, Tapline would pay for "all reasonable and necessary expenses" incurred by the government for protection, administration, customs, health, and municipal works and establish schools and hospitals in the area of the pipeline stations. The company paid a security fee and extended the provision of water and services in the newly established administrative Northern Frontiers Province—originally referred to as the Tapline Governorate. The company drilled fifty-two groundwater wells and provided medical services in its clinics along the right-of-way. It planned the towns adjacent to the pumping stations of Turaif, Rafha, Ar'ar, and Qaisumah; built their public facilities and schools; and supported a home-ownership plan for its employees.

Although the interests along the northern boundary might have been partially shared by the transnational oil corporation and the state, the two were not in consensus over all operations. The space of flow was actually a site *through* which involved actors negotiated their political rationalities, whether claims for higher transit revenues, labor strikes, or interruptions of flow.

Section drawing illustrating the flow of water into water troughs from Aramco wells.

Water troughs were a microcosm of the political process. International Tapline officers made available the "hidden natural resource," local emirs regulated access, and different tribes, no longer confined to their territorial boundaries and water wells, negotiated, sometime violently, for access to water. From its early days of exploration, Aramco made a policy of drilling wells in isolated areas for Bedouins. Water wells drilled for company use were left as public water sources, and Aramco's annual reports to the government between

1947 and 1960 regularly referred to this program of water development.[13] Tapline's public relations with the Bedu and the governor of the Northern Province were sometimes mediated as "water-shows." Tapline's contribution to water development in the northern region was highlighted in company reports and during official visits to the province. For example, during his visit to Turaif, the minister of defense "expressed pleasure at seeing a filled camel trough and complimented the company for looking after the Bedu so well."[14] Through these early encounters, Tapline managers emphasized that they were making "every conscientious effort" on water supply, as outlined in the convention. To get some statistics into the files, aerial photographs were taken of the Bedu area to get a tent census. Also, at the company's request, the police made a list of all tribes represented, with the names of the headmen and with some guesses as to population, both human and animal.[15]

Tapline had a first taste of the "Bedouin problem" when newly drilled water wells became sites of conflict among the different factions that had come to depend on company wells as permanent water supplies during the summer months. A slowdown in water production, or a change in the well-head fixtures, resulted in appeals for more water. Formal tribal delegations would report local delays and incidents to Tapline and to the Saudi governor of the province. A 1950 report entitled "Bedouin Survey Rafha" recounts the disputes that occurred when a tribal emir who claimed prior right to the water because Rafha fell within his normal range asked that other Bedouins be stopped from using the water.[16] Other tribal factions contended that they had been encouraged by the king to camp near Rafha rather than cross the Iraq border to reach the water of the Euphrates.[17] When the emir's letter to the relations representative at Rafha proved of no avail, he attempted to frighten off the other factions. In the process, the emir of the Northeast Border Force was wounded along with some of his men, and one soldier was killed. Tapline's representative in Jeddah soon after received a telegram from King Ibn Saud "protesting the incident and alleging that it would not have occurred but for the presence of Tapline operations in the area...that the shooting had occurred as a result of a dispute over water furnished by Tapline in a company trough, and that therefore there was need for a large protective force of Saudi soldiers such as has been advocated by the Government for the past four months."[18] The Tapline representative responding pointed out that such shooting scrapes had characterized the uncontrolled border areas for many years, and he did not think the presence of Tapline was a contributing factor. However, the incident left the representative with the difficulty of planning for the future at Rafha in the presence of multiple factions. It became evident that an "efficient" provision of water required regulation by a local government authority.[19]

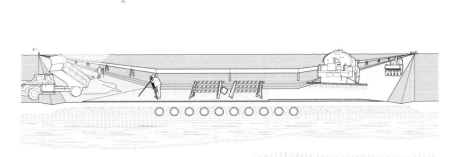

Drawing of grading and paving of Tapline Road, a project funded by the Saudi government as part of a development agreement with Tapline.

A second friction-vignette reveals contradictory interests between the transportation and concession departments of an oil company through the story of the Tapline Road. The convention terms had obligated the Tapline company to construct, maintain, and grade the road along the pipeline at its own expense. During initial construction, an earth road was surfaced with decomposed limestone and marl, and crude oil, rather than asphalt, was used as a binder. The practice continued until the renegotiation of the convention terms in 1963.[20] In these negotiations, Aramco was most concerned about the repercussions of Tapline's choice to capitalize rather than expense the program on its own infrastructural obligations toward the kingdom. Aramco had been expensing its roads on the grounds that once a road was built, the oil company lost control of it and it in effect became public property. Aramco communicated to Tapline its concern that the government's approval to capitalize the road program set a precedent that Aramco would have to comply with on similar roads, past and future. Also at stake were schools and other community development projects, which Aramco expensed but which the company feared the Saudis might pressure them to capitalize in the future. "Any arguments that we might use for capitalizing the Tapline road can probably be turned against Aramco by the Government... The potential savings to Tapline shareholders by capitalizing the road must be compared with very much larger amounts which Aramco would have to pay the Government if forced to capitalize roads, schools, etc."[21] The road was eventually expensed. In this case, its status as a sister corporation and commitment to the larger financial interest of Aramco influenced Tapline's decision to meet the kingdom's developmental requests, despite its initial efforts to limit its commitments to the Saudi government.

Drawing of the Sidon oil spill and the fisherman it affected.

At a regional scale, the political dynamics between Nasser's pan-Arabism and the pro-Western allies of the Baghdad Pact unfolded around oil spills and labor dynamics in Tapline's Sidon Terminal, the end station on the Mediterranean, the setting of the third friction-vignette. King Saud's visit to Lebanon in 1957 symbolically marked the convergence of regional economic interests and American foreign policy. During this visit, John Noble, president of Tapline, welcomed the Saudi king and Lebanese president Camille Chamoun to Sidon Terminal, declaring, "This is an added source of pride to both Tapline and Medreco that they are a means by which the mutual interests of these countries are being served through the transportation of crude oil from Your Majesty's Kingdom."[22] At the same time, Sidon, home to the terminal, was growing into a stronghold for Nasserite affiliations, particularly with the 1957 parliamentary election of Ma'rouf Saad, a Sidon deputy with socialist labor claims and close ties to the local fishermen. Minor oil spills had begun to pollute the Lebanese coast, attracting the attention of the government, press, and the Sidon labor union under the leadership of Ayoub Shami. Tapline's management feared a strike and labor unrest in Lebanon: "just as the University of California at Berkeley has its Mario Savio, we have our Ayoub Shami."[23] After a major spill in 1961, the company's fears were confirmed when a court order sided with local landowners and fishermen affected by the pollution.[24] Sidon fishermen contended that chemicals the company used to disperse the oil resulted in damage to aquatic life. The Lebanese government had signed the international treaty protecting a zone extending 100 nautical miles from the coast, within which it was illegal to dispose of oil-contaminated ballast or bilges. While no legislation to support the treaty had been passed, the Lebanese government stressed to Tapline and other countries that the country intended to comply with the treaty. At the same time, in "a gesture of goodwill toward the Sidon community," the company built two fishermen's storage buildings in the port area at a cost of about $10,000. During the inauguration ceremony in April 1961—in the presence of Ma'rouf Saad—John Noble called this "philanthropic undertaking by Tapline" a "symbol of the mutual friendship and respect which exists between the community of Sidon and Tapline."[25] The cover of the "Season's Greetings" issue of *Periscope*—the company publication—is charmingly illustrated with a color photograph of the Sidon storage facility. Later that year, in another sign of rapprochement with the fishermen, Tapline entered Sidon's Second Spring Festival with a gigantic fish float adorned with carnations, chrysanthemums, gladioli, and marguerites.[26]

Throughout the twentieth century, the growth of oil into a global commodity has transformed the Middle East into a hotspot of foreign policy and geopolitical negotiations between producing and transit states, both in peace and war times. Across the region, oil delineates territory through extraction fields, along transportation routes, and at terminal ports. From celebrations of abundance in the postwar *Felicia Arabia* to the anxieties of the 1973 Arab oil embargo through to the nationalization of oil resources and the Gulf Wars, the subject of oil has all but defined the region in newspapers and policy reports. Yet the profuse literature on oil and the Middle East has mostly addressed the geographies of oil as the exercise of diplomatic power over space. Left out of that narrative are the materialities, scales, and social processes necessary for the establishment and maintenance of oil flows. These three episodes in the life of the Tapline retrace the spatial configurations of such political and economic projects. They narrate how the pipeline has embodied a zone of friction, a zone in which various actors negotiated their overlapping and differing interests.

The Tapline narrative is also relevant to contemporary conversations on energy and infrastructure. At a time when the environment is at the forefront of design concerns, it is imperative that we not bracket out the politics of geography—that its frictions, alliances, and material realities are not ignored when lamenting the "energy crisis" or searching for renewable resources. Many contemporary energy projects continue to be presented as a set of technological artifacts in some faraway, scarcely populated desert. Such images are reminiscent of earlier environmental imaginaries, such as those that inspired the Tapline itself, in which the systemic attributes of the technology remained outside geographic examination. As we transition to new modes of energy, we must examine the geographies of new technological systems; if we fail to do so, we miss any opportunity for political and social transformation. The wind farms, solar fields, and offshore wells that will be our new energy landscape carry their own geographic narratives, their own frictions. It is the role of designers to make those visible.

1   John Cadman, "Middle East Geography in Relation to Petroleum," *Geographical Journal*, vol. 84, no. 3 (1934): 201–12.

2   Michael Clarke (dir.), *The Third River* (Iraq Petroleum Company, 1952), 29 min., 16mm film.

3   Daniel Da Cruz, "The Long Steel Shortcut," *Saudi Aramco World*, vol. 15, no. 5 (September 1964): 16–25.

4   Manuel Castells, *The Rise of the Network Society* (Cambridge: Blackwell, 1996), 412.

5   David Harvey, *Spaces of Capital: Towards a Critical Geography* (Edinburgh: Edinburgh University Press, 2001), 328.

6   Richard Sennett, *Flesh and Stone: The Body and the City in Western Civilization* (New York: Norton, 1994).

7   Erik Swyngedouw, "Circulations and Metabolisms: (Hybrid) Natures and (Cyborg) Cities," *Science as Culture*, vol. 15, no. 2 (2006): 105–21; Erik Swyngedouw and Maria Kaika, "Fetishizing the Modern City," *International Journal of Urban and Regional Research*, vol. 24, no. 2 (2000): 120–38.

8   See Rania Ghosn, "Where Are the Missing Spaces? The Geography of Some Uncommon Interests," *Perspecta* 45 (2012): 109–16.

9   Anna Tsing, *Friction: An Ethnography of Global Connection* (Princeton, NJ: Princeton University Press, 2005), 4.

10   Much of the discussion here draws from my dissertation: Rania Ghosn, "Geographies of Energy: The Case of the Trans-Arabian Pipeline" (DDes diss., Harvard University Graduate School of Design, 2010).

11   Timothy Mitchell, "Carbon Democracy," *Economy and Society* (2009): 399–432, 422.

12   Andrew Barry, "Technological Zones," *European Journal of Social Theory*, vol. 9, no. 2 (2006): 23–53; Gavin Bridge, "Global Production Networks and the Extractive Sector: Governing Resource-Based Development," *Journal of Economic Geography*, vol. 8, no. 3 (2008): 389–419.

13   J. P. Mandaville, "Bedouin Settlement in Saudi Arabia: Its Effect on Company Operations," report by Arabian Research Unit, December 1965, box 7, folder 15, William E. Mulligan Papers, Georgetown University Library Special Collections Research Center.

14   Turaif, June 13, 1951, box 6, folder 2, Mulligan Papers.

15   Turaif, July 25, 1951, box 6, folder 2, Mulligan Papers.

16   Rafha, July 13, 1950, box 11, folder 21, Mulligan Papers.

17   "The 'abdah section consistently claims that Rafha fell within its traditional range… the Aslam and Tuman from the larger section of the Shammar known as Sinjarah took the position that they had been encouraged by the King to camp near Rafha rather than to cross the Iraq border to reach the water of the Euphrates river." "Camel Trough Troubles," Rafha, June 18, 1950, box 11, folder 21, Mulligan Papers.

18   "Shooting Incident May 2 at Rafha Pump Station on Tapline Route," Foreign Service of the U.S. Rafha weekly report, May 3, 1950, box 11, folder 21, Mulligan Papers.

19   "Bedouin Survey Rafha," Rafha, July 13, 1950, box 11, folder 21, Mulligan Papers.

20   "Schedule of General Specifications Attached to Letter Agreement Dated 24 March 1963 between Government and Tapline," in "Tapline," n.d., Al Mashriq, http://almashriq.hiof.no/lebanon/300/380/388/tapline/tapline-road/html/56.html.

21   "Pipeline Road," April 26, 1963, William Chandler personal papers, Boise, Idaho, courtesy of Blaine Chandler and Gail Hawkins.

22   "King Saud Visits Sidon Terminal," *Pipeline Periscope*, vol. 5, no. 7 (November 1957): 1.

23   "Labor Situation, Lebanon," December 2, 1966, Chandler papers.

24   "Oil Pollution of the Sea," September 20, 1966, Chandler papers; "Oil on the Beaches," *Pipeline Periscope*, vol. 16, no. 7 (August 1966): 2.

25   "Sidon Fishermen Facilities Inaugurated," *Pipeline Periscope*, vol. 9, no. 4 (May 1961): 6–7.

26   "Tapline Float Scores Hit at Sidon Spring Festival," *Pipeline Periscope*, vol. 11, no. 6 (July 1963): 2.

Remarks on the Production of Representation
REINHOLD MARTIN

The title of the conference that gave rise to this book, "Architecture and Representation: The Arab City," seems to suggest that representation—for the time being: culturally specific symbolism and/or its antithesis—is an essential ingredient in thinking and making the modernity of recently decolonized societies, or those still colonized, the architecture of which, over the past fifty years or so, has laid claim to some kind of culturally, religiously, or nationally recognizable expression. Far from being all that the conference was about, you could say that this question, the question of representation, was its remainder, what was left after the conference was over. As we know, longstanding debates concerning representation in architecture, which have drawn on and contributed to the so-called linguistic turn in the humanities and the social sciences, have been complicated and challenged in recent years by what is sometimes called a materialist—or "new materialist"—turn. We should really call this turn a *return*, and if it constitutes a scholarly formation of sorts, then I confess membership. But by the same token, we should not be satisfied with simply turning or returning; that is, we should not be satisfied with simply exchanging language and its questions for materiality and *its* questions.

One way to think of this is to watch architecture, and the aesthetic domain more generally, including cities, operate along at least two axes or on two levels simultaneously: an axis of representation and an axis of production. This does not mean we need to choose between the two, or indeed that we have any choice at all. It means that the thing called architecture, as well as the thing called a city when thought in terms that include aesthetics, sits at the intersection of these two axes. You might think of these as the x- and y-coordinates of a Cartesian system. Two properties (rather than two quantities) coordinate to produce a point.

At that point, that intersection, little stays put. Things float. In the language of language, floating things cast about by societal forces like our minimally defined x,y point are called signifiers. In the particular cases addressed by some of the essays here, we might also call these signifiers domes, villages, oil, parks, pipelines, skyscrapers, and so on. In that same language, we can ask what these things mean, what meanings they carry or convey. Even so, I insist on calling them "things" as that is what they are; they are dense, obdurate artifacts. And if we learned anything from all those years of calling architecture a language, it is not *what* things mean but only *that* they mean.

This, minimally, is what the axis of representation can teach us. From it traditionally flows the critique of ideology, the permanent deferral of meaning that is sometimes called textuality, and the enigmatic persistence of the icon. But things like buildings or cities don't just mean; they produce meaning. That is, as elements in a sociocultural and socioeconomic field, they produce a real, tangible effect, a force even, which we call meaning. Which suggests that even when we bracket out the decoding of representations or the reading of signs, "meaning"—as the set of effects to which the subset "representation" belongs—cannot be taken entirely out of circulation from among the domes, villages, parks, oil fields, labor camps, skyscrapers, and other things that the contributors here argue belong to the Arab City.

Understood pragmatically, as an effect that is produced rather than as a category of being, representation thereby also acquires a slightly different political valence. For example, a dispossessed people may lay claim to what Henri Lefebvre famously called a "right to the city" from which they have been expelled, or, in the case of Palestine as addressed by the work of Suad Amiry, what we can call a "right to the village." Likewise in the contested case of the Sayyida Zeinab Cultural Park for Children in Cairo, as explained by Ashraf Abdalla, in which both the material and symbolic aspects of the space become sites in a struggle over what we can call more generally the "right to representation." In both examples, this claim divides into two competing possibilities: representing (oneself, or ourselves) and being represented (by others, such as the state, the party, a nongovernmental organization, and so on). Architecture and urban space straddle these possibilities, uncomfortably.

On the other hand, though quite asymmetrically, there is the spectacular theater of representation built on expropriated labor through which power flows, as in the case of Dubai discussed by Ahmed Kanna. Correspondingly, there are the infrastructures through which the material that seems to supply that power—oil—runs, as analyzed by Rania Ghosn. But theater is not to infrastructure as superstructure is to base, namely, a straightforwardly "ideological" expression that disguises or distracts from the productive, inexorable force that pulsates below, reorganizing the land as it goes. The theater of representation—Dubai, let's say—is also an infrastructure of sorts. Its material existence is secured by a division of labor that depends on a logistics of exploitation. In fact, we are dealing with infrastructures all the way down, from the gridded, mirrored glass to the labor camps to the oil wells. Add in the parks and the villages, variously adorned by culturally specific but thereby also contingent signifiers, and you have an infrastructural ensemble—a machine for producing meaning. In other words, you have a city.

This is why turning away from language and toward materiality does not consign representation to the dustbin of history. Nor does it treat iconology or the study of symbolism as errant distractions from the productivist path. On the contrary, it asks us to take the representation effect more seriously and more literally than ever. Rather than see architecture or urban space as a network of meanings, we might pay closer attention to how architecture or urban space *makes* meaning. Spectacular skylines, pipelines, parks, camps, and villages: all of these operate infrastructurally, as representation machines. The question is not what they mean but how they mean.

Remarks on the Production of Representation

Context

A Stone of Contention:
The New Town Hall of Byblos, Lebanon

HASHIM SARKIS

Set in a sandstone cliff overlooking the Mediterranean about 40 kilometers north of Beirut, Byblos is one of the world's oldest continuously inhabited places, with a constant human presence since 5,000 BC. Its archaeological sites bear evidence of civilizations stretching from the ancient neolithic to the early bronze age, and it is home to the world's oldest Phoenician inscriptions. Originally known in Phoenician as Gebal, Byblos has been ruled by the Egyptians, Assyrians, Greeks, Persians, Romans, Arabs, Crusaders, Ottomans, and French, until Lebanon gained its independence in 1943. All of these civilizations have left their marks in the soil and, significantly, in the popular imagination that determines the town's identity.

Byblos's archaeological wealth is a boon, making it Lebanon's most visited town. When the political situation is stable, it can receive upward of one million visitors each year. There is much to see—pre-Phoenician sites, Phoenician temples, Crusader castles, a medieval city wall, Mamlouk-era mosques, and a picturesque harbor that predates the arrival of the Crusaders. The town's ancient Roman axis is still visible in its street layout. Yet Byblos's history is also a burden. During the French Mandate, the excavations that uncovered the pre-Phoenician sites essentially gutted the historic city, leaving only a small remnant standing. The city is now a UNESCO World Heritage Site, which can be both a blessing and a curse. History has also distorted development and planning during Byblos's often sporadic growth. Facile concessions are made to fuel a swelling religious tourism. Many of the Old City's mosques have been spruced up, and its churches restored. The town's old bazaar has been revamped, hastily and several times, to make it more appealing to tourists.

The eagerness to attract ever more visitors has transformed the entire appearance of the city. Planners and architects cater to the tourist industry with an inarticulate, stereotypical aesthetic. Everywhere you look there are sandstone façades and elements intended to evoke a vague and romanticized pan-Arabic past. As if this superficial veneer weren't already confused enough, it is then clumsily spiced with the decor of a global patois. But there is hope. A succession of active local governments have worked to improve the overall urban planning of the city and to diversify its economy beyond tourism. The current Byblos Municipal Council is a young and dynamic group, headed by the energetic Ziad Hawat.

In 2012 Byblos held a design competition for its new town hall. The structure was to be situated in the highway interchange separating the historic city from its suburbs, an area surrounded by a patchwork of incoherence: filling stations, an isolated bank, and undercultivated agricultural tracts. Hashim Sarkis Studio's proposal (which went on to win the competition) consisted of three different volumes floating above a park inside the interchange. We aimed to reconnect the zones severed by the highway with bridges to the old city and the new.

Despite the important development initiatives under way in the town, Byblos lacked, at the time, an original and effective framework to implement them. Part of the town hall project included drafting a framework and identifying certain elements—a metropolitan transportation plan, a land use plan for the old town, key public places and sites—that could be packaged and presented to local and international donors. We also helped the council to compile a list of priorities for their initial investments and to develop design strategies for each. The list included the highway frontage, the main entrances to the city, and, of course, the town hall and its site plan, which would incorporate both the city's complex history and its future.

Like most projects in historic cities, the town hall faced several challenges. The municipal documents available were dated—looking more like sketchy collages than detailed drawings. But they did represent the hodgepodge urban fabric and enabled us to identify the major barriers that halted continuity within the city and stemmed connectivity beyond the urban center. First among these was Byblos's chaotic road system. The east-west mountain road, the north-south coastal road, and a series of *étroits droits* formed a redundant hierarchy that rarely corresponded to the needs of commuters, commerce, and tourism. Circulation in and around the town was spasmodic and inefficient.

By introducing a ring road that connected an existing infrastructure loop and then widening the passages under the highway to connect with a municipal transportation network (an expanded version of the network currently used by visitors in high tourist season), the proposal was able to unify the fragmented but overdetermined plan. In order to reduce pressure on the city's inner interchange, we proposed a campaign of landscaping and signage to draw attention—and traffic—to other entrances and exits around Byblos. To revitalize the east-west passages across the city's challenging topography, we suggested a series of paths, many of which would be built around streams and lead to historic or mythological sites, like the path that leads to the source of the Adonis River. We also proposed using abandoned railroad tracks along the coast as the base for a light surface rail system that could link Byblos with its surrounding municipalities.

The highway interchange site presented several hurdles but also the opportunity to restitch the "amputated" historic core back into the larger urban fabric and flow. The project creates three volumes along the highway that seem to hover when viewed from passing cars. The park beneath the structures creates a continuum that flows beneath and through the new site. Widened paths and pedestrian bridges, expanded parking, and a noise barrier help transform the previously indeterminate zone into protected and useful public space.

The three volumes house the three programmatic elements of the town hall: the administration, the presidency, and a museum of the Phoenician alphabet. The park flows under the three buildings and the ground floor consists of a common lobby. The upper levels of the administration and the presidency are connected by bridges. The newly widened pathways in the park and a new pedestrian bridge that extends the Roman axis will improve the connection between the historic city and the nearby commercial hub to the east of the interchange.

Site plan of Byblos Town Hall, Hashim Sarkis Studios, 2011.

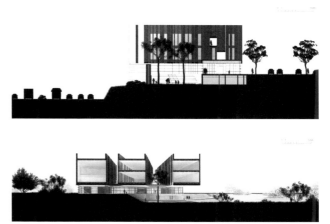

Section rendering of Byblos Town Hall, Hashim Sarkis Studios, 2011.

Yet one element left us perplexed and somewhat uneasy: the sandstone. The initial proposal included renderings with sandstone façades. It was an image of convenience, a look that might suffice until a more suitable material was found. Sandstone is a problematic material that should really not be exposed to the elements—it stains easily, its color is inconsistent, and it is very soft and vulnerable.

Particularly since the reconstruction following the Lebanese civil war, sandstone has come to evoke a sentimentalized, Lebanese/Arab muddled past that never was. It has sprouted up everywhere in Lebanon, Byblos being no exception. The city is plastering sandstone on surfaces around its downtown—along the Roman axis, on the temporary town hall, and, despite our reservations, along the highway. The use of sandstone is obligatory in the old souq and, while not specifically required elsewhere, is "strongly encouraged." Byblos seems so obsessed with the material that in many historic interiors it has been dug out from under a protecting plaster layer, leaving the stone exposed to moisture. Some public monuments that were originally built of limestone have been restored with sandstone, much of which is already rotting. Yet the obsession persists.

So for the town hall, the Byblos municipality bought a stock of sandstone and asked us to determine the best use of the material. All along we had envisioned three blocks that would look like large megaliths rising along the edge of the highway. Only when you got close to the volumes would you realize they were made of smaller pieces of stone. This was difficult to achieve with the 30-by-40-centimeter stones we had; the difference in color between the stones would make the pattern visible from a distance.

We tried different patterns, but none worked. Finally, a piece of yellow travertine provided the solution. The pattern of the travertine has similar colors to the sandstone was but organized in long veins. If we could only separate the colors of the sandstone and organize them in a similar pattern as the travertine, they would read almost as monolithic. Using strips approximately 40 centimeters long by 7 centimeters high and 2.5 centimeters thick, we were able to separate the stones into four shades, from yellowish to reddish. We then took the picture of the travertine, blew it up to the scale of the façades, and made it turn the corners so that the façades would read as one block. We also "posterized" it into four colors and pixelated its pattern into seven-by-forty-bit sections. We painted the pattern on the façades, and slowly the masonry team filled it in with sandstone. The pattern is carried across the three blocks so that from afar they read as if they were cut out of the same stone. As one draws closer, one sees that each is composed of a thin veneer.

While the current interpretation of Byblos's history may have compelled us to use a less than optimal material for our façade, it also inspired us to reach for new techniques and expressions in the design of the town hall's interior façades. The original design had imagined a kind of curtain wall covered with a striated screen and a similar pattern for a horizontal pergola covering the spaces between the blocks and their underbellies. We decided to seek a structural and decorative scheme that could unify these horizontal and vertical elements. We found a modern-day analogue for the Phoenician alphabet in bar codes—the composite lines of varying thickness used worldwide to identify retail products, track airport luggage, verify concert tickets, and monitor hospital patients, among countless other applications. We built a curtain wall with an aluminum lining anodized in Prussian blue and mounted it vertically onto a black background. The barcode construction, this digital "alphabet," establishes a thematic dialogue with its Phoenician forbearer, emphasizing the universal importance of language, and of Byblos's role in its development.

The municipality is still waiting to finish the Alphabet Museum and to program its different elements, including the long exterior wall that defines the

Byblos Town Hall, Hashim Sarkis Studios, 2011.

Byblos Town Hall, Hashim Sarkis Studios, 2011.

Hashim Sarkis

Curtain wall, Byblos Town Hall, Hashim Sarkis Studios, 2011.

Interior rendering of Byblos Town Hall, Hashim Sarkis Studios, 2011 .

edge of the park under the complex, so we proposed to paint a mural, which we imagined as a sort of wallpaper that could be covered by future art pieces. This decorative scheme was composed of gradual abstractions of Phoenician letters into geometric figures, applied horizontally in several distinct patterns that appear to the viewer to move at different rates as one walks along the wall. These patterns, visible from the lobby, complement the patterns formed by the aluminum barcode scheme and the color patterns we had achieved in the stone façade. In this way, the project becomes a broader experiment, an attempt to use architectural surfaces as a place of exchange—surfaces that can host diverse languages, symbols, and signs, and that can support forms of art and communication. Identity, in the building, is constituted by this exchange, not by the prevalence of one denotation or image. No matter how much we might try to keep it at bay, the question of identity permeates every architectural project. It certainly infused our work in Byblos, yet by avoiding the question of identity in a calculated way, we reached solutions that revealed how identity is constituted in architectural terms and how therefore it could be actively negotiated, questioned, and reconstituted.

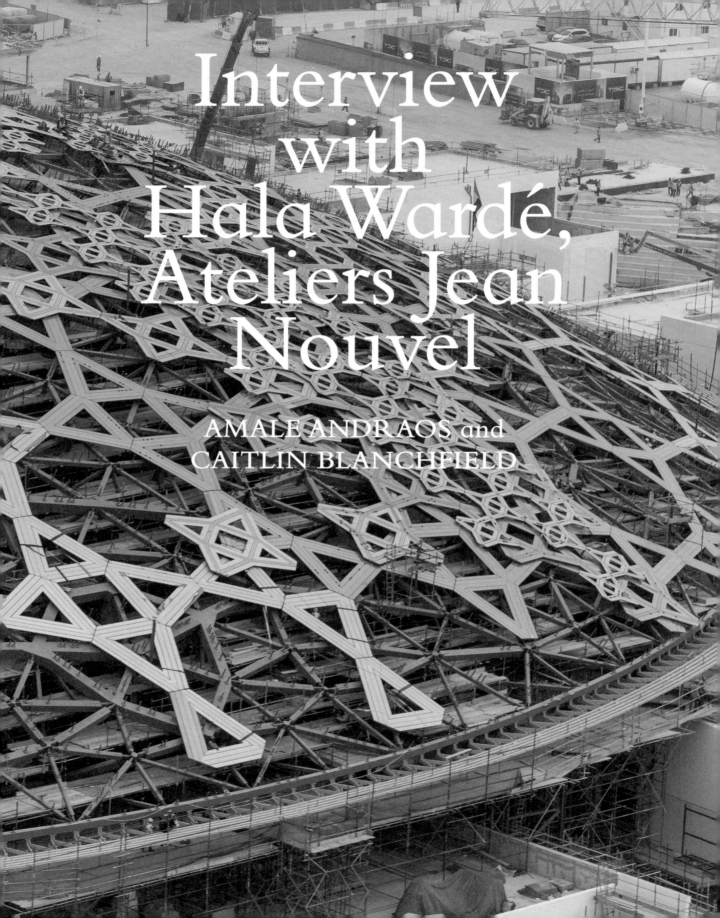

Interview with Hala Wardé, Ateliers Jean Nouvel

AMALE ANDRAOS and
CAITLIN BLANCHFIELD

AMALE ANDRAOS   The Louvre Abu Dhabi will be not only an exquisite piece of architecture, but also an anchor of the Saadiyat Cultural District. As the project's manager for Ateliers Jean Nouvel, can you discuss how the museum fits within the overall master plan and vision for the Cultural District?

HALA WARDÉ The Emirati authorities were in the process of designing a master plan for Saadiyat Island and sought advice from Tom Krenz, the former director of the Guggenheim. Tom suggested that the island should be conceived as an international cultural destination with five major museums designed by five renowned architects forming the basis for a cultural district. It's the interface between and around these museums, including the canal, the landscaping, residential and hotel amenities, etc., that makes this place a new or real destination. There is a vision that goes beyond the museums included in the master plan. The design of the surrounding urban environment puts this museum in a context, even if it is still under construction.

AA   You use the word "context," and it's a word you have used to describe the project in the past. Do you consider yourself, or does the office consider itself, contextual?

HW   Absolutely. Jean Nouvel defines himself as a contextual architect. He wrote *The Louisiana Manifesto* in 2005, in which he explains his theory of contextualism as something that goes beyond the physical context. Architecture belongs to a moment, a culture, and a place; it is a form of dialogue. As Jean says, we are not building a space but *in* a space. Jean would never design the same building in two different places; project specificity is vital.

CAITLIN BLANCHFIELD   That is interesting because you're working on a building that is, to a certain extent, the replication of something very famous that exists elsewhere. I'm curious how you're able to navigate working with the Louvre but also creating a structure that does feel responsive to its locality.

HW   What's interesting about this project—and very unusual for an architectural process—is that we designed the concept for a "classical museum" before the brief had been developed and before knowing who the museum operator would be. There were negotiations taking place between the French and Emirati governments in 2006, but when we were commissioned to design the building we didn't know it was going to be the Louvre until the intergovernmental agreement was signed in 2007. So the museum was conceived as an urban plan, prioritizing flexibility, as it is built of several individual buildings that have evolved over the years as the curatorial program has developed, while retaining their original integrity. The idea behind the concept was ultimately to adapt for whoever would operate this museum. It was, in a very real sense, a universal museum. When it was announced that the Louvre would be the operator of the museum, we were of course very pleased with the choice of this great institution and the harmony of a French architect for a French museum.

Interestingly, because the architectural concept was already in place, the curators developing the scientific and cultural program were inspired by the architecture, creating a continuity of discourse between the place and the content. We designed the museum so there would be many ways to *use* the space—to enter, to exit, and to explore it. By choosing

Aerial view of dome construction, Louvre Abu Dhabi, Ateliers Jean Nouvel, 2015.

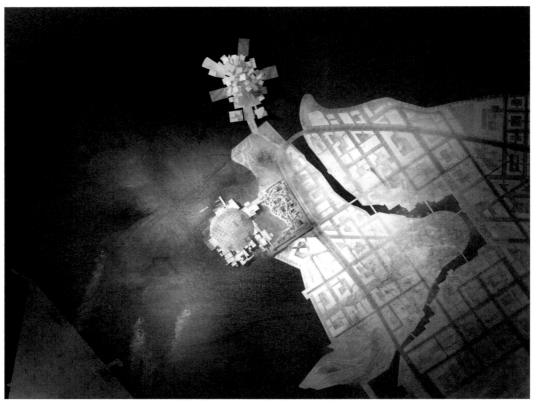

Louvre Abu Dhabi site plan, Louvre Abu Dhabi, Ateliers Jean Nouvel, 2014.

Louvre Abu Dhabi roof plan with dome, Louvre Abu Dhabi, Ateliers Jean Nouvel, 2014.

Rendering of exterior of the Louvre Abu Dhabi, Ateliers Jean Nouvel, 2014.

Concept rendering of gallery areas, Louvre Abu Dhabi, Ateliers Jean Nouvel, 2014.

Hala Wardé

Aerial view of construction, Louvre Abu Dhabi, Ateliers Jean Nouvel, 2015.

Site view with dome under construction, Louvre Abu Dhabi, Ateliers Jean Nouvel, 2015.

Interview

to enter the museum at one point and exit at another you have the possibility to read the cultural narrative not just in one order but in two or three different orders. This is how this architecture has influenced the *fil du discours*, the outline of the brief. The building participates in this idea of crossing a civilization organized chronologically: that you could not only view it from the beginning to the end, but you could read it in different ways or in different directions. This is where something very engaging happened between the architecture and the structure of the architecture and the content and the structure of the content.

We have also been able to go beyond the building structure itself and design the museography and interior fit-out. It's a total design project, which we are trying to keep as a coherent entity by designing all aspects of the museum with the context in mind, right down to the furniture.

CB I was struck by the way you articulated how the building evokes the presence of time, how it evokes the history and duration of the context you're working in. But in this case you're designing for a very newly built city. Could you talk more about the relationship between the museum and Abu Dhabi and what it was like building in a place that has such a strong recent architectural history?

HW It is always difficult when working in a young city to design a building that has roots in its locality. In this instance we were interested in creating a *lieu de rencontres*, a museum city. The organization of the buildings is a microcosm of an urban environment that could have always existed. To do this, we researched different urban plans, whether from traditional Arab cities or modern plans from

European and American towns, or even imaginary plans from Piranesi, for example. All of these references together become the basis for a new urbanism that took place naturally, as if a preexisting, multilayered archaeology could have always been there and has risen to the surface from the sand and seabed. The dome that partially covers this city is an obvious reference and homage to Arab culture.

AA I want to push that a little bit because, as architects, we understand this is a kind of mat. The mat has a long history. Even though it isn't a direct translation of the kind of traditional Islamic city, the mat presents a kind of typology that's been used in many, many different places. We understand that it goes beyond cultural specificity.

If the desire for an expression of a certain Islamic identity is coming from the client, then do architects have some agency to approach that obsession with specificity in a more sophisticated way? I think this building manages to do that, but that desire comes from the client, right?

HW The client wanted a museum that would be a landmark and would become a real destination, not necessarily that it should be an expression of a certain Islamic identity. If the museum had been in London or Berlin or São Paulo we would have questioned the context in the same way. Jean does not believe in general solutions; his architecture is specific and singular. Identity is something that exists already beyond form; it is much deeper. I know there was a lot of debate on this subject during the talk: What does it mean to bring Nouvel from Paris to interpret Arab identity? What does identity mean really? If we look at contemporary architecture in the UAE built by

Construction view of dome structure, Louvre Abu Dhabi, Ateliers Jean Nouvel, 2015.

Construction view of dome structure, Louvre Abu Dhabi, Ateliers Jean Nouvel, 2015.

Arab architects, it does not necessarily convey an Arab identity but rather European models.

AA   I don't think that the debate was ever that there's an issue for a Parisian architect to come and work in the UAE. That's not at all the question. And I totally agree with you. If as architects right now we are working to construct an identity, at a time where Arabs are constantly being reduced to the narrowness of their beliefs—and I'm talking personally—do we have a kind of responsibility to move beyond these narratives? That's more my question. If we are in fact helping construct an identity, do we encourage the construction of something much more hybrid, much more complex?

HW   You are completely right. And I think, yes, we should help to go beyond this. But at the same time, I think that we as architects should still build on contextual and cultural specificity. In this project, it's the light and the geometry. We have taken these two notions and addressed them in a much more nuanced and contemporary way that goes beyond everything that has been done before.

Interview with Ali Mangera, Mangera Yvars Architect

AMALE ANDRAOS and CAITLIN BLANCHFIELD

AMALE ANDRAOS The Qatar Faculty of Islamic Studies (QFIS) building, which your firm, Mangera Yvars Architects designed in Doha, Qatar, brings together a contemporary architectural language and traditional Islamic motifs. Can you speak about that?

ALI MANGERA We were quite keen on exploring ideas of contemporary visualization, let's say, of Islamic architecture. It's a very broad term. I'm not sure I should use that term, Islamic architecture. For too long there has been a kind of pastiche approach to what these sorts of buildings are or should be. And quite often it upsets people.

I'll give you a good example. Abdel-Wahed El-Wakil is a contemporary of Hassan Fathy and was involved with QFIS in a teaching capacity. He looked at our building with utter contempt. It really caused an extreme reaction, which is unbelievable.

But what we're trying to do is look at some of the historic buildings in Islamic civilization and understand how they operate from the point of view of plan. So in the case of QFIS, we were looking at the Sultan Hassan Mosque in Egypt and essentially how teaching space and prayer space can be combined.

From the beginning, we were interested in the interface between learning and faith and how these components have been woven together in buildings historically, but also how that connection might be made effectively by using more contemporary strategies. Essentially the building is very clean and simple, although it looks complicated. In this way it allows the audience, the students, to interface with their faith in an unhindered way rather than encountering embellishments that might distract from the purpose of learning and from the purpose of gaining faith.

Initially, Arata Isozaki was asked to do the project. Though he proposed some interesting ideas, like mixing the male and female prayer space, in the end he made an odd choice. He essentially proposed a cube. And if you look at this cube as a Muslim, it looks very familiar, just like the famous cube that everyone prays toward. The fundamental idea of his proposal, to redeploy this icon, had alienated him. You can't do a building that looks like Mecca in Education City. It might be misconstrued.

Anyhow, then they came to us. After an informal interview, we presented three very different options to Sheikha Moza. She wanted the building to be a statement, a building that could articulate the faith in a very positive way while still embedded with those Islamic references.

We have some very important Islamic scholars involved with the project, like Sheikh Yusuf al-Qaradawi, one of the preeminent Islamic scholars, who is from Egypt but now living in Qatar. He's a purist but at the same time very open to the idea of including women, for example. It's a very positive message he's giving about Islam, and that message resonates well with Qatar. On the other hand, detractors like El-Wakil feel that what we're doing is not Islamic architecture. He understands it to be completely different.

AA It's as if there is such a thing as an authentic interpretation versus inauthentic interpretation or pastiche. Is what he does pastiche? Or is your building pastiche, and according to whom? I think that debate is very interesting. If you start to make references, how do you choose to make them? Is it the plan, the form, the kind of calligraphy? Where do you say the references played the biggest role?

The roof terrace of the Qatar Faculty of Islamic Studies, Mangera Yvars Architects, Doha, Qatar, 2013.

199

Qatar Faculty of Islamic Studies, Mangera and Yvars Architects, Doha, Qatar, 2013.

Interior spiral stairway, Qatar Faculty of Islamic Studies, Mangera and Yvars Architects, Doha, Qatar, 2013.

AM   The plan is a simple way to identify pathways between knowledge and light. For example, the plan of the Sultan Hassan is a square plan with prayer in the center and with *Hanafi, Shafi'i, Maliki, Hanbali* (the four schools of Islamic thought) around the corners. The scholarly program is on the perimeter, and the center is prayer space. We looked at alternate ways of doing this in different universities and different institutions, understanding that the students are there to gain knowledge and at the same time to enlighten themselves. That enlightenment happens in the mosque. The idea of traveling from outside the campus and also within the building itself is this continuous spiral movement between knowledge and light, and an oscillation between the two. The whole building is connected on different levels back to the mosque, so there are many pathways. That's loosely the concept of the project, one that originates in the plan.

It's not called a mosque, by the way. It's not allowed to be called a mosque because the religious authority that approves mosque designs in the Middle East won't necessarily approve a building of this type to be a mosque. Officially, it's a high-capacity prayer room. The main function of the building is the university, but the prayer room figures prominently in the whole formal arrangement, and deliberately so. While it can't be officially recognized as a mosque, that's what everyone calls it.

While the figuring of this prayer space responds to certain historical arrangements, there are obviously some environmental factors to consider. The big volume of the mosque is placed to the south, to provide a lot of shadow on other parts of the building. That's one of the main factors for the scheme's orientation. And then of course you have the requirement to face Mecca, along with the logistical need

to direct people off the main campus, so the building ends up facing the main campus.

CAITLIN BLANCHFIELD   I'm curious how you considered the positive representation of Islam through these references within the specific context of Education City, which is a twenty-first-century university model. How did you navigate both this desire to express tradition and the need to locate that tradition in a contemporary center of knowledge production and learning?

AM   I think in order to express tradition, let's say, there are some clever or perhaps more obvious ways of doing it. The minute you start using scripture, texts from the holy Quran, suddenly the building takes on a layer of meaning beyond its form. People reading the text on the wall of the mosque, for example, can directly identify with the spiritual reference. The calligraphy in the courtyard in particular is an element that is meant to engage more traditional visitors. The building itself can take them back to the Quran, which I think is quite important.

We have made an effort to provide a space for Islamic scholarship but in a contemporary way. We've implemented some of the latest ideas that you have at Harvard, in terms of how you create formal and informal teaching spaces. The corridors are outfitted to perform both as teaching spaces and outdoor spaces. So all of the features that you would normally find in contemporary universities are in that building.

What is also interesting is that a lot of the universities in Doha are imported. There's a Texas A&M campus, one from Cornell, and others. QFIS is the first indigenous Qatari university on the now-renamed campus, Hamad

The open floor of the high-capacity prayer room, Qatar Faculty of Islamic Studies,
Mangera and Yvars Architects, Doha, Qatar, 2013.

Interview

campus. I think that's quite positive, that we don't only need foreign universities to come in and launch a campus like this.

CB   Did you think the prospect of building the first indigenous campus in Qatar created a desire in the client for a certain kind of Qatari representation in relation to, for instance, the image of Texas A&M in Doha?

AM   I don't know if they were interested in whether it was specifically Qatari. I think the client's concern was if it was contemporary or could be something that talks about contemporary Islam. The Qatari vernacular is a very strong idea, and it is being executed in Msheireb, which is a downtown Doha project. But it does have its limitations, so to speak. In this case, I think the Qatar Foundation just wanted something emblematic that could help launch the campus or give it another orientation.

AA   But if the new image of Qatar is in fact able to merge tradition with an image of modernity, how does that extend to labor practices? Were you as an architect part of the conversation to determine the contractor or the means by which a contemporary project should be constructed in Qatar?

AM   This is a very familiar stick to beat Qatar with, to be honest. We were also asked to work on some of their World Cup projects, and what's new—to be completely open—is that they're sending to all the design teams the policies with regard to labor, with regard to how labor should be treated and so on. There's a kind of a manifesto being circulated now. Obviously, the media has made it something that they're now quite conscious of.

But the work on our site predated all of that. I know we had four thousand people on the site during its peak. As designers, we're not party to how contractors manage their labor. For me it's interesting on a personal level because all of these immigrants are migrant Indian workers. And here I find myself originally from South Africa but originally-originally from India, having relocated to the UK, designing a building in Qatar as the architect, and seeing workers who are from probably the same region where I come from. So it's kind of a strange place to be in.

AA   I don't think the issue has been that they are migrant workers. I think its just been, in some cases, how they've been treated. So Qatar is now reacting to the labor issues on construction sites, in your mind?

AM   Oh, definitely. As I said, we're working on some of the FIFA-related projects. So we are quite conscious of how things are proceeding. I think it's something that cannot be sorted out overnight. It's just the way things are when you're moving from one system to another.

But I'm quite confident that from the highest level, I'm talking from the Emir downward, there is that motivation. And if you look at what Sheikha Moza is saying, it's apparent that they are very conscious of image and want to be seen in a generous way in regard to these issues. This is something that is strangely absent in other Middle Eastern countries where we're also working.

AA   It's interesting you should say that because I'm not sure that the labor condition has improved relative to the '50s, the '60s, or the '70s.

Calligraphy inside the prayer room of the Qatar Faculty of Islamic Studies, Mangera and Yvars Architects, Doha, Qatar, 2013.

Interview

Calligraphy inside the mosque and on pillars that create an entry sequence into the school, Qatar Faculty of Islamic Studies, Mangera and Yvars Architects, Doha, Qatar, 2013.

Informal spaces for teaching and working, Qatar Faculty of Islamic Studies, Mangera and Yvars Architects, Doha, Qatar, 2013.

Ali Mangera

Education City campus under construction around the Qatar Faculty for Islamic Studies, Doha, Qatar, 2013.

Interview

CB I'm curious about this manifesto that you mentioned. A statement about labor conditions does seem like something new. Do you know if that's a response to concerns raised by architects, or the media, or something else?

AM No, it's a political move, of course. It's a response to what's happening in the press. It's a response to outside pressure. I don't think Qatar went into this World Cup blindly. I think they would have expected this kind of scrutiny, and they would have been prepared for it.

Obviously, things are not going to change overnight. But I think this scrutiny is a bit unfair. It's very easy to bash Qatar, for example, when equally troubling things are probably happening in China that no one knows about. Even projects in African countries funded by the US government—how they are procured and how they are developed deserves the same scrutiny. How is Apple and how are other private companies doing procurement and managing labor forces? This is a global problem. I think we need to consider where this comes from, who's saying it, and what is the subtext. How, for example, are Palestinians enjoying their working conditions? No one really bats an eye.

AA Why do you think the UAE and Qatar have been so attacked?

AM Well, because they're small enough to be attacked without major political consequences. If the World Cup was taken away from Russia, there might be another war. But if FIFA took the World Cup from Qatar, well, there might be an economic impact, but who knows? The region is falling apart. It doesn't take much for something to go off, you know, for situations to change. And I think whoever is saying whatever they're saying, they need to think very carefully about the impact that it might have in Qatar and elsewhere. It's just too easy to single out some nations and not others.

AA I have a question that's less specific to Qatar but concerns global practice. As the practice of architecture has become increasingly global, architects have tended to ask the question of identity. Is it important that architecture participates in some kind of construction of identity?

AM Of course, whether you do so consciously or unconsciously, you're participating. The minute you make a statement, any statement in built form, you're participating in the making or reinforcement of an identity. Particularly in the Gulf, there is a kind of pursuit of identity at the moment, which is a nostalgia for an era that's gone missing. Phenomenal change has occurred in the last fifty years in the move from Bedouin culture to contemporary society.

But I have to ask, what is identity? Whose identity are we talking about? Is identity itself American? Is it kind of pan-European, pan-global? Is it modern? What are we all aspiring to? Shops are selling the same products in all these different countries. The remnants of identity in the case of Qatar, the historic vernacular of one- or two-story houses, are reconfigured in projects like Msheireb to make twenty-story buildings. So it's a different way of looking at identity.

And I think a lot of that has been caused by the huge kind of building boom that happened in the '70s and '80s. A willing destruction is carrying on in a place like Mecca now, with the replacement of the old city with absolutely vulgar statement buildings, which are completely out of scale and purely about

The Qatar Faculty of Islamic Studies building alit at night, Mangera and Yvars Archiects, Doha, Qatar, 2013.

A worker walks in front of the Qatar Faculty of Islamic Studies construction site, Doha, Qatar, 2013.

generation of income. I think people are just fed up with that.

Mecca is an interesting case because many people go there, some of them from the Third World who might be spiritually uplifted by its architecture but who are not compelled, or even able, to read its particular identity. But in cities like Jeddah this same postmodern architecture imparts no identity, and there are no redeeming qualities that place it in Jeddah, which make it specifically Saudi. Look at what is happening in Palmyra now. It is the same ideology that has been used to destroy Mecca and parts of Medina. They've done that to their cities, and it's because those few people who are in charge just don't get it. Countries like the UAE and Qatar, and Iran to some extent, are smaller, and they have a much-better-educated public. Those countries are not so isolated.

Identity is still a question. I don't think we've got the answer. But I think it has been the cause of a lot of destruction, primarily by Western architects.

Juxtopolis Pedagogy

MAGDA MOSTAFA

THE CAIRO STUDIO

Today, perhaps more than any time in the recent history of the Arab City, architects, scholars, and educators are compelled to review our perceptions, reassess our roles, and redefine how we choose to address the urban environment. Recent events across the Arab region have necessitated this form of introspection. It is partially in response to the dynamic changes taking place on the ground in cities such as Cairo during social and political unrest, and partially in support of the socially conscious role of the praxis of architecture in bringing to the forefront of current debates issues such as the right to the city, the role of public space, the definition of ownership versus control, and the growing need for the basic human right of shelter.[1] Across all sectors of architecture we have responded to these issues through advocacy, scholarship, and alternative modes of teaching and practice.[2] The Juxtopolis pedagogy presented here is a response to these events and forces of introspection.

This pedagogy, like many things, was born of necessity—a necessity to bring the urgencies of the January 25th uprising to the forefront of architectural education in Cairo. In addition to the above-mentioned debates, a relative absence of regulation—or at least its implementation—between 2011 and 2014 caused a dramatic rise in informality and illegal, speculation-driven demolition.[3] These factors threw our metropolis into a rapid state of flux, necessitating an alternative methodology to the current top-down planning and aesthetic romanticism in our city—one that is more rooted in the harsh realities of the city and its current and continuing fluid state.

This pedagogy begins with a specific view of Cairo that goes beyond the reductive binaries that have been used to define it: black or white, planned or unplanned, rich or poor, us or them. Instead, it defines Cairo as a series of layers and a series of juxtapositions. Cairo, like many other cities to varying degrees and through different manifestations, is a city stratified on the horizontal plane as it sprawls outward.[4] At the same time, it is stratified vertically, through parallel street networks and roofscapes that are disconnected from one another and from the ground plane of the city. Across both these axes and throughout our formal city are mixed-use pockets of informality. This is captured visually by the work of Hamdy Reda, photographer, artist, and activist, as well as through literature and cinema, especially in Alaa Al-Aswany's *Imarat Ya'qubiyan*.

The juxtaposition of heritage and modernity in Islamic Cairo.

These seemingly binary conditions exist in a symbiotic but tenuous coexistence and are completely juxtaposed. These juxtapositions include issues such as heritage and modernity, great wealth and extreme poverty, agriculture and urbanity, commerce and revolt, permanence and temporality, and formality and informality. Cairo's roofscapes present the perfect backdrop for this complex milieu: a parallel world of occasional poverty, often illegal activity, occasional glimpses of freedom and escape, and even religious symbolism.

Vendors at a protest in Tahrir Square, Cairo January 2011. Juxtapositions are also found in the more intangible and include sociocultural practices such as the juxtaposition of commerce and protest.

The juxtaposition of formal and informal at the margins of the urban core and informal belt of Cairo.

Possibly the most critical and prevalent juxtaposition addressed through the Juxtopolis pedagogy is that of the formal and informal, whether it is one of ownership, operation, or urban condition. This dialogue invariably begins with the question of what defines informality. The term has, until recently, carried negative connotations in relation to urban development. And over the past

The roofscape of Cairo's Garbage Village at the foothills of Mokattam.

The parallel city of pigeon breeders on the roofscapes of Cairo.

A church precariously built on the roof of what seems to be an administrative building in the El Daher downtown area of Cairo. The image prompts us to ask what in our city's urban and social density and dynamics would force a building off the street and onto the roofscape in this sort of way.

Juxtopolis Pedagogy

decades, informal development in cities has incited, to varying degrees, negative reactions—from quiet but limited tolerance to indiscriminate evacuation and demolition of informal urban settlements. In Egyptian colloquial Arabic, the word commonly used to refer to these informal settlements is *ishwai'yat*, which literally translates into "chaoses" or "disorders." As the Cairene activist Yahia Shawkat states in a documentary on the right to housing, "these [informal settlements] are not chaoses, they are self-reliance."[5] Beyond this negativity, we must begin by asking ourselves what it is specifically that distinguishes formal from informal. Is it about legality? Ownership and security of tenure; access to infrastructure; poverty versus wealth; permanence versus temporality; pre-determinism and planning? Or is it really about form?

The surprisingly modular and regulated spatial form of informal trade
on Twenty-Sixth of July Street in downtown Cairo.

In our early definitions and investigations of informality, we found that this urban condition that we call "informal" is actually highly organized and concerned with form.[6] In a robust response to actual needs, this process of self-organization, self-regulation, and continuous negotiation results in an urban form, capable of replication and mutation to adjust to change and growth. This is the case at various scales and though various functions, from commerce to housing to mobility.

It is through this process of negotiation that we unfold one of the values of studying and understanding informality. Hubert Klumpner states, "architecture and urbanism are frozen politics."[7] In tune with this notion, the Juxtopolis pedagogy views informality as a manifestation of a community's needs and the social structures that exist to enable or disable them. This self-reliant urbanism currently comprises the vast majority of our built environments. Yet our educational institutions do very little to address the fact that 90 percent of the world is built without architects.[8] We continue to educate future architects only to participate and constructively engage in that minority 10 percent.

NEGOTIATING THE JUXTAPOSITIONS

In this alternative, multilayered vision of the city, every design begins by determining the juxtapositions in play. Working within the city of Cairo, these projects start with a search for contestation and friction between two seemingly opposite forces. Focusing on navigating and negotiating, the design task is invariably to find a way to mediate in between these layers and juxtapositions, seeking middle ground between the typical top-down and bottom-up approaches. These two processes—navigation and negotiation—are ever more relevant in institutionally fluid cities such as Cairo, where the various poles of these binary relationships are in an almost perpetual state of change, and where the implementation of top-down strategies becomes next to impossible when the top is fragmented among various bureaucratic entities, which are often dysfunctional or, more recently, nonfunctional.

Often complex and multilayered in themselves, proposals using this approach must determine the contradictory forces requiring mediation and negotiation through design. Over the past four years, studio projects at the American University in Cairo have used this pedagogy to approach the city's architecture with increasing complexity.

THE GARBAGE CITY OF CAIRO

Primarily carried out by Coptic Christian migrants from the villages of Egypt's south, garbage collection in Cairo is mostly performed by legions of young male workers who use horse-drawn carts and small trucks to gather solid waste from the doorstep of almost every home in the city. Since its establishment in the 1960s in the informal settlement of Manshiyet Nasser at the foothills of the Mokkatam plateau east of the city center, this community has been largely segregated and ostracized.[9]

The "Garbage Village—Social Integration through Quarry Architecture" project addresses both the geographic and cultural isolation of this community from the greater city to which it provides an infrastructural service. Given that the economic return for these workers is primarily the inherent value of the garbage itself, not a monthly wage or salary, they have developed a highly efficient low-tech recycling process. In a manner similar to how the community identifies value in what is discarded, the design identifies a potential discarded site and proposes how it can reconnect the garbage village to the greater Cairo population by providing social gathering spaces and linking nodes and by utilizing Coptic carving methods.

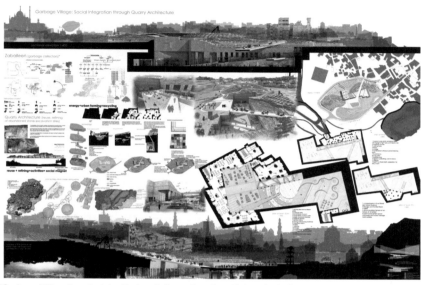

"Garbage Village" project, by Mariam Zaitoun, American University in Cairo architecture program, 2013.

HERITAGE AND MODERNITY:
RECONCILING HISTORY AND PROSPERITY

Cairo offers emblematic examples of the polarity between urban modernity and heritage: informal settlements and the Great Pyramids, high-traffic vehicular roadways and centuries-old mosques, metro stations and some of the world's first churches, and more specifically, a Mamluk aqueduct and an informal tannery district.

Earmarked to be relocated miles away as part of the Cairo 2050 vision, *el dabbagheen* (the tanners) settlement is an extension of Cairo's slaughterhouse district. Pressing against the historic aqueduct, this community is slowly being disenfranchised by the neoliberal policies of the city. A thesis project for the Juxtopolis program—"Rehabilitation of the Tannery District"—uses an urban husbandry program to create a mixed-use live-work community. This resource-driven approach looks at both the human and physical potentials of the site, within an effective policy framework. Keeping in mind the possible gentrification and soft-eviction its realization may produce, the project proposes a more participatory design process that includes issues of tenure security for its inhabitants.

Photomontages from "River Park of Ather El-Nabi" project for the American University in Cairo architecture program's senior thesis studio, 2013.

RECONCILING THE CITY AND THE NILE:
STEP BACK, RECLAIM, AND RECONNECT

Cairo's history is built along the Nile. Various periods throughout the city's development have witnessed significant changes in the relationship between city and river, the most darastic of which followed the opening of the Aswan Dam in 1970, which brought an end to annual flooding. This dramatic shift allowed the city a more permanent edge and a more deterministic relationship with the river—a condition not always managed to the advantage of Cairenes.

The relationship between Cairo and the Nile today seems to be one of coexistence, as opposed to connection and symbiosis. A recent study from the College of Environmental Design at the University of California, Berkeley, looked at that relationship in depth and identified ways to make it more vital and productive for both the river ecology and the residents of Cairo.[10]

Located in the abandoned port of Athar El-Nabi, the Juxtopolis thesis project "River Park of Ather El-Nabi" looks at the highly polarized coexistence of an informal settlement that lies parallel to and behind an almost impermeable wall of upper-class residential and mixed-use towers along the eastern bank of the Nile, stretching south between the neighborhoods of Misr El-Qadima and Ma'adi. Since its establishment in 1960, residents have been exposed to tenure insecurity and general urban disenfranchisement, with the most recent regulations proposing their removal and relocation to a desert city miles from their current homes. "River Park of Ather El-Nabi" identifies three core interventions: developing underused pockets of land to serve social functions, such as a women's empowerment center and wholesale produce market; establishing circulation arteries and vistas to pierce the Nile-front urban wall and connect the informal community to the river; and creating a riverside public park with floating structures.

A collage by Mohamed Badawy showing the juxtaposition of history and the chaos of the modern city, developed as part of the "Ramses Culture Hub" project for the American University in Cairo's architecture program's senior thesis studio, 2013.

THE STATIC AND THE MOBILE:
RENEGOTIATING CAIRO'S GATEWAY

Possibly the most ambitious of the Juxtopolis projects attempted to date, the "Ramses Culture Hub" project looks at the urban gateway of Cairo—Ramses Square. Named for the pharaoh whose statue once stood at its center, this square is home to Cairo's central train station. Formerly an epitome of "Paris on the Nile," it now stands as a highly congested, polluted, and contested battleground between authorities, transit users, pedestrians, cars, and informal traders. It has recently become too congested and polluted for even the granite statue for which it was named, which has been moved to a storage facility outside of the city for fear of the long-term effects of the vibrations and smog it endured on a daily basis.

The Culture Hub proposes to revive Ramses Square by removing traffic from its core and creating three pedestrianized urban plazas. The proposal looks at absorbing Sixth of October Bridge, which bisects the square, and it introduces new functions as a densified mixed-use ring around its periphery, including a deconstructed *wekala* to give agency to the informal traders, legitimizing their presence and defining their domain, which currently sprawls unchecked across the square. These three elements—plazas, bridge, and ring—are connected by a new form of urban space that wraps up, through, and around the buildings in the form of public walkways, bridges, circulation skins, elevated plazas, and accessible rooftops.

The development of this complex and composited way of seeing the city responds to the demands to shift and change the status quo of architectural education. A widespread adoption of this approach will help cultivate a generation of architectural practitioners able to deftly negotiate, mediate between, and connect the contradictions and multiple layers of the contemporary city—Arab or otherwise—as opposed to imposing design across them. This type of practice is represented in the work of art activists during the aftermath of January 25th, where they used art to negotiate and dissolve even the harshest and sometimes deadliest collisions.

An image of the bedoun *hawa'et* (without walls) art activist movement's mural on security blockades off Tahrir Square.

1   Discussions and documentation of Cairo's state of flux can be found in Omar Nagati and Beth Stryker, "Archiving the City in Flux" (2013), http://issuu.com/clustercairo/docs/archiving_the_city_in_flux.

2   Many lessons on this subject came out of the south-south dialogue initiated in 2013 at the American University in Cairo's symposium "Learning from Cairo." For a compilation of these dialogues, see Beth Stryker, Omar Nagati, and Magda Mostafa, eds., *Learning from Cairo: Global Perspectives and Future Visions* (Cairo: Cluster; American University in Cairo, 2013), http://learningfromcairo.org/publication/epub. For more discussion on the impact of this introspection on teaching see Magda Mostafa, "Learning from Cairo: What Informal Settlements Can (and Should) Teach Us," *ArchDaily*, March 14, 2014, www.archdaily.com/486294/closing-the-loop-learning-from-cairo-s-informal-settlements.

3   The most reliable estimate available to date of the prevalence of informality in Cairo is found in David Sims, *Understanding Cairo: The Logic of a City Out of Control* (Cairo: American University in Cairo Press, 2010), which states that approximately 64 percent of the urban population lives in informal settlements. This work does not account for the increase of informality following the January 25, 2011 protests. Further discussion of his estimates of rate of informal growth post–January 25th can be found in Sims, "Understanding Cairo's Informal Development," in Stryker, Nagati, and Mostafa, *Learning from Cairo,* 38–41.

4   David Sims describes this stratification as the "urban core, informal belt, and desert city." Sims, *Understanding Cairo.*

5   "Right to Housing" documentary series (2012), produced by the Shadow Ministry of Housing, http://blog.shadowministryofhousing.org/2012/05/blog-post_28.html.

6   Stryker, Nagati, and Mostafa, *Learning from Cairo.*

7   Velux Group, "Learning for the Unknown," *Daylight and Architecture* 21 (Summer 2014): 32.

8   Cynthia E. Smith, *Design with the Other 90%: Cities* (New York: Cooper-Hewitt, National Design Museum, 2011).

9   Further discussion of the state of Cairo's solid waste management community can be found in Petra Kuppinger, "Crushed? Cairo's Garbage Collectors and Neoliberal Urban Politics," *Journal of Urban Affairs* 36 (2014): 621–33.

10   George M. Kondolf et al., "Connecting Cairo to the Nile: Renewing Life and Heritage on the River," IURD Working Paper no. WP-2011-06, Department of Landscape Architecture and Environmental Planning, University of California, Berkeley, with the American University in Cairo and Cairo University, 2011.

Architecture and Representing

LAURA KURGAN

Architecture never stops representing. From documenting the preexistence of the building, to embodying its role in the city, to inscribing its formal language in states of economic boom as well as conflict, architectural drawings are representation in an active form, in the present tense. In fact, nothing changes in architecture without changes in modes of representation; new ways of not only seeing but also of making images lead to different kinds of interventions in the built environment. What architects should be thinking about, and what many of the practitioners included in this volume speak to, are the instruments and tools of representation—how they are used to make architecture and how they can change the perception of what architecture does. How does architecture represent? What does architecture represent? Who does it represent? And, most importantly, how can we change what architecture represents through the instruments of representation?

The work and ideas presented in the conference, and in this publication, cover an incredible spectrum, but one through-line connecting many of these projects, both scholarly and design-based, is their response to situations of conflict. We have seen architecture as a witness to conflict, as well as architecture that operates in cities that are in a permanent state of conflict. The work of Eyal Weizman and Forensic Architecture demonstrates how architecture may be mobilized as evidence, be it through reading the fragmented remains of urban warfare or using analytical drawing to reveal how urban violence is perpetuated.

At times it is the persistence of architecture, and the obdurate designers who continue to reimagine the city even in midst of violence, that is itself a response to conflict. Bernard Khoury, for instance, stayed and built in Beirut during the civil war and in its aftermath. Beirut, I think we can agree, is not the best example of how to resolve conflict, and the history of conflict, through architecture. After the war the government completely dictated how the city center would be rebuilt, commissioning one private developer for its master plan and thereby foreclosing opportunities for many Lebanese architects concerned with Beirut's reconstruction. Yet Khoury found novel ways for the war to allow him to build and gain commissions, through interacting with the cast of characters that remained in the city and continued to shape it.

In the work of Senan Abdelqader, there is an almost quiet way of addressing conflict through the small scale of a house and the small changes that you can make to shift patterns in the way we live. It is architecture as a cultivator. Design can be a catalyst for negotiation, for people to demand their rights. This process is a slow one, and it seems to entail a certain commitment to permanence in places that may feel quite volatile. It requires staying in one place and addressing the architecture of conflict. It insists on seeing binaries that conflict inscribes and also seeing around or through them. Infrastructure can become a means of crossing physical divides; informal interventions can slowly chip away at exclusionary structures; and design language can change the image of certain spaces within a city and among its residents.

Practice is one site from which to address conflict, which can be difficult, gradual, and piecemeal. Another is pedagogy, which also operates through the construction and transmission of images and evolves on a different time scale. The work of Magda Mostafa and her students at the American University in Cairo is one example of this approach—architecture as a response to extreme juxtapositions. Through the work of her students we can see not just urban continuities or ruptures but also the juxtapositions, particularly between the formal and the informal, that have become so prevalent in many cities.

It seems architecture is increasingly in states of permanent conflict, a condition of the origins and futures of many cities. Take Aleppo for example, where the conflict began long before the war—and now during the middle of the war, in another city, developers and planners are talking about its reconstruction. Conflict takes many forms and leaves many traces on the city, as the work in this book makes evident. So the question is, is architecture enough? Is architecture enough to do what each of these people is trying to do? With these questions in mind, it is also crucial to see how architecture may be one tool among many to address conflict and to participate in the documentation and mediation of it.

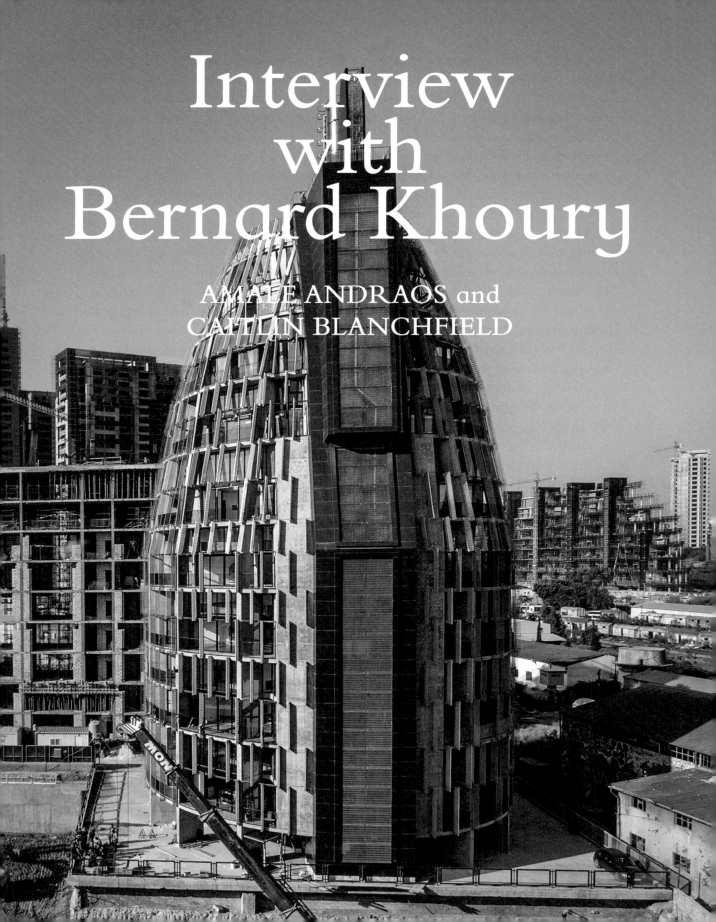

Interview
with
Bernard Khoury

AMALE ANDRAOS and
CAITLIN BLANCHFIELD

AMALE ANDRAOS Your work embraces narrative to generate architecture, and I think the centrality of the story is related to your intimate knowledge of, and participation in, a highly specific context. Do you think that engaging personal stories allows you to access a level of specificity in relation to context?

BERNARD KHOURY Architects can have a very particular sense of duty when it comes to their relationship with context. The same kind of orthodox accountability to employ impartial or more correct definitions drives the wise researcher to produce 2-kilogram books based on an accumulation of endless data and generic papers drafted by experts and historians, only to breed fictitious definitions of territories and dangerous oversimplifications of history.

The narrative you refer to is a constructed reality that takes shape at a given moment in time in a given place, with very specific protagonists. I choose to understand this given place through a very intimate and sometimes very intense relationship with these protagonists, who become heroes around which I then construct extremely particular yet unexpected situations. This specificity creates a sense of place that transcends the more consensual definitions of context and allows for instinctively sincere contradictions from one street corner to another.

CAITLIN BLANCHFIELD Can you offer an example of those contradictions or the relationship between two buildings in which you have had to navigate these contradictions?

BK I have long been a prisoner of a sensationalist label, resulting from critics' recurrent recuperation of my early work for the entertainment industry, in which there were obvious references to our difficult recent past and my reaction to the collective amnesia of the postwar period. However, concurrently and within the same city, I have developed an important number of residential buildings alongside developers, with completely different agendas. The most fundamental contradiction I still navigate in today lies in the stark contrast between the nature of these two contrasting types of commissions, both set against what could have been the same consensual backdrop.

On one front, I resolutely plotted a building not intended for families, children, nannies, or school bus pick-ups in the morning. My experience with the developer of this particular project generated what could seem to be an unreasonable scenario, an instrument of selfish pleasure, which at the outset does not respond to the parameters of the traditional real estate residential models. The spatial configuration of Plot #4371, also referred to as Artist Studios, incites instances of debauchery, which could allow for the culmination of an inebriated night at the driver's seat smack in the middle of your living room, indulging that all-too-familiar illusion that the minuscule front seat of your car is the winning alternative over the discomfort of having to get out and walk to your bedroom.

Simultaneously, a little further into the city and with a different developer accomplice, another scheme seeks to challenge the traditional developer's typology of deep slabs, blind central cores, and a segregation of public and private functions. These conformist residential models usually seal family dwellings from the outside, as if the streets and surrounding neighborhoods were hostile territory.

In resistance to these imposed standards, I attempted to revive, through my plans, an almost carnal relationship with the surrounding

Plot # 4371, Bernard Khoury, Beirut, 2015.

Plot #183, Bernard Khoury, Beirut, 2009.

B018 nightclub, Bernard Khoury, Beirut, 1998.

territory by drawing conceived trajectories which inscribe my buildings into the fabric of their environment, rendering them bare and in direct rapport with the street. Plot #183 is a very literal illustration of this desire to reconnect the urban habitat to its urban surroundings. The façade of the building is drawn by a promenade that links families' internal functions of each apartment through an exterior path. This circuit allows you to literally hug your house and travel around it. You are no longer living inside the walls but in these passages around the apartment, which are simultaneously part of its internal functioning as well as the urban fabric.

Both situations are constructed within the same supposed Mediterranean tableau, presenting very specific yet radically different stories as a result of two very different encounters.

AA You've been navigating Beirut for over two decades now, so how has your relationship to that context evolved? I think the reason why your work sometimes unnerves and annoys, especially people in the West, is because you send back an image of Beirut and of the Arab world that is not what they like to see or want to imagine. But the question remains for me if you are writing a scenario and if the architecture is helping to construct an identity.

BK My relationship to my context has evolved in the sense that I no longer seek to base my projects on certitudes. What unnerves and annoys the West is the fact that they fail to categorize me within a frame that confirms their predisposed expectations of my territory. Situations that I deal with do not imply accountability. They have, at the onset at least, primarily financial agendas, not political ones, and this has allowed me to take radical stances.

Our cities are now, and have been for quite some time, in the hands of the private sector. In this part of the world, it becomes necessary to recognize this sour reality and work from there. This does not mean that one cannot produce relevant meaning out of these situations. Why could it not be more relevant than acting on more conventional institutions such as memorials, museums, or other public buildings? Public commissions, in my opinion, lead more often to consensual political stances due to their accountability.

AA This is where I think your work starts to invert expectations. Typically we think that designing for institutions, building cultural centers: this is where architecture can be expressed as capital-A Architecture. But what you're saying is that the possibility for relevant meaning today can actually be found in working with a developer.

BK This is actually the only way I can survive, and the only way I am able to intervene. But this was not always the case.

Back in the early nineties, we all hoped that we were going to be part of rebuilding the nation, and making supposedly meaningful interventions through institutional projects, through Architecture with a capital A: museums, public schools, public housing, hospitals, opera houses, and so on. Obviously this never happened, and we saw the notion of the nation-state completely collapse. So what do you do in this situation? It took me a few years to realize that Beirut would never be rebuilt in the way we were naively expecting it to be.

Instead we have had to adopt strategies of survival that are of a completely different nature. Practicing in these conditions that are unstable and problematic requires confronting

Plot # 7950 residence, Bernard Khoury, Faqra, 2010.

"The Landowner," one of Bernard Khoury's clients.

Interview

the fact that the most basic notion of the state no longer exists. I want to believe that the sour realities of our environments could produce another kind of modernity, one that comes from within.

I see my colleagues, particularly those practicing in the secure territories of Europe, for instance, where the state is far more present in the making of the city. I do not envy them because at the end of the day, their margin of operation and the political relevance of what they are doing are, in my opinion, very limited. Sometimes I ask myself if this is the fate of public architecture in the civilized world. Maybe I prefer to work with pirates, sons of dictators, and my local heroes here in Beirut.

AA   Actually, in the last ten to fifteen years, I think a lot of architecture has happened at the hands of the developer. But because your work, which is often quite critical, is enabled through these kinds of alliances, you are at the same time participating with and also critiquing certain expectations about the private sector client. The characters here are meaningful, and your relationship to them is quite personal.

BK   You are absolutely right. In fact, I pulled out of a large-scale project a few months ago. The project was driven by a large corporate machine with set recipes and very little margin for critical elaboration.

I am in opposition to the stiff schemes that are dictated by these professionals and specialists, the preachers of archaic urban planning methods. I choose not to conform with their conventional definitions of space.

I want to eschew the specialty consultants who in all legitimacy can dictate what to do and what not to do when we are commissioned to plan a hotel, a school, a prison, a stadium, a hospital, a train station, an airport, a museum, a concert hall, a shopping center, an office tower... Circumventing them could give way to more spontaneous spaces.

Interview with Senan Abdelqader

NORA AKAWI

NORA AKAWI You operate in a context where architecture and planning have been, and continue to be, strategically activated as tools in the occupation of Palestine. Palestinians in Jerusalem continuously face obstacles designed to obstruct their livelihood, with the aim of controlling demographics in favor of a Jewish-Israeli majority. We see this executed through zoning and planning regulations and the construction of infrastructure that fragments Palestinian neighborhoods in East Jerusalem and suffocates their foreseen growth, and through systematic home demolitions. You explained that as a result of these obstacles, only 30 percent of the need for housing for Palestinians in Jerusalem is met and that the eastern part of the city was largely developed informally. The urban planning project you did in Arab Al Sawahreh was entirely shaped by this condition. And its outcome, although it can be described as a success, reveals the system set in place by the Israeli authorities to render Palestinian planning in the city impossible. How did your involvement in this project begin?

SENAN ABDELQADER We started working on this project in 2009. At the time there were many isolated efforts by residents of Arab Al Sawahreh, who were submitting plans to the municipality. They were trying to change the zoning of their lands from non-constructable areas, to be able to build with permits, and to avoid facing demolition. As you mentioned, one of the many obstacles Palestinians in Jerusalem face is the suffocation of urban growth. This agenda has been clearly introduced into master plans ever since Israel occupied the rest of Palestine in 1967 and annexed East Jerusalem to the Israeli municipality's jurisdiction. The majority of Palestinian-owned land in East Jerusalem

was designated as "open public space area" to make the development of these areas illegal. Since 1967, the population of East Jerusalem grew enormously, especially in Jabal Al Mukabber. People started leaving the denser areas and building in the outskirts of Al Mukabber, in Arab Al Sawahreh. Of course, many faced the demolition of their homes and other forms of military and legal prevention of construction by Israel. They started working on master plans as a response. The municipality accepted a small number of these projects. But as the municipality officials were receiving more and more of these plans, they resorted to another way of stopping this planned development. They made the pseudo-professional claim that with the growing number of isolated master plans being submitted, a larger plan needed to be put in place for the entire area.

Of course we know that when the Jerusalem municipality crafts a condition of this sort for the Palestinian neighborhoods in the city, it's certainly not with the intention of developing and planning the area, but the contrary. We expect that the goal is to delay the process, to create more obstacles. It's at this point that I was approached for the project. We had many meetings with the residents and landowners of the area, at first to discuss whether or not we should accept this task at all, with the knowledge of it being part of the Israeli plan to construct yet another hindrance. It wasn't an easy decision to make. After much discussion we reached a consensus that we should accept the project and develop much-needed plans for this part of Jerusalem, which has never been planned before. It was important to us because it's the natural extension of the neighborhood Jabal Al Mukabber, south of Silwan, and very close to the Old City. Our main goal was to transform these lands from being labeled as

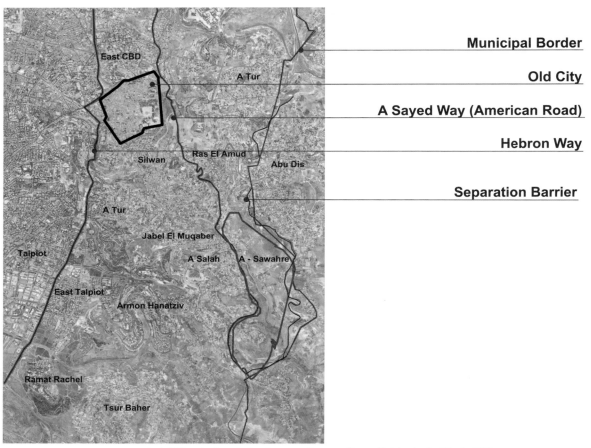

Municipal Border

Old City

A Sayed Way (American Road)

Hebron Way

Separation Barrier

Arab Al Sawahreh project and surrounding area, Senan Abdelqader Architects, 2009.

open areas, inaccessible to their Palestinian owners, to lands they can develop and live in, in the heart of Jerusalem.

NA   You've mentioned that the planning process was a collective effort that you led in your office with the landowners, and that this transformed your office space into a platform for civic engagement and participation. Can you elaborate on how this took place?

SA   The most important aspect was that we introduced the landowners into the planning process. Of course, we all knew that it would be very difficult, if not impossible, to achieve our goals since the political agenda of Israel in regard to Palestinians in Jerusalem is overtly opposed to these goals. But I explained that our strategy would be to set high aims, and whatever fraction we were able to achieve, we would see as a victory. This was the optimistic beginning of the project, especially as residents were facing obstacles repeatedly and systematically. As I mentioned, before I was introduced into the project, people had already begun isolated planning efforts in order to define their plots and change the designation of their lands from non-constructable to constructable areas. What we aimed for was to bring these efforts together in an urban collective project. One of the interesting challenges was to introduce local modern concepts in order to meet the needs of a highly urbanized society, while at the same time maintaining the social and cultural agreements according to which they had started developing the plans for the area. We developed a housing project in which we considered the social implications of division and subdivision of plots into parcels, and how to organize the buildings, the green spaces, the public spaces, the residential, etc. We developed

a plan, an urban imagination, with planning guidelines for the area. That empowered the community to submit more detailed proposals for their lands within a larger collective project. And to do more than ask—to demand—their right to build and develop their lands after having a more complete understanding, from an urban point of view, of what they need and how they want this area to develop: a local modern urban space with public facilities, cultural institutions, and commercial activity. Not only residential.

NA   How did Israeli officials and decision-makers at the municipality receive your proposal?

SA   At first we were aiming for 7,500 housing units. It was a high-density proposal, but also a direct response to the housing needs for Palestinians in Jerusalem. In 2009, during a key meeting at the municipality that was attended by the city engineer and his deputy, the proposal was immediately dismissed. They asked, "Are you planning on bringing a million Arabs to this area?" In that exact language. This was the beginning of the process. At one point we were being forced to reduce the proposal to 2,500 housing units. We had two options. The first was that we would decide to stop the work entirely and return the situation to the status quo. The second was that we would continue to work with the main purpose of changing the zoning of the area from non-constructable to allow for construction. At the conclusion of one of our discussions with the landowners and the residents, we decided to proceed on the basis that at least changing the zoning of the land would allow them to build, even if at a lower density than we had initially aimed for. Of course, as soon as land is rezoned

Community meeting for Arab Al Sawahreh project, 2009.

Interview

from "open," "public," or "green" to constructible, its value is raised drastically. But more importantly, as soon as Palestinian landowners in Jerusalem have the possibility to build legally, even if at a lower density, this solidifies the fact that their lands can be developed and solidifies their right to construct and live on those lands.

NA   So did the process play out as you had anticipated? Was it indeed merely another plot for the further hindrance of Palestinian growth in the city?

SA   Absolutely. We have opposed goals. Ours is to secure the infrastructure that would allow Palestinians to remain, live, and grow in Jerusalem, and the Israeli municipality's goal is to limit this infrastructure to the point of death by suffocation. In the planning process, there were conditions that we were aiming to achieve that we deliberately kept ambiguous—in the ratios between construction percentage, numbers of housing units, and land area. They introduced personnel—arbitrators—whose sole role was to double-check the numbers and do the math three to four times after us. We continued to have meetings on the planning through 2014, and the relationship went from one of suspicion to one of antagonism. At that point they decided that they would accept our proposal not as a master plan, but as guidelines.

On the one hand, though collective planning work, in the infamous 2020 plan for Jerusalem, this land in Arab Al Sawahreh was rezoned from open non-constructable to residential, constructible land—on paper. For reasons I mentioned before, this is important as a political planning statement. On the other hand, further conditions were crafted and put in place by the municipality and the

District Committee for Planning and Building to make this plan unachievable, impossible to realize. With our proposed plan introduced as the planning guidelines for the area, landowners in Arab Al Sawahreh can now submit master plans for a particular zone in order to complete the approval process for construction. This is where the trickery begins. Master plans covering an area that is smaller than 50–100 dunams [around 12.5–25 acres] are not even considered. Landowners are required to approach the municipality with plans only once they have reached a consensus with all of the owners of at least 50 dunams combined. Consider that the largest ownership of land in that area is 3–4 dunams, and even those are usually shared among a number of family members. They're being asked to bring ten to twenty families together in order to work on one collective, detailed plan. This is impossible anywhere in the world. This is just one example of how we are forced to work within a system designed to lead to failure, cornered into states of indefinite suspension, working toward plans that are impossible to implement. This is a very frustrating reality, and a destructive condition, representative of the mode of operation and mentality of the occupier.

NA   During the conference, you explained that the situation in Jerusalem is radically different, even isolated, from other Arab cities: it is under occupation, controlled by a continuous settler-colonial military regime, and as a result the architecture you produce is about existing, surviving, and above all resisting all of the very powerful forces attempting to push you out. You also said that while all of those forces and conditions are designed to limit the local Palestinian aspirations for the city, still you work to bring them a kind of representation through

Arab Al Sawahreh site, 2009.

Interview

architecture. And in more than once case, your architecture is also representative of repressed and silenced local, collective, Arab, Palestinian aspirations for the city. This is true for the Arab Al Sawahreh planning project, but it's also true for others like the Mashrabiya House or the sports and cultural center in Beit Safafa. How can you, through design, begin to employ your architecture for criticism?

SA   Shortly after I moved to Beit Safafa, in several informal conversations with friends, neighbors, and members of the community, the need for a cultural and sports center repeatedly came up. We drafted a proposal that was immediately rejected by the municipality on the basis that the residents of Beit Safafa don't need a center of this sort. For sports facilities, they should use the center in the neighborhood of Sur Baher, six kilometers away. Ten years later, the project was later revived, and we began the design process. We designed a space that would host cultural, educational, and sports activities for the youth of the neighborhood, and conceptually, the project was designed as infrastructure, not as a conventional building. After many revisions, we reached a design proposal that met all of the technical requirements for the project to be approved, but that wasn't enough. There is a very specific Israeli typology for a sports center, the *matnas*, that we were expected to replicate. We did use some of the characteristics of this typology, like standard dimensions of particular programs, but we reinterpreted the program and the organization of the various functions to fit our goals for this facility in our particular context. The municipality officials wanted to see an Israeli *matnas* with the standard two to three stories, standard openings, windows, and doors. We are interested in a local cultural,

educational, and sports center for the population of Beit Safafa, one that grows from within, that's open and acts as infrastructure for the neighborhood. Municipality officials even advised some community members that if they wanted to have a center approved, they should hire a particular Israeli architecture office, which happens to produce a very large percentage of the municipality-approved designs for educational and public sports facilities in the city. The emergence of a local interpretation of an architectural program, with an Arab Palestinian local identity and culture, is threatening to the Israeli bureaucrat.

NA   Although a private project, the Mashrabiya House has also gained local public significance in Beit Safafa. It has become a collective statement and political critique. How did you develop this critique through design?

SA   The building stands as a critique against several impositions on the local Arab culture and livelihood in the city. An important element in the building is a reinterpretation of the traditional *mashrabiya*, rethought to respond to its specific local political, social, cultural, and environmental contexts. In Jerusalem we are forced to build with stone, a law that was passed on from the British Mandate to the Israelis. The seemingly seamless material continuity of the city, from the old to the new, is meant to symbolize a connection to the place. This form of colonial cultural appropriation of Arab Palestinian culture and building technique is of course deceptive, particularly since the use of stone in building has become a thin 3–5 centimeter layer that wraps around the building, where the stone loses its functionality altogether. Addressing the loss of the value of the stone as a building material in this

Mashrabiya House, Senan Abdelqader Architects, 2011.

cladding technique, we reinterpreted the wooden *mashrabiya* using traditional stone-cutting methods to build a stone envelope around the building, offset by 1–2 meters.

Through this critical act, the design responds to the requirements for a stone façade while also fulfilling the traditional function of the *mashrabiya* as an architectural element that creates the threshold between public and private, and provides climate control. The stone envelope protects the internal spaces from the harsh summer sun and the winter rain and winds, while allowing for a constant flow of fresh air through its gaps. It is also designed to operate a passive cooling system. It is left open toward both the bottom and the top edges of the building in such a way that it operates as a chimney, pushing the hot air upward and replacing it with cool air sucked in from the gap at the base of the ground floor.

Another important aspect in the design responds to the discriminatory planning regulations we discussed earlier, which are aimed at maintaining the Palestinian population in Jerusalem at a low 30 percent, in favor of a Jewish-Israeli majority. In the Arab neighborhoods in Jerusalem, the construction percentage is limited to 50 percent of the land. While the stone envelope responds to building regulations, the gap between the outer and inner envelopes provides us with the flexibility for expanding the living spaces in the building. Instead of the allowed 500 square meters of built space, we can use around 2,000 square meters of living space, thanks to the interplay between the indoor and outdoor spaces around the two envelopes. Others are now following this kind of response to the limitations imposed by regulations, and the Israeli authorities are forced to deal with them since the building has become quite representative of the neighborhood.

NA   In our recent conversations, you suggested that the most dominant factor shaping architecture for Palestinians in East Jerusalem is the absence of a certain sentiment: *yaqeen* (which in Arabic is the combination of trust, knowledge, and certainty). Your practice, both in the office and in your teaching and other work with academic institutions, is a continuous investigation of, and is largely shaped by, these questions. Is it possible to plan for the future in a political context where the asymmetry of power and violence entraps people in an endless present? Or can we, as a group or individuals, who act from within this field of power relations between occupier and occupied, establish an architecture that is capable of reflecting our own subjectivities and aspirations? And, finally, can we construct imaginaries under occupation?

We've learned more about how these questions shape your design practice, but can you tell us more about how they affect your teaching?

SA   For about a decade, I've been running a research unit at Bezalel on informal architecture, investigating the ways in which the unplanned development of the eastern part of Jerusalem took place. We explored the particularities of neighborhoods like Beit Safafa, Silwan, and Jabal Al Mukabber, and developed urban planning and architectural design responses that took into consideration the complex political and social specificities of these sites. But the situation has become much more difficult in Jerusalem in recent years. Of course, we're also facing an Israeli government that has absolutely no intention to change this condition—one that intensifies the violence and oppression at every turn. Jerusalem is at the heart of this, and so is Bezalel. On the other hand, the curriculum, faculty, and

Mashrabiya House, Senan Abdelqader Architects, 2011.

the students (with a few exceptions of course) remain entirely oblivious to their political surroundings. The introduction of more complex and politically charged issues into the classroom is met with resentment and discomfort. And in our design and planning work at the office, we are pulled into constant, everlasting delays, sometimes even reaching open confrontations with a municipality and a planning department that is commanded by a military mentality. On the one hand, this liberates and motivates us to fight for our demands and our rights openly, in a transparent way, discarding any diplomacy and discretion. On the other hand, staying and continuing the work, especially in Jerusalem, is itself a struggle.

One important answer to your question, particularly in regard to teaching Palestinian students in Israeli institutions, is language. What does it mean when Palestinian students come from their homes straight out of high school to the university and the language they have to learn in is Hebrew—a language that for them has been the language of the military, of war? And within a social and political context where Arabic, and their Palestinian identity in general, is not only repressed but even often met with oppression and hostility? Now imagine that the Palestinian students come to learn in an Israeli academic institution and attend lectures in Arabic, their mother tongue. All of their understandings, emotions, and approaches change. This is something that I'm working on. What happens now is that when the Palestinian students come to Bezalel, for example, they are handed a constructed understanding of what it means to excel in that context, and it's to excel on the Israelis' terms. Unless they break out of this, which is no easy task, everything they are able to produce from within that position is produced from within a colonized mentality—there is no possibility for anything other than that. But when you speak and work with Palestinian students in their language—the language of their homes, their mothers, their fathers, their families, their streets, their friends—they begin to confidently produce from within their culture and its locality and specificities. It becomes a collective realization that says, *wait a minute, I—and we—exist*. Only then can Palestinian students begin to critically examine the concepts and notions that they are internalizing, that are external to them. Take the concept of *du-kium* (Hebrew for coexistence), which we sometimes see surfacing in studio design projects. Where did this come from? Nowhere in our language, in our conversations at home, among family or friends, does the question of *coexistence* come up. *Du-kium* is an Israeli construct, in line with the fabrication of a seemingly even playing field, in a context of asymmetrical power. For a people under occupation, it's not simply a question of tolerating the other but a struggle for liberation. I think this is essential, and I'm continuing to fight for this issue of the language of learning and teaching. It's not about language as external to production; it's about the construction of a body of knowledge and of work that is coming from a local Palestinian thinking process.

The Nakba Day Killings
EYAL WEIZMAN

On May 15, 2014, two Palestinian teenagers, Nadeem Nawara and Mohammad Abu Daher, were shot and killed in the town of Beitunia, near Ramallah in the West Bank, after a protest marking the sixty-fourth anniversary of the *Nakba*, the Palestinian exodus caused by the war in 1948. Their deaths sparked a sequence of events that escalated into the Gaza War of 2014.[1] Forensic Architecture, a research agency based out of Goldsmith's University, London, undertook an investigation of the Nakba Day killings on behalf of a Palestinian nongovernmental organization, DCI-Palestine, and the parents of the teenagers. It sought to help uncover not only the perpetrators of a double murder but also the entire web of mechanisms set up to deny that those murders happened. The events of the Nakba Day killings involved various forms of denial. On the individual level, it was a security guard attempting to conceal a murder he had committed. On the institutional level, the case showed how Israeli politicians and security personnel automatically deflect all accusations of their wrongdoing, a form of denial that also relates to the facts of the occupation. Israeli society is made to believe that dominating an entire people can be achieved without violence and repression, that the occupation is a "situation" rather than a crime, and that violence only starts with acts of resistance that disturb the situation. Significantly, because the events took place on Nakba Day, they also intersect with historical forms of denial and negation that are at the foundation of the state of Israel. In each of these forms, denial is not simply a rhetorical or cognitive position of refutation, suppression, or evasion, but an active physical practice that involves specific techniques, technologies, and legal regimes. Denial on all of these levels is crucial to Israeli domination because it enables the ongoing perpetration of violence. If one has done no wrong, one can simply go on without changing.

—

The "Nakba Law" that the Israeli parliament passed in 2011 imposed harsh fines on public organizations that refer to Israel's Independence Day as "a day of mourning."[2] Every May 15, the *Nakba* and its state-sanctioned denial is countered by protests throughout Palestine, from the Galilee through to Gaza, the Naqab, the West Bank, Syria, Lebanon, Jordan, and other diasporas. These protests often lead to clashes with Israeli security forces.

On the morning of Nakba Day 2014, one of the protest locations was near the Ofer military prison and took place in solidarity with over 100 detainees on a hunger strike there. After the main part of the protest was aggressively dispersed, witnesses heard three distinct gunshots separated by roughly one hour. The first, at around 12:20 p.m., wounded Muhammad 'Azzah, 15, with a shot to the chest. The second, at 1:45 p.m., killed Nadeem Nawara, 17, with another shot to the chest. The third, at 2:58 p.m., killed Mohammad Abu Daher, 16, with a single gunshot to the back. All three teenagers were hit along the same patch of pavement, right in front of a small carpentry workshop.

Dozens of Palestinian teenagers have been similarly killed or wounded by Israeli soldiers and other security personnel in the West Bank in recent years. Most of these killings take place off-camera, and a very small minority are investigated. The bodies of victims are buried hastily, by the same evening if possible, according to Islamic laws, and almost always without a pathological investigation—certainly without later exhumations allowed. Youth leave the house in the morning, disappearing into the ground before sunset.

On that day, however, the killings were captured by multiple cameras. Footage relevant to the fatal shootings of both Nadeem Nawara and Mohammad Daher was recorded by security cameras installed by the owner of the carpentry workshop. Furthermore, because it was Nakba Day and clashes were expected, there were several media crews on site, both local and international, shooting stills and video. The Israelis on site were also recording, all within a relatively confined space of several hundred square meters.

The security camera footage is chilling. It shows both Nawara and Abu Daher walking casually and alone just before they are shown suddenly collapsing to the ground. The silent video makes their falls appear soft. Their bodies remain face down and motionless for several seconds until people are seen rushing in to evacuate them.

In addition, there was another crucial bit of evidence available. After the funeral, Siam Nawara, Nadeem's father, received his son's backpack and other belongings. Within the bag he found a 5.56 millimeter bullet, the standard ammunition used by Israeli security forces. In a rare decision, Siam gave permission for the exhumation of Nadeem's body. An autopsy confirmed that it was this bullet that had killed Nadeem before exiting his body.[3]

In the weeks after the fatal shootings, protests escalated and Israeli forces were firing live ammunition and rubber-coated steel bullets at youth, resulting in injuries to over one dozen other children.[4]

Those investigating and reporting on the shooting did not immediately realize that it had been captured by security cameras. On May 19, four days after the shooting, while surveying the site for physical evidence, DCI researchers noticed CCTV cameras outside the carpentry workshop of Fakher Zayed.

The CCTV camera in location.

Zayed was wary about handing over the footage, fearing military retalia-
tion, but he finally allowed DCI to examine the files. Going through hours of
material, DCI's researchers identified relevant footage in four of Zayed's eight
cameras. After receiving both parents' permission, DCI posted short segments
of this material online.[5] The footage was picked up almost instantly and went
viral on social media, gathering more than 700,000 views. This resulted in con-
demnation of the killings from many states, the UN, and human rights groups,
as well as an "expression of concern" from the Obama administration.[6]

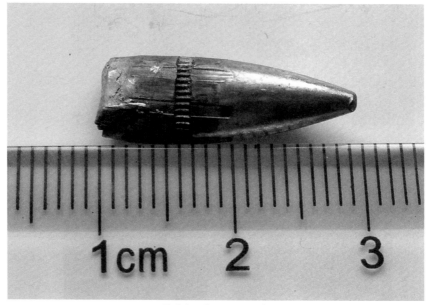

Bullet casing, measured.

In response, Israeli spokespeople stated that their "preliminary report concluded that there had been no live fire" and that the forces on site deployed only non-lethal means—rubber-coated metal bullets and tear gas—and further suggested that "the chances of fabrication were high."[7] The Israeli minister of defense, Moshe Ya'alon, pursued two contradictory lines of explanation. In remarks delivered at an event in a West Bank settlement, he claimed that the Beitunia killings were the result of a violent encounter in which the youth were engaged in throwing Molotov cocktails at the soldiers, who felt at risk for their lives and acted properly.[8] Referring to the videos showing the youth shot while walking along, he sarcastically added that he was "familiar with the ways videos are edited," alluding to them as malicious and fictional constructions of the growing cottage industry of "Pallywood."[9] Other Israeli spokespeople explained that the CCTV videos showing the boys collapsing were "tendentiously edited."[10] A senior officer briefing journalists cast doubt on the idea that the two were even dead. Michael Oren, former Israeli ambassador to the United States, told CNN that the manner in which the boys were seen falling— Nawara had his hands stretched forward to soften his fall—was inconsistent with shooting.[11] Others claimed that the youths seen in the videos were not the same as the two boys whose deaths were registered.[12] A post by Danny Ayalon, another former Israeli ambassador to Washington, called for DCI-Palestine's tax-exemption status in the United States to be revoked because it was fabricating the truth.[13] Israeli security forces were seen filming the clashes, but all requests to examine their footage were denied.[14]

The media attention, and persistent Israeli denials, led CNN producer Kareem Khadder to look again at his own footage recorded that day. He

Ya'alon issuing a denial.

realized that his camera had captured the moment of the shooting of Nadeem Nawara from a different angle. On May 22, CNN released Khadder's video.[15] It showed a group of Israeli border policemen (an enlisted unit under police control rather than military command, recognizable by their darker uniforms) aiming their rifles toward the place where Nawara was hit, and firing twice.

The camera then pans to the right to show the evacuation of the body; the footage ends when an ambulance arrives at the scene. Earlier that day Israeli forces raided Fakher Zayed's wood workshop and confiscated some of the security cameras and the computer on which the video files were stored. Two weeks later, on June 13, as the story gathered momentum, Israeli Israel Defense Forces (IDF) personnel returned to confiscate all other CCTV cameras and computers in the area, returning them only a few days later.[16] On June 17, Zayed was taken for military interrogation.[17] Officers berated him for sharing the security videos with human rights groups, claiming he had lied and fabricated evidence. They threatened that if he did not remove the security cameras within twenty-four hours, they would "crush" him and unleash dogs on his children. "They told me that the video I gave to the press was fabricated, that everything I said and all my testimonies are a lie, that this is a serious violation of the law, and that I made the IDF look bad and caused a lot of problems," he reported.[18]

On June 6, 2014, three weeks after the incident, DCI-Palestine commissioned Forensic Architecture to investigate the case based on available material. The aim of our investigation, which was coordinated by Nick Axel, was to cross-reference all the video and image material together with other testimonial evidence that was provided to us by DCI as well as by Sarit Michaeli, an indefatigable researcher for B'tselem (the Israeli human rights organization), in order to counter Israeli official accusations and to establish who shot Nadeem Nawara and Muhammad Abu Daher, and what mechanisms of denial were eventually employed in the aftermath. We agreed with DCI-Palestine that the material would not be provided to the Israeli police, the same body that had perpetrated this act, but rather released publicly and incrementally in response to developments on the ground.[19]

We began by synchronizing the relevant bits of footage from CNN and the CCTV. To generate a synchronization point, we had to find the same visual marker in both sources. There are twenty-four frames per second in these videos. To find the overlapping frame it was not enough to look at the same figures in continuous movement; rather, we had to identify distinct shifts in the direction of movement. In both sequences we see a man in a white shirt running toward an ambulance. He makes two distinct turns. The first turning point allowed us to synchronize the videos and the second to confirm that we had done so.

Rewinding both videos at the same speed, we stopped at the moment the CCTV footage shows Nawara starting to fall. At that moment the CNN footage captured the sound of a gunshot. There is also a faint smoke cloud seen next to a border policeman behind a small bush. He is likely the shooter.

When the CNN camera captured the sound of the second shot, fired by a person on the right side of the image, Nawara was already being carried toward the ambulance. The shooter in this instance is a soldier from the military communications unit. His information was never made available. This soldier later took one of the border policemen's guns and shot a rubber-coated bullet at the people evacuating Nawara.[20] This soldier was the first to be investigated and was suspended on May 28, 2014, for unauthorized use of firearms. At the moment the communication unit soldier is seen shooting, the CCTV footage shows a man with a video camera next to the helpers that carry Nawara to the ambulance. Samer Nazzal, a photojournalist standing near them, took a high-speed, high-resolution photograph at the very same moment. His photograph shows the same cameraman at the same position and moment as both the CCTV and the CNN footage. Upon closer inspection, we noticed that the photograph captured the rubber-coated steel bullet in mid-flight, just before it hit the head of a Palestinian paramedic wearing a bright orange vest. This photograph confirmed that the military was shooting at first responders for no apparent reason and that the second shot seen fired in the CNN footage was indeed a rubber bullet.[21] This allowed us to mark the sound sample of this shot as referring to rubber-coated steel munitions.

Israeli sources claimed that there was no sightline and thus no fire trajectory between the border policeman and Nadeem Nawara when he was shot. To examine this statement, we undertook a ground survey of the site and constructed a virtual model based on all available sources, including a measured plan provided by the municipality of Beitunia, as well as satellite imagery and ground-level photographs. On the model we marked the location of both the CCTV and the CNN cameras.

We modeled the trajectories from each of the shooters to Nawara. A direct line of sight and fire to Nawara did exist, but only from the border policeman, the same one we saw shooting when Nawara was falling. The line of fire grazes the corner of the building. Nawara's direction of movement confirms that he had just entered the border policeman's line of sight when he was shot. The shooter could not, despite claims by Israeli spokespeople, have responded to anything he had seen Nawara previously doing.

A person identified as an Israeli "fire-arms ballistic expert," filmed on Israeli TV Channel 2, claimed that the rubber bullet extension visible on the weapon of the communication unit soldier cannot be used to fire live ammunition: "The thickening that we can see here around the barrel is not intended for firing of live ammunition, only for firing of rubber [coated steel] bullets."[22] In contradiction to that statement, we saw that the border policeman we had established

Synchronization of video.

CCTV footage showing Nawara starting to fall at the moment the CNN footage captured the sound of a gunshot. There is also a faint smoke cloud seen next to a border-policeman behind a small bush, he is likely the shooter.

When the CNN camera captured the sound of the second shot, fired by a person on the right side of the image, Nawara was already being carried towards the ambulance. The shooter is a soldier from the military "communications unit"; his information was never made available.

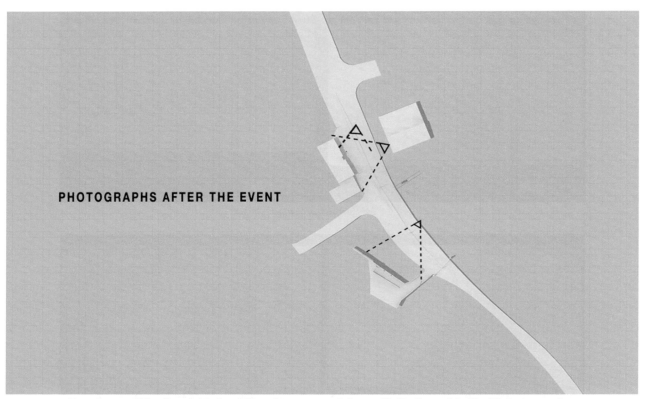

Ground survey of the site and virtual model based on a measured plan provided by the municipality of Beitunia, as well as satellite imagery and ground level photographs. On the model is marked the location of both the CCTV and the CNN cameras.

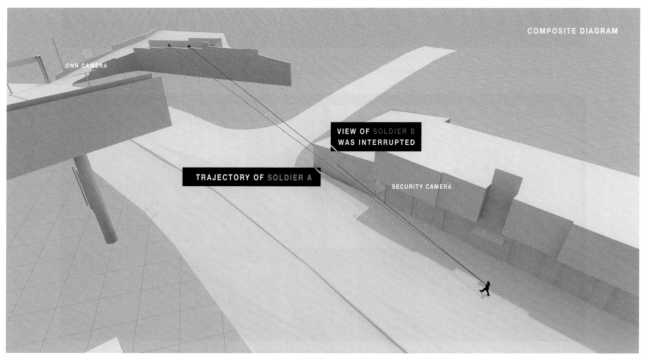

Model showing the trajectories from each of the shooters to Nawara.

as the shooter had a similar extension mounted on his gun. In the product's catalogue, the manufacturer, Israel Military Industries, advertises the possibility of shooting live fire through the rubber bullet extension.[23]

A person identified as an Israeli "fire-arms ballistic expert," claimed that the rubber-bullet extension visible on the weapon of the "communication unit" soldier cannot be used to fire live ammunition.

Israel Military Industries product catalogue.

To determine whether the soldier had actually fired live ammunitions through the rubber-bullet extension it was necessary to examine the way an M16 rifle works. When live ammunition is fired, the gas pressure in the gun is strong enough to automatically and immediately eject the spent cartridge from the chamber and to reload the weapon. To fire a pack of three rubber-coated steel bullets, a blank cartridge needs to be loaded into the rifle's chamber. The pack is inserted into the end of the extension. The explosive power pushes the munitions out. But because there is not the same amount of firepower in the blank cartridge as in a live round, there is not enough pressure in the gun to automatically discharge the blank cartridge and reload. Reloading has to be done manually.

Looking carefully at the first shooter, we could identify a single brass-colored pixel flying out of the gun. This is the spent cartridge, and we can see it was automatically ejected, indicating that a live round was fired and that no rubber-coated munitions were put in the extension. If a live round were discharged into a pack of rubber-coated bullets loaded at the end of the extension, the gun would likely explode and cause serious harm to the soldier. This means that the act has to be carefully planned. The shooter is seen cocking the gun. This could be consistent with the firing of a rubber bullet. But given that the spent cartridge has already flown out and that the gun has reloaded, the border policeman's actions could be explained as an attempt to conceal, from the camera crew he must have noticed, or from anyone else, the fact that he shot a live round.

A blog used for soldiers' communication describes a similar practice. The text reads, "When I was in Gaza I met somebody that told me about a common trick…you shoot the rubber bullet and then you are left with the empty extension

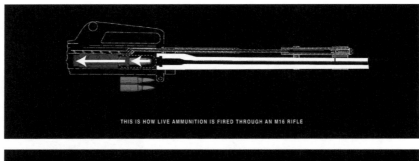

THIS IS HOW LIVE AMMUNITION IS FIRED THROUGH AN M16 RIFLE

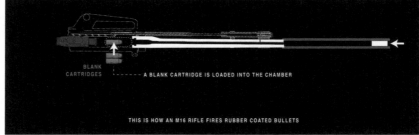

BLANK CARTRIDGES

----- A BLANK CARTRIDGE IS LOADED INTO THE CHAMBER

THIS IS HOW AN M16 RIFLE FIRES RUBBER COATED BULLETS

Weapon analysis of rubber coated steel bullets.

on the rifle. Then you shoot live fire when the officer next to you thinks that you are shooting rubber..." In any case, "the Palestinians take the body and there is no investigation so who cares."

About an hour and a half later, at the very same location, Mohammed Abu Daher was shot and killed while walking home. The same CCTV camera recorded footage of his death. The CNN camera crew had already left, and the other film crew on site, from Palestine TV, was not aiming their camera at the soldiers when the second lethal shot was fired. They did, however, capture the sound of the gunshot and a group of Palestinian protesters ducking for cover. A few seconds later the camera pans to find Abu Daher on the ground, tended by his friends, who proceed to carry him away.

We collected available sounds of gunshots captured by the Palestine TV camera throughout the day. Then we compared them to the sound of the shot that killed Nadeem Nawara, which we now knew to be that of live fire shot through a rubber bullet extension.

Lawrence Abu Hamdan of Forensic Architecture's team processed these shots through a software offering spectrograms to identify their distinct visual patterns. When we visualized the sonic frequencies in a spectrogram, we could compare the distinct sound signature of live rounds shot through rubber bullet extensions with these of rubber-coated bullets. The difference is clear—live fire is louder in higher frequencies and softer in the low frequencies.

Ramallah journalist Samer Hisham Nazzal from *Raya News*, who was at the scene, explained that most participants in demonstrations can hear the difference between rubber bullets and live fire.[24] Protesters captured on the Palestine TV cameras when Abu Daher is shot are seen ducking for cover and

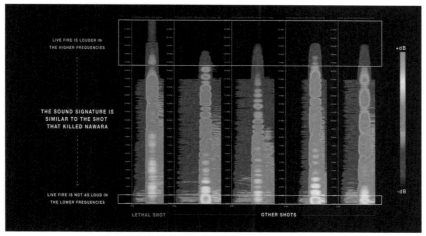

Nawara and Abu Daher sound signatures comparison.

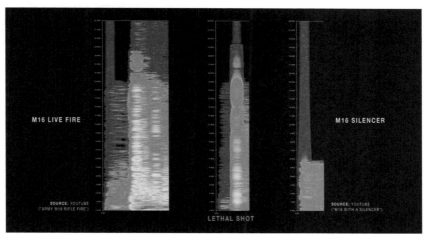

Silencer and M16 sound comparison.

fleeing, indicating they heard the sound of live ammunition. As Abu Hamdan explained, "These Palestinian teenagers can exactly identify a tiny distinction in the frequencies and react accordingly. Those are the real acute expert listeners in this case."[25]

To confirm the source of the fire, we compared this sound to the sound of an M16 rifle shooting without an extension, as well as an M16 gun shooting with a silencer. The signature of the shot we identified falls somewhere in between these extremes. The sound of live ammunition becomes suppressed and disguised when shot through a rubber bullet extension—the extension acts like a silencer, but not to the same extent. This specific sound signature indicates that it is likely that Abu Daher and Nawara were both killed by an Israeli security person using the same method, and possibly the same gun.

The story was kept alive throughout May and June because the footage evidence contrasted sharply with the narrative of Israeli spokespeople. In July

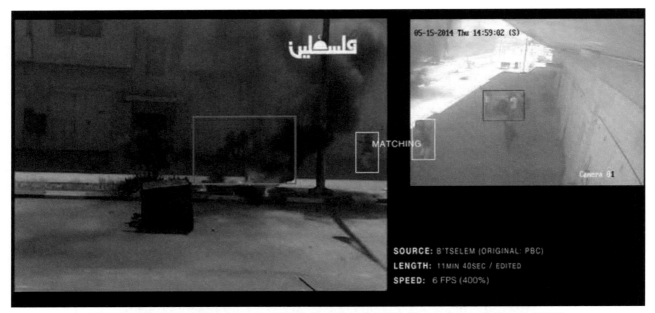

Video still of Abu Daher falling, captured on CCTV (left), and Palestinian TV still capturing sound of gunshot (right).

and August, attention shifted to the Gaza War. It felt strange to work on this case all throughout that summer as hundreds of Palestinian children were being killed in the war, but it was the respect for young life unnecessarily lost that pushed us to continue.

Allegations of Israeli war crimes in Gaza mounted after the war. A UN investigation of the war was under way, and the International Criminal Court (ICC), which had just gained jurisdiction over Gaza, launched its own preliminary investigation. It was then that the police investigation of the Nakba Day murders seemed to gather momentum. International law is bound by the principle of "complementarity." The ICC sees itself as a "court of last resort" and will step in only if states fail to launch processes that address international crimes with their national laws.[26] Demonstrating the competence of national jurisdiction is thus the best way to deflect international process.

On November 11, 2014, the Judea and Samaria District Police arrested the Israeli border policeman. His name—Ben Deri—was also revealed. On November 23, 2014, Deri was indicted by the Jerusalem district attorney's office for the "manslaughter" of Nadeem Nawara. The 5.56 millimeter bullet found in Nawara's bag was traced back to Deri's gun and used as evidence against him.[27] The charges against Deri were the most serious ones levied against an Israeli security personnel in recent times. Most other killings are simply written off as self-defense.[28] Deri, however, was released from police custody to await his trial on house arrest, where public figures associated with the right and settler movement came to show support. Demonstrations and social media campaigns were launched, calling for his immediate release and demanding that the government "untie the hands of the military." Neither Deri nor anyone else was charged with the killing of Mohammed Abu Daher.

The first part of our analysis was delivered to DCI-Palestine as a written report in September. The organization has used it in its campaign in the UN and the US Congress. We also endeavored to produce a more accessible video version. The first part of this analysis was publicly released as a clip on YouTube immediately after Deri's arrest and manslaughter charge. It was used to make the claim that the evidence suggested that the killing was premeditated—a murder—and that prosecuting the case as manslaughter mischaracterizes the event.[29] A video analysis released several weeks later on DCI-Palestine's website and YouTube channel dealt with the killing of Abu Daher. His death was no longer being discussed, probably because there was no autopsy (his family refused on religious grounds), no bullet, and no video of the shooter synchronized with the CCTV footage showing him fall. In this as in other cases, the absence of evidence was used as evidence of an absence. Our analysis of the gunshot sounds helped link the two cases. Abu Daher's body will likely not be exhumed, but the audio signature suggests that the bullet that killed him likely came out of the same gun that killed Nawara. This link also indicates the total absurdity of the Israeli police investigation and prosecution case. Launched only to deflect a potential international process, the case was limited as much as possible, even in the face of two extremely similar killings.

After the war, as calls mounted for Israeli crimes in Gaza to be internationally investigated, Israeli defense minister Ya'alon used the arrest of Ben Deri to claim that the IDF could investigate itself. Because it was capable of charging a soldier, he argued, it could investigate itself in relation to the Gaza allegations, making international inquiries redundant. It is possible that the Beitunia case was investigated and Deri charged in part so that the massacre in Gaza could be silenced. A trial, and even a conviction, might themselves function as forms of denial, masked by the law. This is precisely why our analysis examined both the violence articulated in the case and the violence and denial articulated by the law. And this was also the reason why neither we nor DCI-Palestine ever submitted our report of evidence to the police. Our attempt to "snipe" at the process from the outside sought to expose the legal process for the denial that it was.

On October 12, 2015, Deri's trial began in the Jerusalem District Court. It lasted only one day. The judge disqualified himself from ruling on this matter. The reason given was that he discovered when the trial started that he was a distant relative of one of the expert witnesses. It will take months for another judge to learn the details of the case; it has still not reopened as of early 2016.[30]

On August 18, 2015, our report was presented as part of a special event convened at the US Congress by Betty McCollum, a Democratic representative from Minnesota. Siam Nawara, Nadeem's father, attended the event.

Rep. McCollum had also, in what was described as "probably the statement most in support of Palestinian rights to have been made on the capitol," sent a letter to the State Department, in which she wrote, "The murders of Nadeem Nawara and Mohammad Daher only highlight a brutal system of occupation that devalues and dehumanizes Palestinian children." Her letter called on the State Department to investigate whether this action amounts to the violation of the Leahy Law, which prohibits the United States from providing military assistance to foreign military units that violate human rights with impunity.[31] No such investigation will be undertaken, of course, and no ban of weapon exports will be imposed.

Research and analysis conducted by the Forensic Architecture team:
Eyal Weizman, Nick Axel, Steffen Kramer, and Lawrence Abu Hamdan

1   The murder of three Israeli teenagers in the West Bank in June 2014 was a reprisal for the Beitunia killings. It led to the beginning of the war one month later.

2   Israel's denial of the *Nakba*—translated as the Palestinian "catastrophe" and dating to 1948—has for decades been argued on historical grounds. Official history does not acknowledge the intentional ethnic cleansing of Palestinian areas that became Israel in 1948. The Palestinians—as I was told as a young pupil in primary school—had willingly run away to join Israel's enemies. However, hand in hand with mainstream history and the public acceptance that such ethnic cleansing did in fact take place, the nature of the argument also changed: it was a horrible necessity without which Israel would not exist and a preventative action—undoing it would make it done to us.

3   The autopsy was performed on June 11, 2014, at Al-Quds University's Institute of Forensic Medicine in Abu Dis in the presence of US, Danish, and Israeli pathologists. No bullet was found in the body, but the examination identified both the entry and exit wounds of live fire as the cause of death. "Use of Live Ammunition Confirmed in Nawarah Shooting," DCI-Palestine website, June 12, 2014, http://www.dci-palestine. org/use_of_live_ammunition_confirmed_in_ nawarah_shooting.

4   In Gaza on May 23, Mohammad, 16, was shot by Israeli soldiers as he and his brothers gathered hay 492 feet from the border fence. As he ran to protect his younger brothers, a live bullet entered through his right shoulder and severed his spinal cord, paralyzing him from the waist down. In Hebron, in the West Bank, Yazan, 15, lost an eye after he was struck by a rubber-coated metal bullet fired by an Israeli soldier. He had been running errands for his mother on May 30 when he found himself caught in clashes between the Israeli army and Palestinian civilians.

5   The unedited, six-hour-long footage has been shared with several news agencies and human rights organizations, who have verified the video as accurately portraying events on that day. DCI-Palestine is a children's rights organization, whose first priority is, obviously, the best interests of the child. Publicly releasing the full video could allow others to identify specific children where faces are visible. Given the widespread and systematic ill-treatment that exists in the Israeli military detention system, DCI-Palestine does not feel that it can responsibly release the full-length CCTV footage. Eyewitnesses at the scene, including journalists and photographers, have provided statements that verify that the video accurately depicts the day's events. See "We are @DCIPalestine" video, https://www.youtube.com/user/DCIPS.

6   On May 21, 2014, the Obama administration called on Israeli officials to "conduct a prompt and transparent investigation." See "US Urges Restraint by Both Sides After Killing of Palestinian Teens," *Haaretz*, May 21, 2014. On May 23, 2014, the UN Office of the High Commissioner for Human Rights declared that the killings may amount to "extrajudicial executions" or "wilful killings"

under international law, and Human Rights Watch recently found that the killings constitute an apparent war crime. "Killing of Palestinian Teenagers in West Bank Elicits UN Call for Prompt Investigation," *UN News Centre*, May 23, 2014, www.un.org/apps/news/story.asp?NewsID=47875#.U6Gbm_mSySp; "Israel: Killing of Children Apparent War Crime," Human Rights Watch website, June 9, 2014, https://www.hrw.org/news/2014/06/09/israel-killing-children-apparent-war-crime.

7   Peter Beaumont, "Video Footage Indicates Killed Palestinian Youths Posed no Threat," *Guardian*, May 20, 2014; Mitch Ginzberg and Lazar Berman, "Film of Palestinians' Killing Likely Doctored, Top Official Says," *Times of Israel*, May 21, 2014; Dahlia Scheindlin, "Truth, Tapes, and Two Dead Palestinians," +*972 Magazine,* May 22, 2014, http://972mag.com/truth-tapes-and-two-dead-palestinians/91215/.

8   Robert Tait, "Israel Asked to Investigate Shooting of Palestinian Teenagers," *Telegraph*, May 21, 2014.

9   A report aired on the channel France 2 claiming to show the killing of al-Dura, 10, by IDF soldiers was a rallying cry for the Second Intifada but Israeli officials have disputed the report, some going so far as to say that the video was staged and that al-Dura was still alive.

10   Tait, "Israel Asked to Investigate."

11   "Israeli Border Police Officer Arrested in Palestinian Deaths," *CNN*, November 12, 2014.

12   Avi Issacharoff, "An Itchy IDF Trigger Finger or a 'Pallywood' Movie?" *Times of Israel*, May 23, 2014.

13   Larry Derfner, "Day of Catastrophe for 'Pallywood' Conspiracy Theorists," *+972 Magazine*, November 13, 2014, http://972mag.com/nakba-day-indeed-for-pallywood-conspiracy-freaks/98735.

14   "Israel: Killing of Children Apparent War Crime."

15   Ivan Watson, Kareem Khadder, and Mike Schwartz, "Father Blames Israeli Military in Palestinian Teens' Deaths," *CNN*, May 22, 2014, http://edition.cnn.com/2014/05/22/world/meast/israel-west-bank-shooting.

16   Another resident of the area, interviewed separately, who asked that his name not be published out of fear for his security, told Human Rights Watch that Israeli forces called him and told him to open a shop he owns near Zayed's building.

17   "Israel: Stop Threatening Witness to Killings: Forces Target Man Whose Cameras Recorded Deaths," Human Rights Watch website, June 19, 2014, https://www.hrw.org/news/2014/06/19/israel-stop-threatening-witness-killings.

18   "Israel: Stop Threatening Witness to Killings."

19   See "Nakba Day Killings," Forensic Architecture website, http://www.forensic-architecture.org/case/nakba-day-killngs/.

20   Robert Mackay, "Israel Suspends Soldier in West Bank Shooting Investigation," *New York Times*, May 29, 2014.

21   "Evidence of Wilful Killing at Al-Nakba Day Protest," AlHaq.org, May 24, 2014, http://www.alhaq.org/documentation/weekly-focuses/806-evidence-of-wilful-killing-at-al-nakba-day-protest.

22   See "Israeli TV analysis of CNN Coverage of Beitunia Incident," on YouTube, https://www.youtube.com/watch?v=OgPEhjT5u7k.

23   "Israel: Killing of Children Apparent War Crime." A brochure states that the 22 cm "launcher" can be "'attached to any rifle with NATO flash suppressor' and allows 'immediate 5.56-mm lethal firing capability without removing adapter.'" As Human Rights Watch noted: "The Israeli military has used at least one type of assault-rifle attachment, produced by Israel Military Industries, that allows forces to fire rubber bullets, but also to fire live ammunition without removing the attachment.

24   "Israel: Killing of Children Apparent War Crime."

25   See William Kherbek, "Artist Profile: Lawrence Abu Hamdan," Rhizome, August 21, 2015, http://rhizome.org/editorial/2015/aug/21/artist-profile-lawrence-abu-hamdan/.

26   "Complementarity," Coalition for the International Criminal Court, http://www.iccnow.org/?mod=complementarity.

27   Apparently, based on evidence gathered by the police, including a ballistics report that identified with certainty that the bullet that killed Nawara came from the weapon of a border policeman, other pieces of evidence appeared: Expert reports connected the bullet found in Nawara's bag with the border policeman's gun. Wiretapping of the officer's communications and other persons involved in the incident also reveal that he shot his gun. He later allowed the Palestinian authorities to turn the bullet over to the Israelis for forensic testing. Yonah Jeremy Bob, "Judge Recuses Himself in Ex-border Cop's Manslaughter Trial for Death of Palestinian," *Jerusalem Post*, December 10, 2015.

28   According to the Israeli human rights group Yesh Din, since 2000 only 5 percent of complaints submitted to the Military Police Criminal Investigations Division (MPCID) have led to an indictment. Of the 5,000 Palestinians killed by the IDF since 2000, only seven soldiers have been convicted, and none spent more than several months in prison. "MPCID Investigations into the Circumstances Surrounding the Death of Palestinians: Convictions and Penalties," Yesh Din website, July 2013, https://www.yesh-din.org/userfiles/file/datasheets/data%20sheet%20july%202013/ICAP%20Death%20cases%20investigations%20and%20indictments_July%202013_ENG.pdf.

The only other person ever indicted and tried was in the case of the Gaza killing of journalist, but this is because the deceased was European national and because the shooter was Bedouin soldier.

29   Robert Mackey, "Video Analysis of Fatal West Bank Shooting Said to Implicate Israeli Officer," *New York Times*, November 24, 2014.

30   The first witness in the case, a ballistics expert, turned out to be the judge's nephew. See Bob, "Judge Recuses Himself."

31   Rep. Betty McCollum, Letter to Ambassador Anne Woods Patterson and Assistant Secretary Tom Malinowsky, August 18, 2015, http://mccollum.house.gov/sites/mccollum.house.gov/files/15.0818%20State-Patterson-Malinowski_Palestinian%20Nadeem%20Nawara%20Shooting.pdf.

The Capital City

TIMOTHY MITCHELL

To speak about architecture and representation runs the risk of starting from a simplification: that the world exists as a built environment, on the one hand, and the meaning or significance that we attach to what is built, on the other. In *Colonising Egypt* I asked how modern people had come to experience the world in such stark, binary terms. Here, I want to explore alternatives. There are ways to consider questions of meaning, signification, and representation that resist simple oppositions of the material and representational, that instead allow one to account for all of the ways that forms of inscription, forms of value, and forms of meaning are enfolded into every architectural work. One way the question of representation that informs this volume can be addressed is through a different approach to the history of the Arab City and the political formations that have shaped its built landscape.

To consider this question, I will outline the history of a political-economic institution that has shaped modern cities and modern lives: the corporation. We think of the corporation as a form of business organization, one that has come to play a large role in—among other fields—the building of cities. But the corporation is also a way of organizing the relationship between the future and the present. Through the business corporation, the building of cities can both create the future and appropriate it in the present. This power is simultaneously a question of materiality and of representation.

In *Dubai: The City as Corporation*, Ahmed Kanna describes Dubai as a city-state created and controlled by holding companies. These firms have built its megatowers, its enclaves, its retail malls, its ports, and its artificial islands. There are many similar examples of such corporate development: the Solidere project in Beirut and the Sawiris downtown project in Cairo, to name only two. While the centrality of the corporation to the city is latent in many of the essays in this volume, I want to turn to the history of the corporation not just as a business unit but as a political entity.

Examples of the city-as-corporation in the Arab world date from the colonial period. In Europe, there is a longer history. The corporation originally was the city, or at least the town. Historically, the right to incorporate created a collective entity, a body that could act independently and could survive the death of its founders. The town was the most important example of this power to create an enduring and self-acting agency serving a collective purpose. Other examples in medieval and early modern Europe included the university, religious institutions, and, later, the overseas colony.

Colonies provided the link between older forms of corporation and the emergence of a new model in the late nineteenth century: the profit-making business corporation. Entities like the English East India Company, or the Dutch West India Company, which colonized Manhattan, developed the power to monopolize trade routes and trading settlements. Shares in future profits from these colonial monopolies were sold to investors, creating the joint-stock company.

Toward the end of the nineteenth century, new monopolies were created in the form of railroad companies and large oil firms, and in property companies that organized large-scale urban and rural development. The power of corporate bodies to act collectively, to enjoy exclusive control over territory and resources, and to survive across generations was now harnessed to the selling of shares in the future revenues that such corporate control promised. The corporation had become the large business firm.

If the corporation was always a body that could endure into the future, its transformation into the large business firm reflected a change in the relationship to the future. Beginning with the colonial trading company, then moving to the railroad, the oil industry, and the modern megalopolis, the corporation was fashioned through the building of durable structures. This durability was engineered in the new technologies of ship design, steam power, military hardware, and steel and reinforced concrete. Railroad companies, for example, built a long-term apparatus for revenue out of rail tracks, trusses, viaducts, terminals, and rolling stock. Since it was not just the physical structure but its operation that had to be durable, the apparatus equally required the control of territory, the displacement or elimination of native populations, and command over labor forces. New technical and political powers engineered a new temporal relationship: the future as a durable revenue structure.

The changed relation between the present and the future created a new form of political economy. Corporations could now promise a revenue stream that might flow for ten, twenty, or even fifty years. Entrepreneurs, however, did not have to wait decades to realize that revenue. Anticipated future profits of the corporation could be sold at a discount to investors in the present, in the form of shares. Maintaining the value of those shares, through the dividends they promised, became a "cost" carried by the enterprise.

This cost was a charge on the future. In the case of a railroad, for example, it became an additional expense of operating the rail line, paid for in higher fares and freight charges for users, or in lower wages for employees. In the case of housing, the initial profits earned by property entrepreneurs became the "cost" of renting that housing unit over the following decades. The following generation would carry these growing burdens.

The durability of transport systems, energy networks, and urban structures, and of the political orders built around them, engineered the means for speculators in the present to impose charges on the future. The large wealth of a minority of entrepreneurs in the present was acquired from the increased living costs of a majority in the future. There is a technical term for this process of imposing a charge on the future: *capitalization*. The principal mechanism of capitalization, for moving the future into the present, has been the corporation.

By far the most significant form of capitalization today is real estate. In the advanced industrialized countries, about half of a country's capital exists in the form of productive assets, but the other half is created in residential real estate. Real estate represents the most widespread use of the techniques of enriching a minority of entrepreneurs in the present by taking wealth away from a future generation. The entrepreneur sells a housing unit not at the cost of construction (including profit) but as the discounted value of the rent or mortgage payments that can be charged to its future occupants. Since this future revenue may vastly exceed the cost of construction, the difference is represented as the "value" of the land itself. This structure of space and debt does not operate only at the large, municipal scale; it also infuses all levels of development. Take, for instance, Ashraf Abdalla's description of the children's park in Cairo, which turned out to be a vehicle for drawing small craftsmen into systems of debt.

If residential real estate represents 50 percent of the wealth in countries like the United States, in much of the Arab world it accounts for vastly more, though real estate operates differently in each of the region's cities and countries. For example it has a quite specific role in non-oil states; that is to say in states that acquire benefits from being in an oil region and from the reinvestment of oil revenue, but which are not themselves significant producers of oil. These include Lebanon and Egypt but also Dubai. The Emirate of Dubai is part of the United Arab Emirates, which is an oil-producing state. But 97 percent of its oil comes from one of the other emirates, Abu Dhabi. Dubai has very small amounts of oil. Making these kinds of distinctions and then comparing, in architectural terms, the theme parks of Dubai and the rather different kind of architecture of Abu Dhabi is important.

In what particular ways are durable future revenue streams transformed into current wealth in the urban orders of the Arab world? Thanks to those oil revenues—whether enjoyed directly as an oil producer or indirectly through their reinvestment—most of the well-to-do in the Arab world have not been forced to build their wealth through the rather messy, short-term competitive world of manufacturing material goods. Those who have wealth typically want to expand and reproduce it by creating sources of revenue that will generate income in a much more reliable way over a future. And that's why real estate investment always appears alongside oil revenues. It is the most logical and straightforward way to take extraordinary revenues from oil and turn them into a long-term future that can be capitalized in the present.

Real estate in the Gulf is also informed by another distinct aspect of the region, its desert ecology. If you rapidly build large cities in an arid environment, as tends to be the case not only in the Gulf but also in places like Cairo, potential land for development on the outskirts of the city is almost entirely in the hands of the state. This is different from most other cities of the world, where development land on the city's fringe would already be privately owned. This urban condition creates a relationship between the impulse to transform—to generate much larger possibilities for future wealth through the speculative building of real estate—and a form of politics where the state itself has extraordinary access to sites for development. When we talk about powerful families in the Gulf, that particular relationship—between deserts, the state (or the powerful families that claim ownership of the desert), and the movement of revenues into building the durable structures that we call real estate—has to be understood.

The process of capitalization, of building durable futures and turning them into speculative presents, however, does not characterize all building or all architecture, which is why we should draw a distinction between Dubai and Abu Dhabi. To offer a schematic comparison, because Dubai had very little oil, the strategy employed by the people in power there was to transform the emirate into a port city where capital was amassed through speculative real estate. In Abu Dhabi, however, where there were no concerns about the availability of oil revenues in the coming decades, architectural projects did not have the same mandate to satisfy an immediate return for revenue, which brought a different tenor to the architecture and the speed of construction.

So, finally, to address the theme of representation: the difficulty with any attempt to place architecture within the problems of representation does not lie in thinking about the production of meaning, either because the building itself is to produce meaning or because the building is to reflect some national cultural meaning that already exists. The difficulty is the ease with which we slip into the assumption that there is the building on the one hand and what it represents or what it means on the other.

We are not dealing with two separate axes, the built and the representational. The advantage of placing architecture in the larger history of capitalization is that if we think about an example like the railroad, or parallel examples in urban development, at every single point one is involved in these processes of calculation, of inscription, of planning, of drawing, which have to be understood in relation to the fact that one is trying to build a durable future and at the same time to persuade people in the present of the durability of that future. Representation plays its part not just as some general question as to how the built world creates meaning. It works in very specific ways in relation to the role of architecture in constructing the forms of capitalized futures with which we live.

ASHRAF ABDALLA is a Ph.D student of architecture at the Columbia University Graduate School of Architecture, Planning and Preservation (GSAPP), where he also obtained two Master of Science degrees in Critical, Curatorial, and Conceptual Practices in Architecture (CCCP) and Advanced Architectural Design (AAD). He holds a Bachelor of Science degree in Architecture from Ain Shams University in Cairo, Egypt. Prior to pursuing an academic career, Abdalla worked in architectural offices in both the US and Egypt. He also co-represented Egypt with architect Omar Nagati in the Egyptian pavilion at the 6th International Venice Architecture Biennale. In his doctoral dissertation, he intends to examine the relation between architecture and the political and economic transformations in Egypt during the 1980s and 1990s.

SENAN ABDELQADER is a practicing architect and urban planner, leading his firm Senan Abdelqader Architects (SAA), which he established in 1995. Through work on private and public projects that try to influence and are influenced by social and political variables, Abdelqader has created a public platform in which the planning process is considered a collective act and a space for civil practices. Alongside his practice, he has taught at Tel-Aviv University and founded the "Informal" unit at the Bezalel Academy for Art and Design in Jerusalem in 2006, giving students the opportunity to critically experiment in a space where formality and informality are intertwined. He has also taught at the Dessau Institute of Architecture (DIA) in Germany and has participated in various local and international architectural biennials and exhibitions, including the São Paulo Biennale in Brazil in 2007, where he published the book *Architecture of Dependency*.

LILA ABU-LUGHOD is the Joseph L. Buttenwieser Professor of Social Science at Columbia University. She teaches Anthropology and Women's Studies and is currently director of the Middle East Institute. Her scholarship, strongly ethnographic and mostly based on research in Egypt, has focused on three broad issues: the relationship between cultural forms and power; the politics of knowledge and representation; and the question of women's rights in the Middle East. Among her award-winning ethnographies are *Veiled Sentiments: Honor and Poetry in a Bedouin Society*; *Writing Women's Worlds: Bedouin Stories*; and *Dramas of Nationhood: The Politics of Television in Egypt*. A member of the Center for Palestine Studies at Columbia, with Ahmad H. Sa'di she has coedited *Nakba: Palestine, 1948, and the Claims of Memory*. Her most recent book is *Do Muslim Women Need Saving?*

NORA AKAWI joined the Columbia University GSAPP in September 2012 as the curator of Studio-X Amman, a regional research and programming platform dedicated to the futures of cities, run by GSAPP and the Columbia Global Centers, Middle East. Akawi studied architecture at the Bezalel Academy of Art and Design in Jerusalem (B.Arch, 2009) and pursued her graduate studies in Critical, Curatorial and Conceptual Practices in Architecture at the Columbia University GSAPP (MSc. CCCP, 2011). Her research focused on the role of the archive in visualizing collective spatial narratives and in imagining alternative spatial and political organization. With Nina Kolowratnik she codirects a research and mapping initiative titled Echoing Borders, which proposes alternative visualizations of borders and territories through exploring questions of mobility, access, and human rights, and the representation of migration and time across territories. Echoing Borders is developed with the Studio-X Global Network through international summer workshops and an ongoing seminar course at Columbia University GSAPP.

MOHAMMAD AL-ASAD is an architect and architectural historian. He is the director of the Center for the Study of the Built Environment in Amman (CSBE), a private, non-profit think-and-do-tank that he founded in 1999. He has been writing on architecture and urbanism in the Islamic world for over twenty years. His most recent book is *Contemporary Architecture and Urbanism in the Middle East*, and he has also edited *Workplaces: The Transformation of Places of Production: Industrial Buildings in the Islamic World*. In addition, he has appeared in and led the production of a number of documentary films, the latest of which is *Arab Women in Architecture*.

SUAD AMIRY is an architect and writer, and founder of the Riwaq Center for Architectural Conservation, which is dedicated to the rehabilitation and protection of architectural heritage in Palestine and won the Aga Khan Award for Architecture in 2013. Amiry is the author of numerous books, including *Sharon and My Mother in Law*, *Nothing to Lose but Your Life*, and *Golda Slept Here*.

AMALE ANDRAOS is Dean of Columbia University's Graduate School of Architecture, Planning and Preservation and co-founder of WORKac, a New-York based architectural and urban practice with international reach. In addition to Columbia, Andraos has taught at universities including Princeton University School of Architecture, Harvard Graduate School of Design, University of Pennsylvania Design School, and American University in Beirut. Her publications include *49 Cities*, *Above the Pavement, the Farm!* and numerous essays. WORKac is focused on reimaging architecture at the intersection of the urban, the rural, and the natural. It has achieved international recognition and was named the 2015 AIA New York State Firm of the Year.

MOHAMED ELSHAHED recently completed his Ph.D at the Middle East Studies Department at New York University. His dissertation is titled *Revolutionary Modernism? Architecture and the Politics of Transition in Egypt, 1936–1967*. It argues that 1950s urban and architectural development associated with Nasserism refashioned preexisting architectural production in the service of Egypt's "necessary transitional authoritarianism." Elshahed's research has been supported by the Social Science Research Council and the American Research Center in Egypt. He also holds an MA in Architecture Studies from the Massachusetts Institute of Technology and a Bachelor of Architecture from the New Jersey Institute of Technology. He is currently a postdoctoral fellow at the Berlin-based Forum Transregionale Studien. Elshahed is the founder and editor of Cairobserver.com.

YASSER ELSHESHTAWY is Associate Professor of Architecture at United Arab Emirates University, Al Ain, where in addition to teaching he also runs the Urban Research Lab. His scholarship focuses on urbanization in developing societies, informal urbanism, urban history, and environment-behavior studies, with a particular focus on Middle Eastern cities. He has authored a series of books and publications, including *Dubai: Behind an Urban Spectacle*.

RANIA GHOSN is an architect, geographer, and partner of Design Earth. She is currently assistant professor at the Massachusetts Institute of Technology School of Architecture + Planning. Her work engages the geographies of technological systems to open up a range of aesthetic and political concerns for architecture and urbanism. Rania holds a Doctor of Design from the Harvard Graduate School of Design, a Master in Geography from University College London, and a Bachelor of Architecture from the American University of Beirut. Prior to joining MIT, she was an Assistant Professor at the University of Michigan and a Mellon Postdoctoral

Fellow at Boston University. Rania is founding editor of the journal *New Geographies* and editor-in-chief of *NG2: Landscapes of Energy*. Some of her recent writings have been published in *New Geographies*, *San Rocco*, *Journal of Architectural Education*, *MONU*, *Thresholds*, *Bracket*, and *Perspecta*. Her current book project, *Oil Across the Middle East: The Trans-Arabian Pipeline*, traces the system of a transnational oil infrastructure to document territorial transformations associated with the region's incorporation into a global fossil fuel economy.

SABA INNAB is a Palestinian-Jordanian architect, urban researcher, and artist practicing out of Amman and Beirut. She holds a Bachelor of Architecture from the Jordan University of Science and Technology. Her work was shown in various exhibitions, most recently in the 2016 Marrakesh Biennial, Home Works 7 in Beirut, in the Museum of Modern Art in Warsaw in 2015, and in Darat al Funun-Amman in 2014. She has worked as an architect and urban designer with UNRWA on the reconstruction of the Nahr el Bared Camp in the North of Lebanon, a project

nominated for the Aga Khan Award for Architecture in 2013. She received the visiting research fellowship initiated by Studio-X Amman in 2014. Through painting, mapping, sculpture, and design, her work explores the suspended states between temporality and permanence, and is concerned with variable notions of dwelling, building, and language in architecture.

ZIAD JAMALEDDINE holds a Bachelor of Architecture from the American University of Beirut and a Master of Architecture from the Harvard Graduate School of Design. He worked for Steven Holl Architects for five years where he worked on the Simmons Hall dormitory at MIT (winner of an AIA National Design Award in 2003 and an AIA New York award in 2002), and was the project architect for the design and development of the Beirut Marina project in downtown Beirut. Jamaleddine has taught design studios and seminars at Cornell University, PennDesign, the Yale School of Architecture, the University of Toronto, the MIT Aga Khan Program, and the Columbia University GSAPP. His architecture firm LE.F.T is the recipient of the

2002 Young Architects Forum Award and the 2010 Emerging Voices Award from the Architectural League of New York, His firm was the 2009 Finalist in MoMA's Young Architects Program, a member of *Architectural Record's* 2010 Design Vanguard, and a finalist for the 2010 Iakov Chernikhov Prize.

BERNARD KHOURY studied architecture at the Rhode Island School of Design and received a Masters in Architectural Studies from Harvard University. He began an independent practice in 1993. Over the past fifteen years, his office has developed an international reputation and a significant portfolio of projects sited locally and abroad. He was awarded the honorable mention of the Borromini Prize in 2001 and won the Architecture + Award in 2004. He is the co-founder of the Arab Center for Architecture and has been a visiting professor at the Ecole Polytechnique Federale de Lausanne, L'Ecole Speciale d'Architecture in Paris, and the American University of Beirut. He has lectured and exhibited his work in Europe and the US, including a solo show in the International Forum for Contemporary Architecture at the Aedes gallery in Berlin, and numerous group shows, including YOUprison at the Fondazione Sandretto in Torino and SPACE at the opening show of the MAXXI museum in Rome. He was the co-curator and architect of the Kingdom of Bahrain's national pavilion at the Venice Biennale's 14th International Architecture Exhibition in 2014. He is the author of *Local Heroes,* published in 2014.

LAURA KURGAN is Associate Professor of Architecture in the Graduate School of Architecture, Planning and Preservation at Columbia University, where she directs the Visual Studies curriculum and the Center for Spatial Research. She is the author of *Close Up at a Distance: Mapping, Technology, and Politics.* Her work explores questions ranging from digital mapping technologies, to the ethics and politics of mapping, and the art, science, and visualization of data. Her work has appeared at the Cartier Foundation in Paris, the Venice Architecture Biennale, the Whitney Altria, MACBA Barcelona, the ZKM in Karlsruhe, and the Museum of Modern Art. She was the winner of the United States Artists Rockefeller Fellowship in 2009.

ADRIAN LAHOUD is an architect and teacher. He is Dean of the School of Architecture at the Royal College of Art. Prior to that, he was Director of the Urban Design Masters at the Bartlett School of Architecture and served as Director of the MA programme at the Centre for Research Architecture, Goldsmiths. In 2012 he was awarded a Ph.D from the University of Technology, Sydney, for doctoral research on a philosophical, scientific, and architectural history of scale. He works on questions of spatial politics and urban conflict with a focus on the Arab world and Africa. Recently, his work has been published in *Textures of the Anthropocene: Grain, Vapour, Ray; The Journal of Architecture; Architecture and the Paradox of Dissidence; New Geographies 5: The Mediterranean;* and *Forensis: The Architecture of Public Truth.*

ALI MANGERA studied structural and environmental engineering at the University of Leeds, United Kingdom, before completing a Masters degree at Pennsylvania State University in Architectural Engineering. Mangera then studied architecture at the Architectural Association School of Architecture in London and has worked at the offices of Skidmore, Owings & Merrill, and Zaha Hadid. In 2007, Mangera and Ada Yvars Bravo formed Mangera Yvars Architects (MYAA), which is based in London and Barcelona. The practice has since worked on major projects around the world, including in the UK, Spain, the Middle and Far East, China, and India. At MYAA, Mangera is involved in the design and development of key projects, particularly in Arab cities where MYAA is keen to address the more fundamental question of culture and identity. Mangera has been a guest critic at the Architectural Association, Cambridge University, Barcelona University, University College London, COAC Barcelona, and King Saud University. He is also a building expert panel member on The Commission for Architecture and The Built Environment (CABE), UK.

REINHOLD MARTIN is Professor of Architecture in the Graduate School of Architecture, Planning and Preservation at Columbia University, where he directs the Temple Hoyne Buell Center for the Study of American Architecture. Martin is a member of Columbia's Committee on Global Thought and was a founding coeditor of the journal *Grey Room*. His books include *The Organizational Complex: Architecture, Media, and Corporate Space*; *Utopia's Ghost: Architecture and Postmodernism, Again*; and *Multi-National City: Architectural Itineraries* (with Kadambari Baxi). Currently, Martin is working on two books: a history of the nineteenth-century American university as a media complex, and a study of the contemporary city at the intersection of aesthetics and politics. An excerpt, *Mediators: Aesthetics, Politics, and the City*, recently appeared as an e-book from the University of Minnesota Press

TIMOTHY MITCHELL is a political theorist and historian specializing in the modern Arab world. Educated at Queens College, Cambridge, and Princeton University, he is Professor and Chair of the Department of Middle Eastern, South Asian, and African Studies at Columbia University, where he also holds an appointment in the School of International and Public Affairs. His books include *Colonising Egypt*; *Rule of Experts: Egypt, Technopolitics, Modernity*; and *Carbon Democracy: Political Power in the Age of Oil*.

MAGDA MOSTAFA is an Associate Professor of Architecture at the American University in Cairo (AUC), Design Associate at Progressive Architects, and Regional Deputy Vice President for Africa in the International Union of Architects' (UIA) Education Commission. Her research interests include design pedagogy and special needs design, particularly for autism. She has recently developed the Autism ASPECTSS Design Index, for which she was awarded the UIA's Architecture for All Research Award at the 2014 World Congress. Her other awards include the International Award for Excellence in Design in 2008, which she was also shortlisted for in 2012. She was also nominated for the 2005 UNESCO Prize for Research and Training in Special Needs

Education for Children. She is coauthor of the recently published book *Learning from Cairo*, and has developed the Juxtopolis Pedagogy that she currently follows in her studio at AUC and has presented internationally.

NASSER RABBAT is the Aga Khan Professor and the Director of the Aga Khan Program for Islamic Architecture at MIT. An architect and historian, his scholarly interests include Islamic architecture, art, and cultures, urban history, modern Arab history, and post-colonial criticism. His most recent books are *Mamluk History Through Architecture: Building, Culture, and Politics in Mamluk Egypt and Syria*, which won the British–Kuwait Friendship Society Prize in 2011; *al-Mudun al-Mayyita* (The Dead Cities); an edited book, *The Courtyard House: From Cultural Reference to Universal Relevance*; and *al-Naqd Iltizaman* (Criticism as Commitment), a book that deals with the roots and consequences of the Arab Spring. Rabbat regularly contributes to a number of Arabic newspapers and consults with international design firms on projects in the Islamic World.

HASHIM SARKIS (BArch, RISD; MArch and Ph.D, Harvard University) is an architect, educator, and scholar. His firm, Hashim Sarkis Studios (HSS), is based in Beirut, Lebanon, and Cambridge, Massachusetts. HSS projects—which include the Housing for the Fishermen of Tyre, the Balloon Park in Beirut, and the Town Hall of Byblos—have received numerous awards and have been exhibited at the Biennales of Venice, Rotterdam, and Shenzhen/Hong Kong, as well as MoMA. From 1995 to 2014, Sarkis was a member of the faculty of the Harvard Graduate School of Design (GSD), where he taught design and the history and theory of architecture. From 2002 to 2014, he was the Aga Khan Professor of Landscape Architecture and Urbanism in Muslim Societies at the GSD. In October 2014, he was appointed Dean of the School of Architecture and Planning at MIT. His publications include *Circa 1958: Lebanon in the Pictures and Plans of Constantinos Doxiadis*; *Projecting Beirut* (coedited with Peter Rowe); *Josep Lluis Sert: The Architect of Urban Design* (coedited with Eric Mumford); and *CASE: Le Corbusier's Venice Hospital* (editor).

FELICITY SCOTT is Associate Professor of Architecture, Director of the Ph.D program and Co-Director of the program in Critical, Curatorial and Conceptual Practices in Architecture (CCCP) at the Columbia University GSAPP. In addition to articles on contemporary art and architecture, she is the author of *Architecture or Techno-Utopia: Politics after Modernism*; *Living Archive 7: Ant Farm*. She recently completed a book manuscript entitled *Outlaw Territories: Environments of Insecurity / Architectures of Counter-Insurgency, 1966– 1979*, to be published by Zone Books.

HALA WARDÉ holds an architectural degree from the ESA School in Paris, where she studied with Paul Virilio and Jean Nouvel. She has been working for almost twenty-five years with Jean Nouvel in the various structures of his offices. In 1999 she became a partner at the Ateliers Jean Nouvel (AJN) and has been responsible for major projects throughout Europe, East Asia, the Middle East, and the US. In 2008 she established HW Architecture, her own practice, and began developing her own projects in parallel to her collaboration with AJN. In the framework of her partnership on AJN projects, she was recently in charge of the One New Change office and retail project in London, delivered in 2010, and the Louvre Abu Dhabi, which she has been leading and overseeing since its inception in 2007.

EYAL WEIZMAN is an architect, professor of spatial and visual cultures, and Director of the Centre for Research Architecture at Goldsmiths, University of London. Since 2014 he is a Global Professor at Princeton University. In 2011 he set up Forensic Architecture, a research agency that provides architectural evidence for violations of international law and human rights. In 2007 he founded, with Sandi Hilal and Alessandro Petti, the architectural collective DAAR in Beit Sahour/Palestine. Weizman has taught at the Academy of Fine Arts in Vienna, the Bartlett School of Architecture, and the Staedl School in Frankfurt. His books include *Architecture after Revolution*; *Mengele's Skull*; *The Least of all Possible Evils*; *Hollow Land*; *A Civilian Occupation*; and *The Conflict Shoreline: Colonialism as*

Climate Change in the Negev Desert. He has also published many articles in journals, magazines. and edited books, and serves on the editorial boards of *Humanity*, *Cabinet*, and *Political Concepts*. He has worked with a variety of NGOs world wide and was member of the B'Tselem board of directors. He is currently on the advisory boards of the ICA in London, the Human Rights Project at Bard College, and other academic and cultural institutions. Weizman is the recipient of the James Stirling Memorial Lecture Prize for 2006–2007, a co-recipient of the 2010 Prince Claus Prize for Architecture (for DAAR), and has delivered the Rusty Bernstein, Paul Hirst, and Edward Said Memorial Lectures, among others. He studied architecture at the Architectural Association in London and completed his Ph.D at the London Consortium/Birkbeck College.

GWENDOLYN WRIGHT is an award-winning architectural historian, author, and cohost of the PBS television series *History Detectives*. She is a professor of architecture at Columbia University, also holding appointments in both its departments

of history and art history. Wright's specialties are US architectural history and urban history from after the Civil War to the present. She also writes about the exchange across national boundaries of architectural styles, influences, and techniques, particularly examining the colonial and neocolonial attributes of both modernism and historic preservation.

Columbia Books on
Architecture and the City
An imprint of the Graduate
School of Architecture,
Planning, and Preservation
Columbia University

1172 Amsterdam Ave
407 Avery Hall
New York, NY 10027

Visit our website at
arch.columbia.edu/books

Columbia Books
on Architecture and the
City are distributed
by Columbia University
Press at cup.columbia.edu

This book has been produced
through the Office of the
Dean, Amale Andraos and
the Office of Publications at
Columbia University GSAPP.

Director of Publications
JAMES GRAHAM

Managing Editor
CAITLIN BLANCHFIELD

Associate Editor
ALISSA ANDERSON

Designed by
NEIL DONNELLY
SEAN YENDRYS

978-1-941332-14-6

Printed by
Die Keure, Bruges, Belgium

Library of Congress
Cataloging-in-Publication
Data

Names: Architecture and
Representation: The Arab
City (Symposium) (2014 :
Columbia University) |
Andraos, Amale, 1973- editor. |
Akawi, Nora, editor. |
Blanchfield, Caitlin, editor.
Title: The Arab city :
architecture & representation /
Edited by Amale Andraos and
Nora Akawi ; with Caitlin
Blanchfield.
Description: New York :
Columbia Books on
Architecture and the City,
2016. Identifiers: LCCN
2016006572 | ISBN
9781941332146
Subjects: LCSH: Architecture
and society—Arab countries—
Congresses. | Identity
(Psychology) in architecture—
Arab countries—Congresses. |
Nationalism and architecture—
Arab countries—Congresses.
Classification: LCC NA2543.
S6 A6274 2014 | DDC
711/.409174927—
dc23 LC record available at
http://lccn.loc.gov/
2016006572